Exploring Entrepreneurship and Economics

Cynthia L. Greene

THOMSON

SOUTH-WESTERN

Australia · Canada · Mexico · Singapore · Spain · United Kingdom · United States

THOMSON

SOUTH-WESTERN

Exploring Entrepreneurship and Economics
Cynthia L. Greene

VP/Editorial Director
Jack W. Calhoun

VP/Editor-in-Chief
Karen Schmohe

Executive Editor
Eve Lewis

Project Manager
Enid Nagel

Marketing Manager
Michael Cloran

Marketing Coordinator
Linda Kuper

Production Manager
Patricia Matthews Boies

Production Project Manager
Jennifer A. Ziegler

Technology Project Manager
Scott Hamilton

Web Coordinator
Edward Stubenrauch

Manufacturing Coordinator
Kevin Kluck

Editorial Assistant
Linda Watkins

Art Director
Tippy McIntosh

Cover and Internal Designer
Grannan Graphic Design, Ltd.

Cover Photo Source
Getty Images, Punchstock

Compositor
Graphic World Inc.

Printer
Quebecor World
Dubuque, Iowa

For more information about our products, contact us at:

Thomson Higher Education
5191 Natorp Boulevard
Mason, Ohio 45040
USA

Reviewers

Nifara K. Ali
Consultant
Evanston High School
Evanston, IL

Connie H. Ballard
Career and Technical Education Specialist
Charlotte-Mecklenburg Schools
Charlotte, NC

Crystal K. Bolamperti
Business/Technology Curriculum Leader and
    Teacher
Westside Middle School
Omaha, NE

Eva H. Chiphe
Director
Marlboro County Youth Entrepreneur Program
Clio, SC

Tammie J. Fischer
Director
Center for Economic Education
University of Nebraska - Lincoln
Lincoln, NE

Douglas A. Haskell
Associate Director
Economics Center for Education & Research
University of Cincinnati
Cincinnati, OH

Jill Heywood
Middle School Business/Computer Teacher
Crete Public Schools
Crete, NE

Kristine M. Labbus
Business Education Teacher
Neenah High School
Neenah, WI

Sherii Farmer
Program Director
Youth Entrepreneurs of Kansas
Wichita, KS

Brendan Landry
YouthWorks Program Director
Micro Business Development
Denver, CO

Monica Schultz
Program Director
YouthBiz, Inc.
Denver, Co

Zachary P. Sepesi
Teacher, Language Arts
United South Middle School
Laredo, TX

Gail A. Tamaribuchi
Director
Center for Economic Education
University of Hawaii-Manoa
Honolulu, HA

Kathy Woodcock
Teacher, Business Department
Conway High School East
Conway, AR

About the Author

Cynthia L. Greene taught business education at the high school level for 25 years. She taught in the Fulton County School System in Atlanta, Georgia, where she was a Cooperative Business Education Coordinator and chair of the business and career and technical education department. She has been active in the National Business Education Association (NBEA), serving on the Entrepreneurship Standards Committee as a writer and reviewer and as a writer for the Entrepreneurship Lesson Plans. Cynthia is the 2005-2006 President of NBEA.

Contents

FEATURES

ASSESSMENT

Checkpoint 6, 7, 11, 13, 14, 16, 19, 20, 22, 31, 33, 34, 37, 39, 41, 45, 46, 55, 56, 59, 61, 63, 65, 67, 69, 71, 80, 81, 82, 88, 89, 91, 93, 95, 103, 104, 105, 106, 110, 113, 116, 117, 118, 119, 120, 131, 132, 135, 137, 139, 143, 145, 146, 157, 159, 160, 163, 165, 167, 170, 171, 172, 173, 174, 184, 186, 188, 191, 192, 193, 196, 197, 205, 207, 209, 211, 212, 213, 215, 217, 225, 227, 231, 232, 235, 239

Let's Get Real 11, 16, 22, 34, 41, 47, 59, 61, 65, 71, 82, 89, 91, 93, 94, 95, 107, 113, 121, 135, 139, 147, 160, 167, 175, 188, 193, 197, 207, 213, 217, 227, 232, 239

Chapter Assessment 23, 49, 73, 97, 123, 149, 177, 199, 219, 241

Welcome to *Exploring Entrepreneurship and Economics!*

You are about to enter the exciting world of entrepreneurship and economics. Using this textbook, you will learn what it takes to participate in the entrepreneurial process. Realistic concepts and activities guide you in building your own business. You will read about the real-life experiences of teenage entrepreneurs and the history of some very successful businesses, as well as learn realistic concepts and processes associated with building your own business. ***Exploring Entrepreneurship and Economics*** provides you with a strong foundation for developing decision-making skills that will last a lifetime. The textbook helps you to build problem-solving skills, learn about economics and personal finance topics, and become more aware of the role of entrepreneurs and free enterprise in the 21st century workplace.

ACTIVITIES CD

The Activities CD contains exercises that help you improve your entrepreneurial and economic skills.

Special Features

Opportunity Knocks begins each chapter with a story about the real-life experiences of successful young entrepreneurs.

TREND SPOTTER

Trend Spotter shows you how businesses follow emerging trends to meet the needs of their customers.

 How They Started

How They Started is an historical look at some well-known, successful companies.

Be Your Own Boss gives you the opportunity to complete the same types of activities that a real entrepreneur might do.

Help You Learn

Project: Making Entrepreneurship Work for You is a cumulative, team-based project consisting of multiple activities that help you develop a complete business plan.

You can say that again! are enlightening quotes from well-known people in the business world.

NET Bookmark provides Internet activities which you will find on exploringxtra.swlearning.com.

Did You Know? introduces you to interesting facts and statistics about entrepreneurship and economics.

Focus on Reading and Ongoing Assessment

Each lesson begins with a list of terms and goals for the lesson to help you focus your reading. Watch for them as you read! Each goal corresponds to a major heading. Ongoing review and assessment help you understand the material.

Working Together

Working Together provides you with opportunities to work with classmates on cooperative learning projects.

CHECKPOINT

Checkpoint enables you to test your understanding at key points in each lesson.

LET'S GET REAL

Let's Get Real contains activities to help you apply what you have learned in the lesson.

Chapter Assessment provides a summary of the main points and contains questions and activities to test your knowledge.

Chapter 1

What Is an Entrepreneur?

© STEPEHN MALLON/PHOTONICA

Take a Load Off

Christen Wooley just wanted to solve an everyday problem. As an 11-year-old, Christen had grown tired of lugging around heavy schoolbooks in her backpack. Her school didn't supply lockers, so she had to carry up to 40 pounds of books and supplies on her back all day. Her neck, shoulders, and spine were beginning to feel the strain. So, when her sixth-grade science teacher at Suwannee (Florida) Middle School assigned her to find a common problem and invent a solution, Christen didn't have to think too hard for an idea.

Christen's parents helped her create a waterproof vest that had pockets in the front as well as storage space in the back like a regular backpack. Christen thought her invention would be a more comfortable way for kids to carry books. When her teacher and everyone else thought so too, Christen knew she had come up with something special. Her school invention became the model for Vestpakz. Vestpakz is a body-hugging, vest-like pack that more evenly distributes the weight of heavy books. In doing so, it helps relieve stress on the back. By the age of 15, Christen had found a manufacturer for Vestpakz and obtained a patent.

Christen also began entering Vestpakz in a variety of invention competitions. In 2003, she appeared on the Oprah Winfrey Show's "Million Dollar Idea Challenge." She also has appeared at events such as the National Science Teachers Convention. In 2005, she was awarded a scholarship from the Guardian Life Insurance Company of America. Publicity from such events helped spread the word about Vestpakz.

Today, Christen markets and sells her Vestpakz through mail order and on the Internet. It comes in four sizes—for kids and adults—and 14 different colors. She also stays busy as a board member of By Kids For Kids, an organization that helps young inventors.

WHAT DO YOU KNOW?

1] Do you think Christen's idea is a good one? How has she created an interest in Vestpakz?

2] How many products do you use every day that were invented just to solve a simple, common problem? Name one.

WHAT DO ENTREPRENEURS DO?

Terms

entrepreneur
entrepreneurship
employee
manufacturing
   business
wholesaling
   business
retailing business
service business

Goals

* **Explain what entrepreneurs do.**

* **Describe types of entrepreneurial businesses.**

* **Discuss the role of entrepreneurs in history.**

© GETTY IMAGES/PHOTODISC

What an Entrepreneur Does

Have you ever been paid for washing a car or mowing a lawn? Have you ever babysat young children? If so, you have a good idea what an entrepreneur does. An **entrepreneur** is someone who provides a product or service for someone else for money. Entrepreneurs are engaged in entrepreneurship. **Entrepreneurship** is the process of running a business of one's own.

The United States has many small businesses. Young people have created some of these businesses. Some young people operate their businesses for only a short time. Others start a small business as a teenager and grow it into a larger business. Their business may help them shape their career. But what makes someone an entrepreneur? How have entrepreneurs changed history? How do entrepreneurs affect today's economy?

Why do some people choose to run their businesses from home?

Entrepreneurs come from all types of backgrounds. People of all ages choose to become entrepreneurs. They create many kinds of businesses. Some may start a pool cleaning service or a desktop publishing business. Others may create handcrafted jewelry or offer a shoe and boot cleaning service. Some entrepreneurs may own huge construction companies. Others may own tiny craft shops. Entrepreneurs try to identify what customers need. Then they meet those needs by offering a product or service. When they succeed, their businesses do well, and they make money. When they fail, their companies do not make enough money to pay their bills. They may have to go out of business.

Employees and Entrepreneurs

Entrepreneurs are willing to take chances to try to create a successful business. Entrepreneurs are different from employees. **Employees** are people who work for someone else. Both may make decisions, but only entrepreneurs are responsible for what happens to the business because of the decisions they make.

Mike Jones manages a video store owned by Felipe Santiago. Mike decides to keep the store open until midnight during the week. He thinks the additional hours will bring in customers and increase profits. If Mike's idea works, Felipe will be happy. He may even give Mike a raise in pay. Mike will not directly receive any of the additional money that is made because he is only an employee. The additional earnings will go to Felipe because he is the owner.

Why Do People Become Entrepreneurs?

People become entrepreneurs for many reasons. Adults may want to leave the business world because they have to travel. They may not like spending a lot of time away from home. Some want to be at home but still earn an income. Others want to do something they have dreamed about doing for a long time. The reason you might become an entrepreneur may be different. Some of the reasons that young people go into business are:

- to be their own boss
- to earn lots of money
- to use their skills and abilities
- to meet a challenge
- to help their community or provide jobs for others
- to build security for their family

These are all good reasons to start a business. Some of these will not be as easy to achieve as you might think. Your hard work will pay off because there are many rewards for entrepreneurs.

CHECKPOINT

→ What does an entrepreneur do?

Types of Entrepreneurial Businesses

Entrepreneurs can choose the type of business they open. The different types of businesses include manufacturing, wholesaling, retailing, and service businesses.

A **manufacturing business** makes the products it sells. Computers are manufactured by companies like IBM, Gateway, Toshiba, Dell, and Apple.

Many manufacturers sell the products they make to a wholesaling business. The **wholesaling business** sells the products it buys to someone

If you run a music store, what type of business is it?

© DIGITAL VISION

Types of Entrepreneurial Businesses

Manufacturing	Wholesaling	Retailing	Service
Clothing and other fabric products	Clothing	Auto and home supply stores	Appliance repair
Chemicals and related products	Electrical goods	Building materials and supply stores	Automotive repair
Electronics and other electrical equipment	Groceries and related products	Clothing stores	Babysitting
Metal products	Hardware, plumbing, heating equipment	Florists	Bookkeeping
Food products	Lumber, construction materials	Furniture stores	Consulting (advising)
Industrial machinery and equipment	Machinery, equipment, supplies	Gift, novelty, and souvenir stores	Dance instruction
Printing and publishing	Automobiles, automotive equipment	Grocery stores	Electrical services
Rubber and plastic products	Paper, paper products	Hardware stores	Pest exterminators
Stone, clay, and glass products	Petroleum (oil), petroleum products	Jewelry stores	Flower decorating
		Retail bakeries	House cleaning
		Shoe stores	Lawn care
		Sporting goods and bicycle stores	Painting
			Plumbing
			Travel agency
			Tutoring

else. For example, IBM may sell computers to a wholesaler. The wholesaler pays less for the product than the final customer will pay. The wholesaler will sell the computers to your local computer store. The computer store will pay the wholesaler a higher price than the wholesaler paid the manufacturer.

Your local computer store is a **retailing business**. It will sell the computers directly to you or other customers. You will be the final user of the computer. You will pay the retailer more for the computers than the retailer paid to the wholesaler.

Service businesses sell services rather than products. Examples of service businesses include lawn mowing services and hair and nail salons.

The chart above shows examples of the four different types of

businesses. Take a few minutes to review the chart. Think about examples of each type of business in your neighborhood.

Other Business Areas

Two other types of businesses are (1) agricultural and (2) mining and extracting businesses. Agricultural businesses provide fresh produce and other farm products, such as wheat. Mining and extracting businesses take resources such as coal out of the ground so that they can be used.

Working Together

Work in small groups. List three local or national businesses for each of the four types of entrepreneurial businesses.

CHECKPOINT

→ If you want to start a pet walking business, what type of business would you be opening? If you own a bookstore, what type of business is it?

Entrepreneurs in U.S. History

During the colonial years, entrepreneurship grew. Entrepreneurs raised crops like rice and tobacco. They also worked as bankers, silversmiths, candle makers, and merchants that traded and sold goods and services. After the American Revolution, the United States began to industrialize. Entrepreneurs invented machines that helped workers do their jobs faster and better and helped the economy grow.

Entrepreneurs Who Changed America

Entrepreneurs change American business decade after decade. They start with ideas that may grow into huge companies. They constantly change how things are done. They contribute to the good of the nation.

Nineteenth-Century Entrepreneurs In 1831, Cyrus McCormick used a machine called the *reaper* to gather crops. The reaper gave the U.S. economy a major boost. McCormick went to Chicago with $60 in his pocket. He opened a factory to make reapers. In time, the company that made his reapers became International Harvester. The company made farm equipment for many years. Today, the company is called Navistar International Transportation Company. It makes International brand trucks.

Lydia Moss Bradley was an entrepreneur from Peoria, Illinois. She made millions of dollars through investments and real estate. She changed unusable marshland into pro-

How did the reaper change the farming business?

© GETTY IMAGES/PHOTODISC

You would like to open your own business some day. To help you prepare, you decide to explore businesses in the four different business areas. These areas are *manufacturing*, *wholesaling*, *retailing*, and *service*. Select a business that interests you from one of these areas. Make a list of questions that you would ask to help you learn more about the business.

ductive farmland. She also founded Bradley University in Peoria in 1896.

When he was 16, John D. Rockefeller worked as a clerk in a small produce company. In 1870, he had saved enough money to enter the oil refinery business. By 1881, his company, Standard Oil, controlled 90 percent of America's oil business. Before long, Rockefeller controlled almost all oil distribution in the United States. Eventually, he became the richest man in America. By today's standards, Rockefeller was even richer than Bill Gates of Microsoft Corporation is now.

How did John D. Rockefeller make his fortune in the oil business?

© PHOTO COLLECTION ALEXANDER ALLAND, SR./CORBIS

1.1 What Do Entrepreneurs Do?

Early Twentieth-Century Entrepreneurs Entrepreneurs were very important in the twentieth century. For example, Henry Ford developed and mass-produced the Model-T automobile. He sold the Model-T at a price many Americans could afford. Ford was a machinist from Detroit. He created one of the largest companies in the world.

During the early part of the twentieth century, Olive Ann Beech co-founded the Beech Aircraft Company with her husband. She managed the finances of the company and took part in major company decisions. She ran the business when her husband became ill in 1940. With Beech in charge, the company continued to be a leader in the aviation industry. In 1980, Beech's company merged with the Raytheon Company, which is still in business.

In the 1920s, Clarence Birdseye developed packaged frozen foods. His frozen foods affected eating habits throughout the world.

Madam C. J. Walker was the first African-American millionaire. Walker began making her own hair treatments in 1905 and sold them door-to-door to other African-American women. In 1908, Walker opened Lelia College, where she trained other women to use and sell her products.

Later Twentieth-Century Entrepreneurs During the latter part of the twentieth century, there were many opportunities for entrepreneurs. The biggest opportunity came in the 1990s when Internet use was beginning to grow. Many people started dot.com, or Internet-based, businesses. However, many businesses were not well planned or researched. Investors lost millions of dollars. Pets.com is an example of a dot.com company that failed. The company had large amounts of funding and publicity. However, it still went out of business in only two years.

Entrepreneurs Today

More than 23.6 million small businesses add billions of dollars every year to the U.S. economy. Small business is very important in America. Small businesses employ more workers than all of the country's large companies combined. The graph on the next page shows that businesses with fewer than 20 employees account for most of the businesses in the United States.

Small businesses are found throughout our economy. Companies such as Microsoft, Intel, and Apple all started as small businesses. These companies have changed the workplace by making computers available to

© GETTY IMAGES/PHOTODISC

How did frozen food change our eating habits?

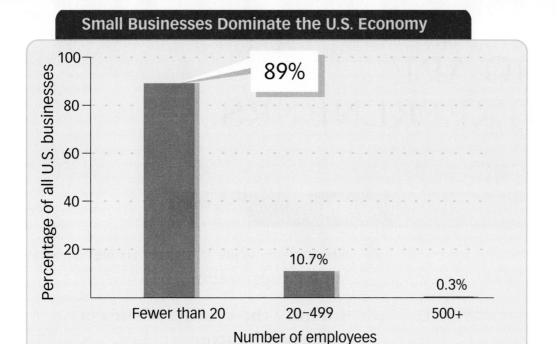

Small Businesses Dominate the U.S. Economy

Percentage of all U.S. businesses

89%

10.7%

0.3%

Fewer than 20   20–499   500+

Number of employees

the world. Other entrepreneurial companies include Southwest Airlines, Mrs. Fields Cookies, and Estée Lauder Cosmetics. These companies make life more pleasant for their customers. They also provide jobs to hundreds of thousands of workers.

CHECKPOINT

→ Name one entrepreneur in U.S. history. Describe what he or she did.

1.1 **LET'S GET REAL**

1 **THINK ABOUT YOURSELF** Why do you want to become an entrepreneur? Do you think all entrepreneurs have the same reasons for starting a business? Are some of your reasons different?

2 **WHAT DO YOU THINK?** What other entrepreneurs in the nineteenth or twentieth century have changed America? How?

3 **MATH CONNECTION** Suppose there are exactly 5,812,000 small businesses in the economy today. Approximately 27 percent of those businesses are service businesses. What is the number of service businesses in the economy?

4 **COMMUNICATION CONNECTION** Clarence Birdseye developed the first packaged frozen foods. Write a paragraph describing what you think a typical family's daily eating habits were like before frozen foods were available.

WHO ARE ENTREPRENEURS?

Terms

consumers
characteristics

Goals

* **Describe what it takes to become an entrepreneur.**

* **Identify the characteristics of successful entrepreneurs.**

* **Discuss the advantages and disadvantages of entrepreneurship.**

What It Takes To Become an Entrepreneur

Many people dream of running their own business. They would like to become entrepreneurs. Entrepreneurship can be exciting. But running your own business is difficult. In fact, many companies that are started by entrepreneurs go out of business. These companies often fail because of poor planning or lack of business knowledge. They also may fail because the entrepreneur chooses the wrong business or does not have entrepreneurial characteristics.

An entrepreneur can be anyone who has a great idea that can be turned into a business. Ideas may come from hobbies or interests. They also

© GETTY IMAGES/PHOTODISC

How could you turn your love of baking into a business?

may come from other work experience, such as a part-time job. Entrepreneurs can be any age and from any educational background. They have good business ideas that meet the needs of customers. They also have the desire and drive to see their idea become a business.

Examples of successful businesses started by young entrepreneurs are:

- car washing or detailing
- t-shirt design
- web site creation and design
- lawn mowing or landscaping
- bakery or catering
- Internet radio station

These are only a few of the kinds of businesses young entrepreneurs have started. These young people saw their ideas as an opportunity and started their businesses!

Entrepreneurs as Consumers

Entrepreneurs also are customers, or **consumers**. As a customer, you know what you like. You know what you want to buy. For example, you may have a favorite restaurant. Maybe it's your favorite because it serves great food. Or, maybe it's your favorite because it has a video game arcade. Entrepreneurs can use this knowledge to their advantage. When thinking about starting a business, you can make a list of the things you like and dislike about similar companies or products. You can think about these likes and dislikes when starting your business. Then, you can offer products or services that will meet your customers' needs better than those offered by competitors.

CHECKPOINT
→ Can anyone be an entrepreneur? Explain.

Characteristics of Successful Entrepreneurs

Characteristics are qualities that make a person different from others. Researchers have found several characteristics that set successful entrepreneurs apart from those who fail.

1. **Successful entrepreneurs are independent.** They want to make their own decisions. They also want to do something they enjoy.

2. **Successful entrepreneurs are self-confident.** Entrepreneurs make all the decisions. They must have the confidence to make choices alone. They also must be able to bounce back if they make a poor decision.

3. **Successful entrepreneurs are determined.** Entrepreneurs will keep trying even in hard times until goals are met.

4. **Successful entrepreneurs are focused.** They know what they want, and they focus on achieving it.

5. **Successful entrepreneurs set high standards for themselves.** They constantly set challenging new goals.

6. **Successful entrepreneurs are creative.** They think of new ways to promote their businesses. They are always looking for new and better solutions to problems.

7. **Successful entrepreneurs are able to act quickly.** They are not afraid to make quick decisions. Acting quickly helps them beat their competitors.

As a high school student, Richard always had a talent for getting things done. He was class president throughout high school. He also helped plan and organize events like the prom and graduation. By taking part in these activities, Richard gained self-confidence. He learned that he had to stay focused to succeed. These experiences led him to open his own floral business. Today he owns and operates Flower Cottage on Main in Atlanta.

© GETTY IMAGES/PHOTODISC

Why must entrepreneurs be determined and focused?

CHECKPOINT

→ Name three important characteristics of entrepreneurs.

Advantages and Disadvantages of Entrepreneurship

There are several advantages to being an entrepreneur. There are also some disadvantages. Before starting your own business, you should think about both.

Think About the Advantages

Many people see major advantages to owning their own business. Advantages include:

1. **Entrepreneurs are their own bosses.** Nobody tells an entrepreneur what to do. Entrepreneurs control their own future.

2. **Entrepreneurs can choose a business that interests them.** Entrepreneurs work in fields that interest them. Many entrepreneurs combine hobbies and interests with business.

3. **Entrepreneurs can be creative.** Many entrepreneurs use their own creative ideas to make a product or offer a service.

4. **Entrepreneurs can make a lot of money.** Entrepreneurs make money if their business succeeds. However, being an entrepreneur does involve risk.

The advantages of entrepreneurship are attractive to many people. Not everyone will have the personal traits and abilities that are necessary to be successful. You may need to work at developing these traits and abilities.

Working Together

Work in small groups. List the advantages and disadvantages of being an employee. Then list the advantages and disadvantages of being an entrepreneur. Compare the lists.

Why is entrepreneurship a good match for those who are creative?

© GETTY IMAGES/PHOTODISC

Think About the Disadvantages

When thinking about becoming an entrepreneur, you should consider the disadvantages.

1. **Entrepreneurship is risky.** All small businesses run the risk of going out of business or losing money.

2. **Entrepreneurs face uncertain and irregular incomes.** Entrepreneurs may make money one month and lose money the next month. Because they often are the sole owner of the business, they cannot afford many losses.

3. **Entrepreneurs work long hours.** Entrepreneurs never really are finished with their jobs. They can work long, unpredictable hours. They receive no paid days off. They may have to work evenings and weekends.

4. **Entrepreneurs must make all decisions by themselves.** Unless they have partners, entrepreneurs must make all the decisions alone. This can be a problem if the entrepreneur does not have the necessary knowledge.

Entrepreneurship is not easy. The business may fail. The entrepreneur could lose his or her investment and possibly more.

> **CHECKPOINT**
> ➡ What are advantages and disadvantages of entrepreneurship?

1.2 LET'S GET REAL

1] WHAT DO YOU THINK? Entrepreneurs can fail even if they are dedicated and have the characteristics needed to be successful. Why do you think this can happen?

2] THINK ABOUT YOURSELF Do you think the advantages of entrepreneurship are greater than the disadvantages for you? Why or why not?

3] MATH CONNECTION One in four small companies that open this year will be out of business within the next two years. What percentage does this represent?

4] COMMUNICATION CONNECTION Rank the advantages of entrepreneurship in order of importance to you. The item ranked "1" is the most important. The item ranked "4" is the least important. Write a paragraph explaining your rankings.

5] COMMUNICATION CONNECTION Choose one of the seven characteristics of successful entrepreneurs. Write a paragraph explaining why this characteristic is important. Give an example of what could happen to a business if an entrepreneur didn't have this characteristic.

The Hershey Chocolate Company

Have you ever unwrapped a Hershey's Kiss and wondered how the candy came to be? In 1894, Milton Hershey was making caramels in Lancaster, Pennsylvania. He started the Hershey Chocolate Company to make sweet chocolate to coat his caramels. In 1900, the company started producing milk chocolate in bars, wafers, and other shapes. Before 1900, milk chocolate had been a luxury for only the wealthy. Mr. Hershey used mass production to lower the cost so that everyone could afford to buy his chocolate.

The early success of the company led Mr. Hershey to expand his business. He located his new chocolate factory in south central Pennsylvania. The new factory was close to the ports of New York and Philadelphia. This location made it easy to get imported sugar and cocoa. There also were many dairy farms nearby to provide the milk needed. Just as importantly, this area provided a local supply of employees that were hard working.

After opening the new factory in 1907, the company began producing a flat-bottomed, cone-shaped milk chocolate candy. Mr. Hershey named the new candy Hershey's Kiss Chocolates. In 1924, the company had the Kiss trademarked.

Through the next two decades, the company added more chocolate products. Some of these products included Mr. Goodbar, Hershey's Syrup, chocolate chips, and the Krackel bar. These new products helped the company survive the Great Depression in the 1930s.

In 1968, the company was renamed Hershey Foods Corporation. It has bought related companies and has added other food products. Today, the corporation has about 13,700 employees and sells its products to over 90 countries. The corporation remains committed to the vision and values of the man who started it all in 1894.

Think Critically

1. Why was Mr. Hershey able to offer chocolate to more people at a lower cost?
2. Why was the location of the new factory important to the growth of the company?
3. What has played a part in the company's continued growth?

SHOULD YOU BE AN ENTREPRENEUR?

Terms

self-assessment
aptitude
resources
commitment

Goals

* **List your interests.**

* **Define your aptitudes.**

* **Identify your resources and commitment.**

Think about Your Interests

Entrepreneurship is not for everyone. Some people lack the qualities needed to become successful entrepreneurs. Others lack the ability to run a business. For others, the advantages do not outweigh the disadvantages. To determine if entrepreneurship is right for you, you first need to do a **self-assessment** by thinking about your strengths and weaknesses. You can do this in a number of ways. You can list your strengths and weaknesses on a sheet of paper. You can ask others what they believe your strengths and weaknesses are. You also can take tests to identify your strongest abilities.

Success as an entrepreneur calls for a strong commitment to a business. It also takes a lot of energy. To be able to commit yourself fully to a business, you should choose a field that inter-

© GETTY IMAGES/PHOTODISC

ests you. You should choose a business that you will enjoy.

Hobbies and Interests

Many entrepreneurs build a business on an interest or hobby. Tricia Johnson loved reading mysteries. She also was interested in collecting books. Tricia created Royal Books. Her company buys and sells new, used, and rare books, especially mystery books. Making a list of hobbies and interests can help you decide what business is right for you.

Past Experiences

Thinking about past experiences and jobs can help you decide on a business you would enjoy. Sam Rodriguez worked as a customer service representative for a large company. From this job experience, he learned that he would prefer a job where he could spend time outdoors. Sam formed his own bicycle messenger service. He now earns less money than he did as a customer service representative, but he enjoys the work that he is doing.

© GETTY IMAGES/PHOTODISC

Why should entrepreneurs know their interests?

CHECKPOINT

➡ List three interests you have. What business idea could come from your interests?

What aptitudes would you need to work with children?

mechanical problems. They also must be good with their hands. People who sell insurance must enjoy meeting people and get along well with others. Answering questions like those in the Job Traits Checklist below can help you find the kinds of jobs that match your aptitudes and interests.

As a middle school student, Sara found that she had an aptitude for working with computers. She learned how to use a variety of software. She also learned how to make simple repairs and how to install disk drivers and networks. In high school, she started her own computer repair and consulting business. Using her aptitudes, Sara was able to earn money to help pay for college.

Think about Your Aptitudes

Different jobs require different job aptitudes. **Aptitude** is the ability to learn a particular kind of job. Auto mechanics must have an aptitude for solving

> **CHECKPOINT**
>
> → What does it mean to have an aptitude for something?

Working Together

As a class, suggest five possible jobs for each item on the Job Traits Checklist. Choose two people to write all the suggestions on the board or on paper.

JOB TRAITS CHECKLIST

☐ 1. I enjoy working with numbers.

☐ 2. I enjoy working outdoors.

☐ 3. I enjoy working with my hands.

☐ 4. I enjoy selling.

☐ 5. I like working with people.

☐ 6. I prefer to work alone.

☐ 7. I like supervising other people.

☐ 8. I like knowing exactly what I am supposed to do.

Resources and Commitment

In addition to your interests and aptitudes, there are other things to consider when deciding whether you should become an entrepreneur. Do you have the resources and commitment needed to succeed?

Resources

Once you come up with an idea for a business, you will have to decide whether you have the resources to carry out your idea. **Resources** are the things used to create products and services. Resources include human resources (people) and capital resources (money, equipment, and supplies). You should ask yourself the following:

- **Can I operate the business myself or will I need help?** In the beginning, you may be able to run the business yourself. As the business grows, orders for your products or services will increase. You may need to hire or enlist the help of others.

- **How much money will I need to get the business running?** The answer to this question will depend on the type of business. Some businesses need little or no money. For other businesses, you may need to borrow money from friends or family to buy the equipment and supplies to get started.

- **Do I have the equipment and supplies needed to run the business?** Different businesses will need different kinds of equipment and supplies. Many businesses will need a computer, printer, and paper. Other companies will need special equipment, such as tools to make repairs in a bicycle repair business.

Did You Know?

Bill Rancic was the first apprentice chosen by Donald Trump from the television series. Bill had his first entrepreneurial experience when he was 10 years old. His grandmother taught him to cook pancakes. Bill then started making pancake breakfasts for his grandmother's friends.

© DIGITAL VISION

Why are tools considered resources?

Commitment

Successful entrepreneurs need commitment. **Commitment** is a pledge to do something. You have to be willing to commit extra time and effort to start and grow your business. You will have to juggle your time between school, social activities, and your business.

You also have to make a commitment to ongoing training and education. You need to grow with your business by learning about new technologies. For example, there may be a new computer software program that could make running your business easier. The program could save you time and money.

Before you start a business, think about how much time and effort you can commit.

NETBookmark

If you are going to start your own business, you will need to find and keep customers. Without customers, you would not have a business. You can win over customers by earning their trust. Access exploringxtra. swlearning.com and click on the link for Chapter 1. Read the article entitled *No Commitment*. List the five tips on how you can earn a customer's trust.

exploringxtra.swlearning.com

CHECKPOINT

→ Why is it important to have enough resources before you start your business?

1.3 LET'S GET REAL

1] **THINK ABOUT YOURSELF** Choose a business idea that you think you would like. Use the Job Traits Checklist found on the *Activities* CD in the Chapter 1 folder. Compare your aptitudes to your business idea. Is this a good choice for you? Why or why not?

2] **WHAT DO YOU THINK** Using the business idea you have chosen, what resources do you think you would need to start that business? Make a list of the human resources and capital resources you have available to you now. Consider the equipment and supplies you would need to run your business. List any additional resources you might need.

3] **MATH CONECTION** You live near the beach and love to snorkel. Your dream is to give snorkeling lessons. You estimate that after expenses, you can earn $10 per lesson. Your income goal is $15,000 per year. How many lessons do you need to give to reach this goal? Is this goal realistic?

4] **COMMUNICATION CONNECTION** Think about where you would like to be in the future. Write at least five goals that will help you get there.

What Do Entrepreneurs Do?

1. An entrepreneur is a person who provides a product or service for someone else for money. Entrepreneurs also take all the risks of the business. Entrepreneurs try to identify and meet a need for a product or service.

2. Entrepreneurs come from all types of backgrounds. They own all kinds of businesses. These may include manufacturing, wholesaling, retailing, and service businesses.

3. Throughout U.S. history, many entrepreneurs have contributed to the economy. Today, more than 26.3 million small companies contribute greatly to the U.S. economy.

Who Are Entrepreneurs?

4. Entrepreneurs can be anyone at any age with a great idea that can be turned into a business.

5. Entrepreneurs are also consumers. As a customer, you can learn what you like or dislike about products and use that information in your own business.

6. Successful entrepreneurs have many characteristics, such as independence and determination.

7. Advantages of owning your own business include being your own boss and working in a job that you enjoy.

8. Disadvantages include risk, uncertain income, and long hours.

Should You Be an Entrepreneur?

9. To decide whether entrepreneurship is for you, you will need to discover your strengths, weaknesses, and interests. A self-assessment can help you do this.

10. It is important to match your aptitudes with your interests. This will help you find the kind of work that suits you best.

11. In addition to your interests and aptitudes, you must consider other things before becoming an entrepreneur. You must consider your resources and your commitment.

Vocabulary Builder

Choose the term that best fits the definition.

1. Person who works for someone else
2. Examining your strengths and weaknesses
3. Person who provides a product or service for someone else for money
4. Ability to learn a particular kind of job
5. Process of running a business of one's own
6. Things used to create products or services
7. Person who is a customer
8. Business that makes the products it sells
9. Qualities that make a person different from others

a. aptitude
b. characteristics
c. commitment
d. consumer
e. employee
f. entrepreneur
g. enfrepreneurship
h. manufacturing business
i. resources
j. retail business
k. self-assessment
l. service business
m. wholesaling business

Review What You Have Learned

10. What is an entrepreneur?
11. What is the difference between a successful business and an unsuccessful business?
12. What makes an entrepreneur different from an employee?
13. What are some of the reasons that people want to go into business for themselves?
14. List the four major types of entrepreneurial businesses. Briefly describe what they do.
15. Name two early American entrepreneurs and explain what they did.
16. What are some reasons that many new businesses fail?
17. What do you think caused the failure of most of the dot.com businesses in the 1990s?
18. Why are small businesses so important to our economy?
19. Explain how being a customer, or consumer, can help an entrepreneur.
20. What are the seven characteristics of successful entrepreneurs?
21. Describe four advantages of being an entrepreneur.
22. Describe four disadvantages of being an entrepreneur.
23. Why is it important for you to examine your interests and aptitudes before deciding to start a business?
24. Explain why resources are important to an entrepreneur.
25. Why is it important for an entrepreneur to be committed before starting a business?

Using the *Activities* CD, open the Chapter 1 folder. Open the activity Entrepreneurship Aptitude Test. Print a copy and complete the activity.

Think About It

1. You use many products each day to make your life easier or more fun. Choose one product that you use daily. Research the history of the company that produces the product. Find out the entrepreneur who started the company. Prepare a report on the company and the product's beginning.

2. Imagine what your life would be like if an entrepreneur had never made the product available. Write a one-page description of how your life would be different without this product.

Project: Making Entrepreneurship Work for You

This activity will help you identify a business opportunity that may be right for you. You will build on your business ideas in the projects at the end of each chapter.

1. Divide a sheet of paper into two columns. In the first column list all your interests. In the second column, list business opportunities that relate to each interest.

2. Make a list of your strengths and weaknesses. Compare this list with your list of business opportunities. Based on your strengths and weaknesses, cross out the business opportunities that no longer seem right for you.

3. Use the Job Traits Checklist in the Chapter 1 folder on the *Activities* CD. Put a check mark next to the business opportunities that match your aptitudes.

4. For the business opportunities left on your list, list the advantages and disadvantages of each one. Cross out any whose disadvantages outweigh its advantages.

5. Use the library or Internet to find sources of information about the business opportunities on your list. Make a list of these sources. For each source, write a sentence about the type of information it offers. Cross out business opportunities for which you could not find any information.

Chapter 2

What Entrepreneurial Skills Do You Need?

© DIGITAL VISION

It Adds Up to Success

A teacher gave eighth-grade student Raynece Leader-Thompson a choice of projects. Raynece could participate in her school's annual science fair, or she could enter the Oklahoma State Inventor's Exposition. Raynece had already built science projects for several other classes. She decided to invent something for the Inventor's Exposition. But what could she build? That was the problem.

Raynece had always loved math. She noticed that some of the middle-school students had problems with basic skills. She and her mom decided that Raynece's invention should focus on math. Raynece wanted to find a way to make math more fun to learn. Since most kids like games, she decided to create a game that would make learning math seem like play. Raynece began creating her math game by using dice and cards she found around the house. She came up with many versions before she finally got it right.

Raynece invented a game called Math-A-Mania. It focuses on addition, subtraction, and multiplication skills. Raynece's teacher was very impressed with the model Raynece submitted for the Inventor's Exposition. She gave the model to the school's sixth-grade math teacher to play in class. The sixth graders liked the game so much that their teacher wanted to buy the game as a teaching aid. As word of the game spread, other local teachers wanted to buy the game too.

Raynece and her mother hadn't planned on making a business out of Math-A-Mania. But the response to the game caused them to think again. They worked with the local chamber of commerce. SCORE, the Service Corps of Retired Executives, also helped them set up their own business. Their new business is called Math Works. It makes, markets, and sells the game. Raynece is vice president. Her mother is president. Three years after it began, Math Works has grown to eight employees. Raynece receives invitations every month to demonstrate Math-A-Mania for school districts across the country.

WHAT DO YOU KNOW?

1 What kinds of skills did Raynece use to create Math-A-Mania? What skills did she use to start her business and sell the game?

2 What skills do you have that would help you start your own business?

WHAT COMMUNICATION SKILLS DO YOU NEED?

Terms

business letter
business e-mail
memorandum
interoffice memo
agenda

Goals

* **Apply good writing skills to business letters and business e-mails.**

* **Describe good speaking skills for meetings and telephone calls.**

* **Explain the importance of using good listening skills.**

© GETTY IMAGES/PHOTODISC

Writing Skills

You and your friends write e-mails and instant messages. People in the business world can communicate by e-mail, but they also write letters and memos. To succeed as an entrepreneur, your writing skills must be very good. You will use these skills every day.

As an entrepreneur, you will need to use writing skills as you work with customers, suppliers, and employees. You will need to develop your business writing skills so that all these people will be able to understand what you are communicating. Good business writing gets ideas across clearly. It helps you get what you want from others.

Effective Business Letters

The most common form of business writing is the **business letter**. You might write letters to ask people to do business with you or to answer customer questions. You might write letters to try to get better prices from those who supply items for your business. Writing a business letter is different from writing a letter to a friend. A business letter is more formal. Certain standards must be followed. But business writing should not be difficult to understand. If it cannot be understood, the desired result may not happen. Good business writing is clear. It makes sense and is concise (short and to the point). It gets its message across simply and positively.

Certain basic rules should be followed when writing business letters.

1. **Key all business letters.** Handwrite letters only when you are writing to friends or family.

2. **Spell all names correctly and use the correct address.** Misspelling a person's name or the name of the company will create a poor impression. Using an incorrect address may cause the letter to arrive late or to be returned.

Sample Business Letter

Andrew's Lawn Services
10 E. 34th Street • Baltimore, MD 21218 • (410) 555-4321

April 11, 20—

Ms. Jane Cartright
6028 Sareva Drive
Baltimore, MD 21209

Dear Ms. Cartright

I would like to take the opportunity to introduce myself to you and tell you a little about Andrew's Lawn Services. I am the owner and am excited to offer my services to you.

I live in your neighborhood and have been providing lawn services for my family and friends for several years. I recently have expanded my business, and I am currently taking on new customers. I provide many different lawn services including, lawn mowing, weed trimming, mulching, fertilizing, and watering. I strive to provide both beautiful lawns and excellent customer service.

I would love the opportunity to talk to you about your lawn needs. Please call me to learn more about Andrew's Lawn Services. I have excellent references, which I'd be happy to provide.

Sincerely

Mark A. Andrews

Mark A. Andrews
Owner

WAYS TO CLOSE A BUSINESS LETTER

Sincerely

Sincerely yours

Cordially

Cordially yours

Respectfully yours

Very truly yours

3. **Always date your business letters.** You may need to refer to this date at a later time.

4. **Use names and titles correctly.** Use the person's first name only if you know him or her well. If you do not know the person or if the letter is formal, use the person's last name along with the appropriate title. Titles may include Dr., Mr., Mrs., Ms., or Miss.

5. **Be direct and positive.** Always use a positive tone. Talk about your business with confidence, even if your letter contains bad news.

6. **Be persuasive and specific.** Make sure readers will understand exactly what you want them to do. Use non-threatening language that will persuade readers that this action or result is the best thing for them to do.

7. **Avoid using fancy language.** Avoid phrases that you would not use while speaking. Use plain, simple language that says exactly what you mean.

8. **Be polite.** Deal with complaints in a businesslike manner. Don't whine or get angry. Never become rude or insulting.

9. **Use a suitable closing.** There are many ways to close a letter. Make sure your closing matches the content of the letter. If you have written a letter to a supplier complaining about poor service, do not use "with warmest regards" in your closing.

10. **Proofread for spelling and grammatical errors.** Even the most persuasive and positive letter can be ruined by a single mistake. Read the letter and correct all mistakes before sending it to anyone.

Effective Business E-mail

A **business e-mail** is different from one that you might send to a friend. A business e-mail should be more formal and written in the same way a business letter is written. Spelling and grammar are important. The e-mail should be written in a clear, concise way. When a quick answer or solution is needed, e-mail can save time.

A **memorandum** is a short written form of business communication. *Memo* is short for memorandum. E-mail is now the most common way to send memos. A memo generally has a set format. The format shows the sender and receiver of the memo. It also shows the date and the subject of the memo.

You can e-mail a memo to people working inside or outside of your company. An **interoffice memo** is a memo from one person in a company to another person in the same company. Interoffice memos can be e-mailed to

DARCI O'DELL

From: Darci O'Dell [dodell@internet.com]
Sent: Monday, January 09, 20— 12:22 PM
To: Jason Baxter; Casey Nelson;
Thomas Riley; Mario Torres;
Jennifer Williams
Subject: December Sales

Thanks to all the employees of Darci's Rings and Things Jewelry Store for making December the best month in our company's history. Sales were 20 percent higher than they were in December of the previous year. I know how hard all of you worked during the busy holiday season and I want you to know just how much I appreciate your efforts. Thank you all for a job well done! To celebrate our success, all employees are invited to a dinner on Thursday, January 12 at the Grande Maison restaurant.

Sample Interoffice Memo

one employee, a group of employees, or everyone in the company.

Interoffice memos are used for many purposes. They may be used to share company policies and procedures. They may be used to assign jobs or to announce a change in an employee's job title or duties. They also may be used to congratulate or motivate employees.

Memos are e-mailed to people you work with outside of your company for many reasons. They are a quick and easy way to communicate. They should be positive and persuasive.

CHECKPOINT

➡ What are some of the characteristics of good business writing?

Speaking Skills

Speaking in a business setting is different from talking with your friends. Much of your communication as a business owner will be done at business meetings or on the telephone. How you present yourself will have a big impact on the people with whom you do business.

Meetings

Some of the communication you will have as an entrepreneur will be in person rather than in writing. Meetings can be formal occasions with handouts and agendas. An **agenda** is a list of things to be discussed or done in a meeting. Meetings also can be informal ways to discuss issues and keep everyone informed.

Good speaking skills are important in meetings. You must be able to communicate clearly. Entrepreneurs sometimes hold meetings to give presentations. You may have to present your business ideas to a banker to get a loan to start your business. You may give presentations to customers to get them to buy your products or services.

Make the most of your meetings with customers and others. Use the following tips when you are in a meeting.

1. **Shake hands and make eye contact with the person you are meeting.** If you know the person's name, use it.

2. **Speak clearly.** Do not cover your mouth when you talk. Speak loudly enough to be heard easily.

3. **Be prepared.** Know what you are talking about. Practice your presentation.

4. **Be enthusiastic.** Make your presentation exciting. Try to get people's attention in the first minute of your meeting.

5. **Show an interest in what the other person is saying.** Ask questions or provide responses to show that you are listening carefully and care about what the other person is saying.

6. **Do not appear rushed to be somewhere else.** If you do not have the time to meet with the person, apologize and schedule another time to meet.

7. **Thank the person at the end of the meeting.** Express your interest in seeing the person again. Be sure you leave your contact information in case the person has a question at a later time.

Telephone Conversations

You will often do business over the telephone. Use the following tips to make the most of your telephone conversations.

1. **Speak clearly.** Talk directly into the receiver.

2. **Be cheerful.** Everyone prefers to deal with a happy person. No one likes to speak with someone who is sad or angry.

3. **Always speak politely.** Don't use improper language or slang. Be respectful. Don't interrupt.

4. **Think about what you are going to say before you make a call.** Write down the

© DIGITAL VISION

Why are notes helpful during telephone conversations?

questions you want to ask or the points you want to make. Refer to your notes to make sure you cover everything.

5. **Take notes.** You may forget important details unless you write them down.

> **CHECKPOINT**
> → Give three tips for conducting a meeting and three tips for speaking on the telephone.

Listening Skills

Have your parents or teachers ever told you that you were not listening to them? Have you ever missed an important assignment in school because you were not listening to your teacher? Listening is an important skill for entrepreneurs. By listening carefully, an entrepreneur can find ways to help the business grow and prevent problems.

Listen to Customers

Entrepreneurs know that the success of a business depends on satisfying the needs of customers. Therefore, it is important to listen carefully to customers.

Coy Funk and Skylar Schipper learned the importance of listening to their customers. They began their business, Manure Gourmet, while in the eighth grade. Manure Gourmet sells soil nutrient products. Their customers were constantly asking them for advice. Customers wanted to know which products were good for certain plants. So Coy and Skylar did research to find the nutrient values of different types of manure. They wanted to know which ones were best for which plants. They also wanted to know how much should be applied. They developed a list that provided their customers with this information. This service helped their business get off to a good start—all because they listened to their customers.

Why is listening important to the success of a business?

Listen to Employees

Problems in business often occur because people fail to listen to each other. Ariel Martin is the owner of a neighborhood bakery. Her employees asked for an air conditioner for the back room. Ariel was busy with other matters and failed to listen to their request. The employees became angry over their working conditions. All four of her bakers walked off their jobs one afternoon. Ariel had to close the shop for a short time to deal with the problem.

Improve Listening Skills

As a business owner, you will need to listen carefully to your employees. You will need to listen to bankers, suppliers, and customers too. You should listen to anyone that may affect your business. What can you do to improve your listening skills?

1. **Focus your attention on the person who is speaking.** Concentrate totally on what the person is saying.

2. **Try to understand what the other person is saying.** Listen carefully and resist the urge to interrupt.

3. **Ask questions to make sure you understand what the person is saying.** After the person is done speaking, ask questions to make sure you have all the information you need.

4. **Take notes to confirm what you are hearing.** Refer back to your notes to help answer questions that may come up later.

> **CHECKPOINT**
> → Why is it important for entrepreneurs to listen carefully?

2.1 **LET'S GET REAL**

1] **THINK ABOUT YOURSELF** Think about your communication skills. Make a list of your strengths and weaknesses in writing, speaking, and listening. Make a plan to improve your weaknesses.

2] **WHAT DO YOU THINK?** Why do you think it is important for an entrepreneur to have good communication skills?

3] **LANGUAGE ARTS CONNECTION** Assume that you own a business. You need to write a letter to a supplier about a shipment that you received late. The late shipment caused you to lose a sale of $2,500. Now you have no need for the shipment. Use the basic rules for effective business letters. Explain to the supplier what happened and ask to return the goods.

4] **COMMUNICATION CONNECTION** You and your friends have started a babysitting service. Your neighborhood Homeowner's Association has invited you to speak about your services at the next meeting. Work with a partner. Prepare a PowerPoint presentation about your services to give to your class.

WHAT MATH SKILLS DO YOU NEED?

Terms

- income
- expense
- profit
- loss
- interest
- markup
- markdown
- transaction
- sales tax

Goals

* **Identify how basic math skills are used in business.**

* **Explain how to calculate percentages for business purposes.**

* **Explain how to calculate markups and markdowns.**

* **Discuss the importance of keeping records of sales transactions.**

Basic Math Skills

The math skills that you learn will be helpful to you if you decide to open your own business. Entrepreneurs use math skills for many things. As an entrepreneur, you should know how to use addition, subtraction, multiplication, and division. You also should know how to calculate simple averages and percentages.

Addition and Subtraction

Addition and subtraction skills are essential to running a business. John Sillay started painting the inside and outside of people's homes during the summers when he was 15 years old. John has been in business for two years. He is now thinking about specializing by offering either inside or outside painting only. He wants to know which of his services has made

© DIGITAL VISION

the most money over the past two years. John knows that he must compare his income with his expenses.

Income is the money made from providing a good or service. **Expenses** are the costs of supplies that are used in a business. If income is greater than expenses, there is a **profit**. If expenses are greater than income, there is a **loss**. John reviewed his business records. Using addition and subtraction, he found the following information.

	Income		
	Year 1	Year 2	Total
Inside Painting	$1,800 +	$1,500 =	$3,300
Outside Painting	$1,500 +	$2,000 =	$3,500

John made more money painting outside than he made painting inside. He also must consider the expenses of the materials that he uses. John found the following expenses in his business records.

	Expenses		
	Year 1	Year 2	Total
Inside Painting	$400 +	$350 =	$750
Outside Painting	$350 +	$450 =	$800

The expenses for outside painting were more than the expenses for inside painting. Comparing the income from inside and outside painting and the expenses for each, John calculated his profit.

	Income	−	Expenses	=	Profit
Inside Painting	$3,300	−	$750	=	$2,550
Outside Painting	$3,500	−	$800	=	$2,700

Based on his calculations, John learns that he made more profit painting outside than he did painting inside. He decides that in his third year of business he will offer only outside painting. By focusing on outside painting, John's profits should increase.

Multiplication

Multiplication is used to solve a variety of business problems, such as figuring expenses. John has found that it takes about one gallon of paint to paint an average-size room in a house. The paint that he uses costs $17 per gallon. If John is going to paint six rooms, he can calculate the expenses for painting the inside of the home.

Number of gallons	×	Cost per gallon	=	Total paint expense
6	×	$17	=	$102

John's total expense for paint would be $102.

Division

John wants to know generally how much money he is making per hour. Using division, he can calculate his wage per hour. John charges $150 for each room that he paints. It takes him about two hours to get the room ready for painting. It takes another six hours to actually paint the room. He calculates his wage per hour using the following formula.

Charge per room	÷	Total hours per room	=	Wage per hour
$150	÷	8	=	$18.75

Averages

It is helpful for entrepreneurs to know averages of such things as expenses and number of hours worked. Averages can help entrepreneurs budget their money and schedule their time. Averages can be calculated using addition and division.

Hope Stallings babysits for families in her neighborhood. She wants to know the average number of hours that she babysat each week for the months of June and July. This will help her estimate her hours for upcoming months. Hope reviews her records and finds the following information:

Hours Worked	June	July
Week 1	32	48
Week 2	39	38
Week 3	41	36
Week 4	40	38
Total	152	160

After she calculates the number of hours she worked each month, Hope adds the hours for June and the hours for July together to find the total hours she worked for both months.

June total hours	+	July total hours	=	Total hours worked
152	+	160	=	312

Hope then divides her total hours worked by the number of weeks she worked to find the average number of hours worked each week.

Total hours worked	÷	Number of weeks worked	=	Average hours per week
312	÷	8	=	39

CHECKPOINT

→ Give an example of when you might use addition, subtraction, multiplication, or division in business.

Percentages

Percentages are used for many business purposes. Working with percents usually requires changing the percents to decimals. Percent means per hundred. To change a percent to a decimal, remember that 100 percent in decimal form is 1.00.

To convert a percent to a decimal, move the decimal point two places to the left. For example, 14 percent is 0.14 in decimal form, and 1 percent is 0.01 in decimal form.

To convert a decimal to a percent, move the decimal point two places to the right. So 0.263 is 26.3 percent.

Rounding

Sometimes it is easier to work with numbers that are rounded. You should round up numbers five or more. You should round down numbers less than five. For example, if you want to round to one decimal place, round 0.66 up to 0.7, and round 0.64 down to 0.6.

Interest

Interest is an amount that can be earned on money that is invested. Interest can also be paid on money that is borrowed. When you borrow money, you pay interest to the bank or person who loans you the money. The interest rate is stated as a percentage. The amount of interest that you pay depends on the length of time for which you borrow the money. The formula for calculating interest paid is:

How are math skills used to calculate interest?

$$\text{Amount borrowed} \times \text{Interest rate} \times \text{Length of time money borrowed} = \text{Interest paid}$$

If you borrow $1,500 at a rate of 4.5 percent for one year, the interest you would pay would be calculated in the following way:

$$\$1,500 \times 0.045 \times 1 = \$67.50$$

You can earn interest on money that you invest in banks and other savings institutions. The way your bank calculates interest affects the rate at which your savings grows.

Chapter 2 What Entrepreneurial Skills Do You Need?

Simple interest is paid at the end of the year. It is paid only one time per year on the average balance of your savings account.

If you invest $100 for one year at 3 percent, using the simple interest method, you would have $103 at the end of the year ($100 + $3), using the following formula.

Investment	×	Rate of interest	=	Interest earned
$100	×	0.03	=	$3

> **CHECKPOINT**
>
> → Using the simple interest method, how much interest will a $1,000 investment earn for one year invested at 4 percent?

Working Together

Work in small groups. List five items sold in your favorite store. Next to each one write its approximate price. Assume the store wants to sell these items to make room for new merchandise. It applies a 35 percent markdown to each item. What is the new selling price of each item on your list? Share your results with the class.

Markups and Markdowns

A **markup** is an amount added to the cost of an item to determine the selling price. Markups allow you to cover expenses and earn a profit. A **markdown** is an amount subtracted from the retail price to determine the selling price. Markdowns are often used to increase sales of certain products, such as seasonal merchandise.

Calculating Markups You make and sell jewelry. You calculate that it costs $14.00 in materials for each necklace that you make. To cover your expenses and make a profit, you estimate that you need to add a markup of 35 percent to determine the selling price.

Cost per necklace	×	Markup percentage	=	Markup amount
$14.00	×	0.35	=	$4.90

Cost per necklace	+	Markup amount	=	Selling price
$14.00	+	$4.90	=	$18.90

Calculating Markdowns You decide that you want to have a sale on the jewelry you made last year that has not yet sold. You are going to offer a 25 percent markdown on necklaces.

Selling price	×	Markdown percentage	=	Markdown amount
$18.90	×	0.25	=	$4.73

Selling price	−	Markdown amount	=	Selling price
$18.90	−	$4.73	=	$14.17

> **CHECKPOINT**
>
> → If the cost of an item is $32 and your markup percentage is 45 percent, what would the selling price of the item be?

Sales Transactions

Entrepreneurs have to keep track of sales transactions so that they will know if they are making a profit. A **transaction** is the exchange of goods or services for money. Sales slips are used to keep a record of transactions when goods or services are sold. Sales tax is often collected on sales transactions and recorded on sales slips.

Sales Slips

You will complete sales slips when goods or services are sold. The sales slip should include a description of the item or service sold. The total amount due is calculated by multiplying the quantity of the item being sold by the unit cost. The unit cost is the cost of one item.

Quantity	×	Unit cost	=	Amount due
5	×	$4.99	=	$24.95

Sales Tax

Retail sales transactions involve sales tax. **Sales tax** is a federal, state, or local government tax charged on goods. Sales tax varies from state to state. It may even vary from city to city. You will need to find out how much sales tax to charge your customers. You will be fined if you do not pay the government this tax.

Sales tax is a percentage. It is calculated using the purchase price of an item you are buying. The sales tax should be added to the purchase price to determine the total selling price. If the sales tax rate is 7 percent, sales tax would be calculated as follows:

Price of purchase	×	Tax rate	=	Amount of sales tax
$24.95	×	0.07	=	$1.75

Price of purchase	+	Amount of sales tax	=	Total selling price
$24.95	+	$1.75	=	$26.70

Cash and Credit Sales Transactions

Eva Sanchez owns Adventure World. It is a retail store that sells sporting and outdoor equipment. She fills out a sales slip form for all of her cash sales. The local sales tax rate is 6 percent.

As her business grows, Eva may decide to let customers pay her with a credit card. Credit card sales are similar to cash sales, but additional information is needed. She will need to record a credit card number and expiration date. A business does not make as much money on a credit card sale as it makes on a cash sale. Whenever a customer uses a credit card to pay for a purchase, the business must pay a fee to the

Cash Sales Slip for Adventure World				
Stock No.	Quantity	Description	Unit Cost	Total
784	2	Skateboard	$32.50	$65.00
912	1	Helmet	$15.00	$15.00
			Subtotal	$80.00
			Sales Tax	4.80
			Total	$84.80

Chapter 2 What Entrepreneurial Skills Do You Need?

Be Your Own Boss

You are going to open a new business. You will make and sell tie-dye t-shirts. You use two different colors of dye to make each t-shirt. You have determined that your expenses will be as follows:

t-shirts	$5.50 each
fabric dye	$2.00 per color

If you are hoping to make a profit of $5.00 on each t-shirt you sell, what price will you have to charge? If you sell, 12 t-shirts at this price, what is your total profit?

bank that issues the credit card. The bank pays the business the amount charged by the customer. Then, the bank collects the payment from the customer.

CHECKPOINT

→ Why is it important for an entrepreneur to keep a written record of sales transactions?

2.2 LET'S GET REAL

1] THINK ABOUT YOURSELF Think about your basic math skills. Have you made good grades in math in school? Are you able to complete simple math problems without using a calculator? Write a paragraph identifying your best math skills and your weakest. List ideas for improving your weaknesses.

2] WHAT DO YOU THINK? What do you think would happen if you made a math error when you were preparing a sales slip for a customer? If the total is too low, what would happen to you? If the total is too high, how would the customer react?

3] MATH CONNECTION You have started a cookie baking business. You have calculated the cost of making each cookie at 23 cents. You want to mark up the cost of the cookie by 45 percent. What would the selling price be?

4] MATH CONNECTION Using the Sales Slip form in the Chapter 2 folder on the *Activities* CD, complete a sales slip for the following items. Add 7 percent sales tax to find the total.

2 bottles of shampoo at $2.45 each
2 bottles of nail polish at $4.25 each
2 tubes of toothpaste at $2.50 each
2 toothbrushes at $1.89 each

WHAT PROBLEM-SOLVING SKILLS DO YOU NEED?

Terms

alternatives
brainstorming

Goals

✳ **Identify the six steps in the problem-solving model.**

✳ **Explain why creativity is important in problem solving.**

Problem-Solving Model

Have you ever been faced with a big problem that you were not sure how to solve? You probably talked to your parents or your friends about what you should do. You may have talked to someone else whose advice you trust. With their help, you came up with the best solution to the problem. When you own your own business, you will have to make decisions and solve problems every day. Many entrepreneurs make decisions carelessly. Sometimes they base decisions on their feelings. As a result, their decisions often are not based on solid facts or on what is best for the business. The best entrepreneurs use problem-solving models to gather information and evaluate different solutions.

A problem-solving model helps businesspeople solve problems logically. The model consists of six steps. The first three steps include defining the problem, gathering information, and identifying different solutions. The final three steps are evaluating the alternatives and selecting the best option, taking action, and evaluating the action taken.

Define the Problem

Before you can solve a problem, you need to define it. Write down what the problem is and why it is a problem. Then try to put a value on it. For example, your store may be out of stock 14 times a month, costing you $102 a month in lost profits. Putting a value on the problem helps you calculate how much it is worth to you to correct it.

Will Peterson knows what his problem is. Will has been operating a pet-sitting service for three summers. He has made over $1,000 each summer. Because Will worked during the past three summers, he was not able to go on family vacations or attend summer camp with his friends. He does not want to turn away customers, but he wants to have time to do some of the things he enjoys during the summer.

Gather Information

Once the problem has been defined, you need to gather information to help solve it. Information may be found in company records and industry data. Industry data includes information about similar businesses. Information also may be obtained from interviews with customers, suppliers, and employees.

To get ideas on how to handle his problem, Will needs to talk to other pet sitters to see how they

Problem-Solving Model

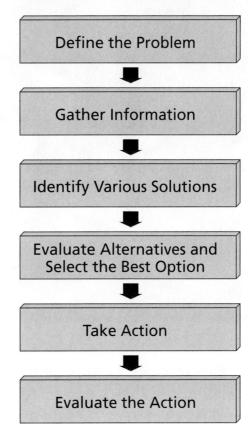

handle this same problem. He knows three other people who offer this service in his area. Will decides to call each one of them for advice.

Identify Various Solutions

Most problems can be solved in a variety of ways. Identify all options before you decide on a solution. Will came up with several possible solutions to his problem.

1. Continue to keep the same work schedule and miss out on family vacations and summer camp.

2. Choose three weeks during the summer and tell customers that he cannot accept any jobs during that time.

How did Will solve his pet-sitting business problem?

3. Hire someone to work with him.

4. Make an agreement with another pet sitter to cover Will's customers when he is away. He then will do the same for the other pet sitter when that sitter is away.

Evaluate Alternatives and Select the Best Option

You next need to evaluate the **alternatives**, or choices, to determine the best solution. In some cases, it is possible to calculate the costs and benefits of each option. In other cases, putting a value on each alternative may not be possible. You may just have to rank each one.

Will ranked Option 1 the lowest since he did not want to continue to miss out on his family vacation and summer camp. He ranked Option 2 next to lowest because he did not want to leave his customers without someone to provide pet-sitting services.

He ranked Option 3 second because it is a practical solution. He is not sure that he wants to hire a full-time employee because it would mean less money for him. Will decides that Option 4 is the best solution. This way he will have someone to help him without having to hire a full-time employee. He then will return the favor when the other pet sitter needs to take time off.

Take Action

Once you have selected the best solution to the problem, you need to take action to apply it. Will contacted Brooke Kato, one of the pet sitters he had talked to when he was gathering information. Brooke was having the same problem that he was. Will suggested to Brooke that they help each other during the summer. Brooke loved the idea. They worked out the dates for the summer. They also made an agreement on how they would pay each other.

Evaluate the Action

The problem-solving process is not done until you evaluate your action. Sometimes even a well-thought-out solution may not work. Will's solution seemed to solve the problem. At the end of the summer, his income was more than it had been last year. All of his customers were happy with the service that he and Brooke had provided during the summer.

Why is it okay for entrepreneurs to make mistakes?

> **CHECKPOINT**
> → What are the six steps in the problem-solving process?

Creative Problem Solving

Entrepreneurs are very creative. They often use their creativity skills to solve problems. Entrepreneurs take an idea and turn it into a product or service that people will buy because it solves a specific problem. Creative entrepreneurs have solved problems in many ways. They learn from their mistakes, look for opportunities, and brainstorm ideas.

Learn from Mistakes

Creative people are not afraid to make mistakes. Entrepreneurs must understand that mistakes are likely to happen in the beginning. Mistakes can help you learn what to do or what not to do. This will help you improve upon your ideas. When you read about some of the nation's most famous entrepreneurs, you will find that many of them failed before they came up with a winning idea.

Colonel Sanders of KFC fame is a good example of this. He held many jobs and owned a motel chain, service stations, and other restaurants that were unsuccessful. While running his restaurant, he developed his secret recipe chicken. In 1952, at the age of 62, he began traveling by car across the country selling his chicken. By 1964, there were 600 KFC restaurants in the United States and Canada, and Colonel Sanders sold KFC for $2 million dollars.

Look for Opportunities

What you know about your neighborhood, your friends, and the things people enjoy doing will help you find ideas for a business. Have you ever heard someone say, "I wish there was a product that…" or "I wish there was someone who would…." Using information like this from people that you know will help

Working Together

Work in small groups. Identify a problem that is common to many teenagers. Brainstorm possible solutions to the problem. Share your problem and list of solutions with the class.

Teenagers often find themselves with a lot of free time without anywhere to go to hang out with their friends. Entrepreneurs who can meet the needs of teens by giving them a place to go other than home or work will attract many customers. Malls are a favorite place for teens to go. Many also go to coffee houses and cyber cafés. However, teens are still looking for places that cater to them. Coca-Cola has tested Red Lounges in malls in Chicago and Los Angeles. Red Lounges have video games, custom-built furniture, and music videos and film previews playing on plasma screens. They do have a vending machine offering Coke and other Coca-Cola beverages, but no other marketing or selling is offered.

Think Critically

1. Do you think your community would be a good place for a Red Lounge? Why or why not?

2. What do teens in your area like to do? What type of hangout do you think your friends would like?

you develop ideas for new products or services. Always be on the lookout for unmet needs and problems. Then, think of creative solutions to meet the needs and solve the problems. But remember, every idea is not going to lead to a business opportunity. The idea must be something that will attract and satisfy customers. In the beginning, it should be an idea that will work in your area so that you can test it locally. It also must be something that you have the time and resources to do.

Brainstorm

Brainstorming is a problem-solving method that involves coming up with a large number of fresh ideas. Brainstorming is often done in a group setting, but you can brainstorm ideas by yourself as well. Think about the problem that you are trying to solve. Write down as many possible solutions to the problem as you can think of. Do not be afraid to write down any idea that you have. The point of brainstorming is not to judge ideas as good or bad. The point is to try to come up with as many ideas as possible. Once you have made a list of ideas, you can use the problem-solving model to decide which ideas could possibly be turned into a business opportunity.

CHECKPOINT

→ Why do you think creativity is important to an entrepreneur?

What is the advantage of brainstorming in a group?

1 THINK ABOUT YOURSELF Think about a problem you have had recently. How did you solve it? Were you satisfied with the way you solved the problem? Do you think using the six-step problem-solving model would have helped you reach a better solution to your problem? Why or why not?

2 WHAT DO YOU THINK? Why do you think brainstorming is a good way to come up with solutions to problems?

3 PROBLEM-SOLVING CONNECTION You own a successful shop that buys, sells, and services bicycles. In January, the owner of the building in which you rent space tells you that she has found a buyer for the property. She plans to sell it in six months. Using the six-step problem-solving model, develop a plan for what you will do.

4 COMMUNICATION CONNECTION Your parents do not think you are old enough to start your own business. Using the problem-solving skills that you learned in this lesson, prepare a presentation that will convince your parents that you can handle the responsibilities and pressures of owning your own business. Give the presentation to your class.

Nike

Just do it! Everyone has heard this advertising slogan. The creative brain behind the Nike Corporation and its advertising is entrepreneur Philip Hampson Knight. As the owner, Knight turned a tiny company called Blue Ribbon Sports into Nike Corporation. Today, Nike is the world's largest athletic shoe and sports apparel company.

Knight was a member of the University of Oregon track team. His coach was never satisfied with the running shoes available. He was always trying to find better running shoes and asked Knight to test them. After graduating from college in 1959, Knight enrolled in the Graduate School of Business at Stanford University. A class assignment led him to the idea of creating a new business. Knight developed a blueprint for superior athletic shoes made inexpensively in Japan.

Knight turned his idea into reality. He began selling his Japanese-made athletic shoes at U.S. track meets out of the trunk of his car. In 1971, as a million-dollar seller of shoes, he renamed his company Nike for the Greek winged goddess of victory.

The jogging craze was just beginning, and Nike rode that wave to incredible success. The company pioneered the trend of signing famous athletes to advertise its products. Signing Michael Jordan to advertise a basketball sneaker in 1984 made Nike a household name. Other more controversial celebrity advertisers included Charles Barkley and Dennis Rodman.

Knight continues to search for new places to sell and new products to make. The women's apparel and outdoors' markets have been profitable for Nike. The company also is opening Nike Town stores. The world market is the next goal for the company as it tries to stay on top. Knight is working to keep Nike's winning tradition. He once said that he didn't want his grandkids to sit on his knee and ask him, "What's a Nike?"

Think Critically

1. What events helped Knight get his company started?
2. Why do you think it is important that Knight has continued to look for new products to make and new places to sell Nike products?
3. Do you think there is any risk involved in asking famous athletes to advertise Nike products?

Communication Skills

1. Communication skills include the ability to write effective business letters, memorandums, and e-mails. There are certain basic rules you should follow when writing letters or memos.

2. Communication skills also include the ability to speak well on the telephone and in person.

3. Listening is a key communication skill for entrepreneurs. It is often more important than speaking.

4. All good business communication is clear, positive, and persuasive. It should ask for a specific result and be persuasive in getting that result.

Math Skills

5. Basic math skills, including addition, subtraction, multiplication, and division, are necessary for business.

6. Finding averages and using percentages are everyday business activities.

7. Sales transactions are a part of all businesses.

Problem-Solving Skills

8. Many entrepreneurs use a problem-solving model to help them solve problems logically. The model consists of six steps. The first three steps are defining the problem, gathering information, and identifying various solutions. The last three steps are evaluating alternatives and selecting the best option, taking action, and evaluating the action taken.

9. Creativity is important to an entrepreneur. Entrepreneurs must be on the lookout for opportunities and for new ways to meet the needs of customers. Making mistakes will be part of the problem-solving process.

10. Brainstorming consists of coming up with a large number of fresh ideas. It can be done in a group setting or alone.

Choose the term that best fits the definition.

1. A short written form of business communication that has a set format
2. Money made from providing a good or service
3. Costs for supplies used in a business
4. A memo from one person in a company to another person in the same company
5. Result when income is greater than expenses
6. An amount that can be earned on money that is invested or paid on money that is borrowed
7. Result when expenses are greater than income
8. An amount added to the cost to determine the selling price
9. A federal, state, or local government tax charged on goods
10. A creative problem-solving method that involves coming up with a large number of fresh ideas
11. A list of things to be discussed or done in a meeting
12. An amount subtracted from the retail price to determine the selling price

a. agenda
b. alternatives
c. brainstorming
d. business e-mail
e. business letter
f. expense
g. income
h. interest
i. interoffice memo
j. loss
k. markdown
l. markup
m. memorandum
n. profit
o. sales tax
p. transaction

Review What You Have Learned

13. Which form of written communication is best suited to communicating with customers and suppliers? Which form is best suited to communicating with employees?
14. Why is it important to use a customer's name when you meet?
15. What four actions can you take to improve your listening skills?
16. What are four math skills you will need to know to operate your business? Give an example of when you would use each of these skills.
17. How do you calculate an average?
18. List at least three situations in which a business owner would use percentages.
19. Why are sales slips important to a business?
20. What are the six steps in the problem-solving model?
21. Why is brainstorming helpful?

Using the *Activities* CD, open the Chapter 2 folder. Open the activity Using the Problem-Solving Model. Print a copy and complete the activity.

1. How would you feel if a business letter was addressed to you but your name was misspelled? What would this tell you about the person who sent the letter?

2. Why are good telephone manners important for an entrepreneur? Why can listening be more important than talking?

3. You deliver newspapers to several customers. What basic calculation will you use to determine how many newspapers you need? Some people have requested that their papers not be delivered next week. What math skill will you use to determine the number of newspapers you will need next week? How should you determine the total each customer owes at the end of the month?

Project: Making Entrepreneurship Work for You

This activity will help you develop the business opportunity that you identified in Chapter 1.

1. Choose one of the business opportunities from the list you made in the *Making Entrepreneurship Work for You* project in Chapter 1. Make a list of the goods or services you will offer.

2. Write a business letter to a new customer introducing yourself. In the letter, describe one or more of the goods or services you will offer. Persuade the customer to call you to talk more about your business.

3. Make a list of everything you will need to start your business. Find a cost of each item on the list. Calculate the total amount of money that you will need to start your business.

4. Assume that you will have to borrow the total amount of money needed to start your business. Calculate the amount of interest you would have to pay the bank if you borrowed the money for one year at a 7.5 percent interest rate.

Chapter 3

What Do You Need to Know about Economics?

They Want It, and He Has It

Cameron Johnson has always loved making money. Even as a young child, Cameron had a knack for selling. Seven-year-old Cameron sold vegetables door-to-door from his wagon. When his elementary school had fundraisers, Cameron usually sold more wrapping paper or raffle tickets than any of his classmates. But when he got his first computer at age 9, Cameron's entrepreneurial passion really took hold. His first business was printing greeting cards and stationery for family and friends.

Cameron's parents soon allowed him to open his own checking account. Keeping track of his income and expenses taught Cameron how to manage money. By the age of 11, he was successfully investing in the stock market.

Cameron also was looking for ways to expand his business. Then he happened upon his sister's Beanie Baby collection and saw a great opportunity. Cameron's instincts were right.

He not only sold his sister's collection, but he also became one of the top Beanie Baby sellers on the Web. Cameron eventually had earnings of more than $20,000 per month. He got out of the business just before the Beanie Baby craze ended.

Since his Beanie Baby success, Cameron has launched more than a dozen mostly Web-based companies. He has sold most of them for a hefty profit. His Internet companies have been largely successful too. In fact, one of them had sales of more than $15,000 per day by the time Cameron was 15 years old. He's been so successful that a biography of his life even became a best-seller in Japan!

Cameron would not have been able to grow his companies without understanding the principles of supply and demand. He also was willing to take risks, and he managed his money wisely. His understanding of the main business functions means that he probably will continue to make money for a long time.

WHAT DO YOU KNOW?

1] How do you think Cameron's money management skills have affected his success?

2] Can you think of any items that currently are in high demand and short supply? How might you use this as a business opportunity for yourself?

HOW ARE ECONOMIC WANTS AND NEEDS SATISFIED?

Terms

economics
wants
needs
command economy
market
market economy
scarcity
utility

Goals

* **Discuss how wants and needs are satisfied.**

* **Describe different economic systems.**

* **Describe the role of business in a market economy.**

Do You Want It or Need It?

Think about your favorite piece of clothing. It may be a shirt or a pair of jeans. Maybe it is a new style of shoes that just came out. Before purchasing the item, you had to think about what you wanted. Then you had to find it and decide if you would spend your money for it. **Economics** is about making choices and satisfying the wants and needs of consumers.

Do you know the difference between your wants and needs? Your **wants** are those things that you think you must have in order to be satisfied. Wants include things like CDs, computers, jewelry, and designer clothes. Your **needs** are things that you must have in order to survive. Needs include food, basic clothing, and a place to live. The role of business is to produce and distribute goods and services that people want and need.

Wants

Individuals have two different types of wants. *Economic wants* are for scarce material goods and services. They are the basis of an economy. People want material goods, such as clothing, housing, and cars. They also want services, such as hair care and medical services. These items are scarce because no economy can satisfy all of the wants of all people for all goods and services. The goods and services that people want must be produced. Clothes must be made. Housing must be built, and cars must be manufactured. Personal services must be supplied.

People also have *non-economic wants*. These are desires for non-material things that are not scarce, including sunshine, friendship, and happiness.

Needs

People have basic needs for food, clothing, and shelter. These needs must be satisfied before any other needs can be met. Once basic needs are met, the mind creates new needs, such as the need for physical security. When this need is filled, then the mind comes up with even more needs. This cycle will continue since people have unlimited wants and needs.

Beyond basic needs, not all people have the same needs. Needs depend on a person's situation. For example, you may live in a house in a safe neighborhood, so your security needs are met. Someone who lives in a high-crime area still may be trying to meet his or her security needs.

CHECKPOINT

→ What role do wants and needs play in determining what is produced in an economy?

The Economics of Wants and Needs

Different countries have different economic systems. An *economic system* affects how an item is produced and distributed. It also affects the demand for the item. An economic system even determines whether an item is available at all. A problem facing economic systems is the unlimited wants and needs of consumers.

Command Economy In a **command economy**, the government determines what, how, and for whom goods and services are produced. Because the government is making the decisions, there is very little choice for consumers. The government sees no reason to have more than one type of the same item.

How do economic wants affect the production of cars?

Working Together

Work in small groups. Make a list of items that group members have bought or received in the last week. Identify each item as satisfying a want or a need.

Therefore, individuals may not always be able to get exactly what they want. There will always be shirts and pants, but there will not be many styles and colors from which to choose. In a command economy, needs may be filled, but wants may go unmet.

Market Economy Market economies are about personal choice. Individual choice creates a market. A **market** includes the customers and the location that a business wants to serve.

In a **market economy**, individuals decide what, how, and for whom goods and services are produced. Decisions about what to buy are made by millions of people, each acting alone. There are many items available that are similar, but each one meets different wants and needs. If a good sells, it will remain on the market. If not, the good will not continue to be produced. For example, a manufacturer will not continue to produce a shirt that no one buys.

Individual choice also exists in how items are produced. A skateboard manufacturer has many choices about the best way to make skateboards. In addition, in a market economy, products and services are always available to those who have a way to pay for them.

Scarcity People are never completely satisfied. Many times there is not enough of a good or service to meet everyone's desires. This is the basic economic problem of scarcity. **Scarcity** occurs because people's wants and needs are unlimited while the resources needed to produce goods and services to meet

Why might there be only one brand of jeans in a command economy?

© GETTY IMAGES/PHOTODISC

these wants and needs are limited. To fill most wants and needs, goods and services of one kind or another must be produced. To produce these goods and services, resources are needed. When your favorite piece of clothing was made, it required fabric and thread. It also required the services of someone who made the fabric into clothing. However, there is a limited supply of fabric and thread. There also are a limited number of people who can perform the service of making the fabric into clothing. This means that there are never enough resources to meet *all* wants and needs.

CHECKPOINT

→ How does a market economy differ from a command economy?

Chapter 3 What Do You Need to Know about Economics?

Business Activities in a Market Economy

Business plays an important role in a market economy. Using resources and knowledge about markets and business, entrepreneurs determine what to produce. They decide how to make the products and services useful to consumers. They also decide the best way to run their business.

Factors of Production

In order to create useful goods and services, a producer uses four basic resources. These resources are land, labor, capital, and entrepreneurship. These basic resources are called the *factors of production*.

Land is a broad term representing all the basic natural resources that contribute to production. The United States has fertile soil, minerals, water, and timber. It also has a mild climate favorable for natural resources. These natural resources help increase production in the United States.

The physical or mental effort that humans put into the production of goods and services is called *labor*. In the early days of America when the country was being developed, physical labor was more important than mental effort. But in today's information age, mental effort has become more important than physical labor.

The buildings, tools, machines, and other equipment used to produce goods and services are known as *capital*. The ovens and grills used to prepare lunch in your school cafeteria are examples of capital resources.

The fourth factor of production is *entrepreneurship*. Entrepreneurs are willing to take the risk to start businesses. They use natural, labor, and capital resources to make final products.

Utility

If a good or service is useful, it has **utility**. The four types of utility are *form*, *place*, *time*, and *possession*. If a good or service does not have all four types of utility, it is not useful.

Lance Armstrong is a cancer survivor and champion cyclist. He believes "unity is strength, knowledge is power, and attitude is everything." The Lance Armstrong Foundation was founded in 1997. It provides information and tools people living with cancer need to live strong. His yellow LIVESTRONG wristband has become a symbol. Over 40 million people wear the wristband to support people in their battle with cancer. Silicone rubber was transformed into a

You can say that again!

No one automatically gives you respect just because you show up. You have to earn it.

—Lance Armstrong, *Founding Director of the Lance Armstrong Foundation.*

What factors of production are shown here?

wristband with LIVESTRONG stamped on it. This transformation gave the product *form utility*. Form utility is the result of using resources to produce a product in its final form.

Making the LIVESTRONG wristbands available in a place where people can get them gives this product *place utility*. The wristbands are available for purchase on the Web.

In 2004, so many people were ordering the wristbands that they were not always available when people wanted them. *Time utility* gets products to people when they want them.

When someone goes to the Lance Armstrong Foundation web site and orders a wristband, pays for it, and receives it, then *possession utility* occurs. Price plays a big role in possession utility. If a product is too expensive, many people will not be able to buy it, or possess it.

Functions of Business

In a market economy, a business is free to produce and offer to consumers any legal product or service. Knowledge of business activities helps entrepreneurs satisfy customers and make a profit. These activities are called *functions of business* and include the following:

- production
- marketing
- management
- finance

Each of these functions depends on the others in order for a business to be successful. When products are produced, marketing must get the word out to consumers. Management must keep everything running well. Financial records must be kept in good order. If these functions are not working properly, the products probably will not be sold for a profit.

Production The main reasons a business exists in a market economy are to provide products or services to consumers and to earn a profit. The *production* function is creating or buying products or services to sell.

Marketing All businesses in a market economy need to complete *marketing* activities to make their products and services available to consumers. The marketing mix is a combination of marketing activities used to reach customers. The marketing mix includes the following:

- *product* is the good or service offered to customers

- *distribution* is the place and method used to get products and services to customers

What functions of business are shown here?

You have decided to open your own snow-shoveling business. Write a plan for your business. Explain how you will perform the four functions of business—production, marketing, management, and finance. Be prepared to present your plan to the class.

- *price* is the amount customers pay for products and services
- *promotion* is how product information is communicated to customers

The goal of marketing is to attract as many customers as possible so that the product is successful.

Management All businesses in a market economy must spend time developing plans and putting them into place. Once they are in place, the plans need to be evaluated to determine if they are working. Then the business must decide what changes need to be made to keep it operating successfully. The role of *management* is to set goals, determine how goals can be met, and decide how to beat the competition. Management also solves problems, manages the work of employees, and evaluates the activities of the business.

Finance In a market economy, the *finance* function plans and manages records and information related to a business's money, or finances. One of the first responsibilities of finance is to determine how much capital is needed for the business and where to get it.

> **CHECKPOINT**
> → What role does business play in a market economy?

3.1 LET'S GET REAL

1] THINK ABOUT YOURSELF Make a list of the things you would do with a large sum of money. Assume you live in a command economy. Would you be able to do or buy everything on your list?

2] WHAT DO YOU THINK? Do you think that entrepreneurs play an important role in a market economy? Why or why not?

3] LANGUAGE ARTS CONNECTION Think of a product that you use every day. Write a paragraph explaining how the four types of utility were applied to the product.

4] COMMUNICATION CONNECTION Ask three friends to name an item they purchase often. Identify the reasons the items were purchased. Write a short paper describing the items and explain how the items met a want or a need.

HOW DO ENTREPRENEURS SET A PRICE?

Terms

monopoly
fixed costs
variable costs
opportunity cost
supply
demand

Goals

* Explain the role of the market in setting prices.

* Identify various types of cost.

* Discuss the role of supply and demand in determining price.

How the Market Helps Set Prices

Choosing the right price to charge for goods or services is important for entrepreneurs. If the price is too low, there may be lots of sales but not enough to cover expenses. If the price is too high, there might not be any sales at all. There are many things to consider when deciding what price to charge. The price must ensure that the entrepreneur will make money. It also must be a price that customers are willing to pay.

A market economy is competitive because people have many choices of the same or similar items. They are free to

decide which item they want to buy and where. Business owners must set their price so that they can compete with others selling similar items.

When There Is No Competition

Not all markets are fully competitive in a market economy. In some segments of the economy, there is little or no competition. AMTRAK is the only train line serving certain routes in the United States. It does compete with other kinds of transportation, such as airlines. However, in many areas of the country, AMTRAK does not face competition from other train lines.

When a company controls all of a market, it has a **monopoly**. A company that has a monopoly is able to charge more than a company that has to compete with other companies. In a competitive market, a company cannot charge prices that are much higher than its competitors. If it does, consumers may switch to the lower-priced good or service. With a monopoly, consumers have nowhere else to go. They will continue to buy a product or service that meets their needs or wants even if the price goes up.

In a command economy, consumers have very little choice. Because the government makes most of the decisions about what is produced, there is no competition. Consumers will pay whatever price is charged.

> **CHECKPOINT**
> → Which type of economy has the most competitive pricing? Why?

Different Costs to Consider

To determine how much profit they are earning, entrepreneurs need to know how much it costs to produce their goods and services. They must consider all the resources that go into producing the good or service. Then they can determine a price to charge.

The Jewel Box is a small company that produces handmade jewelry. It requires office space, materials, labor, management, and other resources to make the jewelry. All of these resources must be taken into account when deciding the price to charge. A company should not price its product based only on the materials needed to produce it. The company would lose money and quickly go out of business.

How does competition affect prices?

Fixed and Variable Costs

Every business has fixed costs and variable costs. **Fixed costs** are costs that must be paid no matter how much of a good or service is produced. Fixed costs also are called *sunk costs*.

Variable costs are costs that go up and down depending on the quantity of the good or service produced.

To understand the difference between fixed and variable costs, consider The Bread and Bagel Shop. This small business is owned by entrepreneur Michael Miller. Whether or not customers buy his baked goods, Michael pays the same rent every month. He also pays the same insurance fee and the same interest charge on the loan he obtained to start his business. Michael must pay these fixed costs even if The Bread and Bagel Shop makes no sales.

The store also has variable costs. The variable costs include the expense of buying flour, sugar, and coffee. These expenses increase with the number of items sold. The more coffee, bagels, and donuts the shop sells, the more resources it must buy to make more goods. But, when customers buy fewer loaves of bread, Michael buys less flour, so his costs are lower.

What are the fixed and variable costs for a bakery?

© GETTY IMAGES/PHOTODISC

Understanding the difference between fixed and variable costs is important. A business with many fixed costs is a higher risk than a business with mostly variable costs. Fixed costs occur whether or not there are sales. If sales turn out to be much lower than expected, the business will be stuck with many bills to pay and little income.

Opportunity Cost

Another type of cost to consider is opportunity cost. **Opportunity cost** is the value of the best alternative you must pass up. When a customer decides to buy an item, the opportunity cost of the item he is buying is the value of the next best alternative. If your grandmother gives you $200 for your birthday, you would have to decide what to do with it. Suppose that you choose to save the money for college. The opportunity cost would be the new iPod, the next best alternative.

Entrepreneurs consider their opportunity costs to help make business decisions. Jamie Cooper, for example, has $2,500 in extra cash that she wants to put back into her cake decorating business. Jamie could invest the money in advertising. She also could invest the money in new equipment. If Jamie decides to use the money for advertising, she will not be able to purchase new equipment. The opportunity cost of advertising will be the value of the new equipment, the next best alternative. Like all entrepreneurs, Jamie will have to choose between various investment options.

CHECKPOINT
→ Explain the differences between fixed, variable, and opportunity costs.

Supply and Demand

In a market economy, individual consumers make decisions about what to buy. Consumers are motivated to buy goods and services that they want or need. Businesses also make decisions about what to produce. Business owners want to make money. Consumers and business owners together determine the prices and quantities of goods and services produced.

Supply

To understand how this decision process works, you need to understand two important concepts—supply and demand. **Supply** is how much of a good or service a producer is willing and able to produce at different prices.

Working Together

Work in small groups. Choose a business in your area with which you are familiar. Make a list of all the fixed and variable costs that you think the business has.

© GETTY IMAGES/PHOTODISC

Why is it important for Jamie to consider her opportunity cost?

3.2 How Do Entrepreneurs Set a Price? 63

Imagine that you supply lawn-mowing services. Suppose that at a rate of $10 an hour, you are willing to spend eight hours a week mowing lawns. If your customers are willing to pay only $1 an hour, you might decide not to bother mowing lawns at all. If, however, the rate for lawn mowing rose to $50 an hour, you would probably increase the number of lawns you would mow. You might even try to get some friends to help you mow even more lawns.

As the price of lawn-mowing services rises, suppliers are willing to mow more lawns. The quantity of lawn-mowing services supplied rises as the price for mowing a lawn increases, as shown on the supply curve graph.

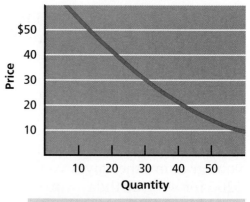

Demand Curve

Individuals are willing to consume more of a product or service at a lower price.

you might decide to have your lawn mowed every two weeks. If the rate fell to just $5 an hour, you might be willing to have your lawn mowed every week.

As the price of the service or product decreases, consumers are willing to purchase more of the product or service. Demand rises as the price decreases, as shown on the demand curve graph.

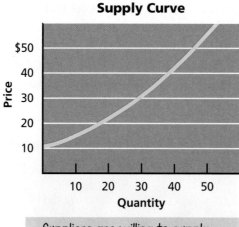

Supply Curve

Suppliers are willing to supply more of a product or service at a higher price.

Demand

Now look at the demand side of the market economy. **Demand** is an individual's need or desire for a good or service at a given price.

Suppose that you are interested in having your lawn mowed. At a rate of $10 an hour,

When Supply and Demand Meet

How do the concepts of supply and demand work together to determine price in a market economy? The point at which the supply and demand curves meet is known as the *equilibrium price and quantity*. This is the price at which supply equals demand.

When the price is above the equilibrium price, fewer people are interested in buying lawn-mowing services than in selling them. When prices are in this part of the graph, suppliers will not be able to sell as much of their services as they would like because they have priced their services too high. When the

Chapter 3 What Do You Need to Know about Economics?

Supply and Demand Curves

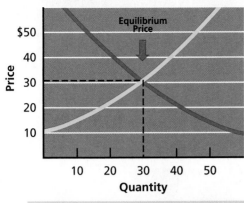

The point at which the supply and demand curves intersect indicates the equilibrium price and quantity. In this graph, the equilibrium price is $30 per unit and 30 units will be produced.

purchase lots of the lawn-mowing service at this lower price. However, suppliers are not willing to supply their services to meet the demand. At a lower price, the supplier may not be able to make enough money to cover the cost of gas for the lawnmower. When the price is too low, the suppliers cannot make a profit. Only at the equilibrium price does the amount consumers want to buy exactly equal the amount producers want to supply.

price is below the equilibrium price, the price is too low. Consumers would be very happy to

CHECKPOINT

→ How is price determined in a market economy?

1 THINK ABOUT YOURSELF Opportunity cost can affect you personally. Name an item that you wanted to buy but did not because you wanted another item more.

2 WHAT DO YOU THINK? How high would the cost of your favorite soft drink have to go in order for you not to buy it anymore? Why?

3 MATH CONNECTION Stephanie makes and sells hats and purses. She has the following costs for her business:

Sewing machine payment	$ 39.00 per month
Rent for space in her cousins' store	$125.00 per month
Utilities	$ 50.00 per month
Cost of making each purse, including labor	$ 12.50 per purse
Cost of making each hat, including labor	$ 14.75 per hat

Identify each of Stephanie's costs as either fixed or variable. Calculate her total monthly expenses for the following months:

January	February	March
10 purses	20 purses	25 purses
12 hats	15 hats	19 hats

WHAT AFFECTS A MARKET ECONOMY?

Terms

subsidies
exports
imports

Goals

* Explain the government's effect on what is produced.

* Identify the different roles the government plays in a market economy.

* Describe how buying and selling in other countries affects a market economy.

© GETTY IMAGES/PHOTODISC

Government's Effect on What Is Produced

In market economies, companies and consumers make decisions about production and spending. But what role does the government play? How do its actions affect entrepreneurs?

Although the U.S. economy is made up of private companies, the government has an effect on what is produced in three important ways—purchases, taxes, and subsidies.

Purchases The government purchases large amounts of goods and services. For example, the aerospace industry is almost entirely dependent on government purchases. The National Aeronautic and Space Agency (NASA) is the sole purchaser of various items produced by aerospace companies. Private companies also supply the government with everything from pens to cleaning supplies.

Taxes The government taxes certain goods and services. Most states charge sales tax on retail sales. Most states also charge extra taxes on certain items, such as cigarettes, gasoline, and alcoholic beverages. These taxes reduce the purchase of these products. In turn, the producers of these products make less money.

Subsidies The government provides **subsidies**, or payments, to producers of certain kinds of goods. U.S. farmers often receive subsidies to encourage them to grow agricultural products such as corn, wheat, rice, and soybeans. The government also pays subsidies to companies that locate their businesses in certain inner-city neighborhoods. These neighborhoods are known as *enterprise zones*. The goal is to help improve the economy in these areas. Entrepreneurs whose businesses can operate in these areas may be able to benefit from subsidies.

How do farmers benefit from subsidies?

Roles of Government

In a market economy, the government plays many roles. The government may serve as a regulator or as a provider of public goods. It also may be a provider of social programs or a redistributor of income.

Government as a Regulator

A market economy is based on private companies producing goods and services to earn profits. Sometimes the strong desire to earn profits causes business owners to take actions that put consumers in danger.

To keep consumers safe, the government regulates certain businesses. The U.S. Department of Agriculture (USDA), for example, inspects meat and poultry plants. Its job is to make sure that proper sanitary steps are being followed. The U.S. Occupational Safety and Health Administration (OSHA) inspects

CHECKPOINT
→ How are entrepreneurs affected by taxes and subsidies?

Why does a beautician have to be licensed to provide services?

factories to make sure that conditions are safe for workers.

The government requires some businesses to obtain licenses. Barbers and beauticians, for example, must complete certain training requirements. They must be licensed by the state in which they work. Entrepreneurs entering fields requiring licenses must pass examinations. They also must pay licensing fees. Licenses help ensure that businesses provide services that meet the expectations of consumers.

Government as a Provider of Public Goods

For most products, the benefits of ownership apply only to the owner of the product. Your next-door neighbor, for example, gets no benefits from your microwave oven. Likewise, you get no benefits from your neighbor's central air-conditioning. A *public good* is a good from which everyone receives benefits, not just the individual using the good. Vaccinations against diseases are a public good because everyone benefits

when other people are vaccinated. It prevents the spread of disease. The country's armed forces are a public good because everyone benefits from the national security they provide. Because the country as a whole benefits from these kinds of goods and services, it is the government's responsibility to provide them.

Many entrepreneurs benefit because the government provides public goods. The government often hires private companies to perform the services needed. For example, engineers are consulted on the building of highways, and construction companies are hired to build schools.

Government as a Provider of Social Programs

The government provides a number of social programs for people. Social security, welfare, medical research, and aid for dependent children and the aged are a few of the many social programs available. The cost of providing these programs is spread among millions of taxpayers. This process greatly reduces the cost to any one person. Although there is much debate over how well social programs work, there is still an overall benefit to society. A large sum of money is spent on cancer and other medical research each year to find cures. Many children and elderly people depend on government aid for their survival. Lower-income individuals benefit from welfare programs designed to help them meet their basic needs.

Government as a Redistributor of Income

The government also affects the economy by redistributing income. People with higher incomes pay more in taxes than people with lower incomes. For example, an entrepreneur who earns a small income might pay only 15 percent income tax. An entrepreneur who earns a high income might pay 40 percent in taxes. In this way, income is more evenly distributed among the population.

Redistributing income is a positive action. Those who feel helpless about their economic situation may have feelings of inequality. They may have a low level of education, or they may be unable to work. By redistributing income, the government tries to reduce social problems due to low income.

How do social programs benefit the public?

Buying and Selling in Other Countries

In a market economy, entrepreneurs are free to buy and sell products to people in other countries. This benefits both consumers and entrepreneurs. As a benefit to consumers, more products are available for sale in the marketplace. As a benefit to entrepreneurs, more opportunities exist to sell goods in new markets. However, there are risks. You may find it difficult to do business in another country because you may not speak the language. You may not be familiar with the customs of the country. You may have to change your product to meet the needs of a foreign market. It also can be very expensive to travel to and ship goods to other countries. As an entrepreneur, you will have to decide if it will help your business to buy goods from or sell goods to another country.

> **CHECKPOINT**
> ➜ Explain the roles of government in a market economy.

3.3 What Affects a Market Economy?   69

Exports

Products and services that are produced in one country and sent to another country to be sold are **exports**. The United States exports agricultural products, machinery, computers, and more. These products are shipped to countries all over the world.

Direct Exporting You can find buyers in foreign markets and ship your products directly to them. This process is called *direct exporting*. You control all exporting activities, but you may need to hire salespeople who live in or travel to foreign countries to help you.

Carmen Wilson owns a midsized flower and garden nursery. Last year, Carmen decided to expand her business internationally. She hired a Dutch sales representative to help her with business in Europe. The sales representative meets with the international customers to answer questions and take their orders.

Indirect Exporting It can be difficult to make contacts with buyers in other countries. You may decide to use commissioned agents. *Commissioned agents* bring together sellers and buyers of products and services from different countries. This is called *indirect exporting*. The entrepreneur is not as involved when this method of exporting is used. The agent does much of the work.

Did You Know?

In 2005, the United States imported goods worth $162.2 billion and exported goods worth $106.9 billion.

TREND SPOTTER

General Motors used the first industrial robots in 1961. They were used to do dangerous, dirty, and difficult jobs. Today's robots are smarter and more capable. Although robots continue to play an important role in manufacturing, they now are being used in other fields. They are used in the medical field to assist in surgeries. They can get into small places that surgeons can't reach. Robots can also be found in homes. Roomba is a robotic vacuum cleaner. It navigates around obstacles, such as furniture, using infrared sensors. You can turn it on and walk away.

Robots have become important tools in helping the United States stay globally competitive. They help improve work processes and keep costs down. Even schools are recognizing the importance of robotics to the world economy. Students at many schools participate on robotics teams that compete nationally.

Think Critically
1. Why do you think robots will help lower costs for businesses and make the United States more competitive in a global market?
2. Can you think of other tasks in the home that robots could do?

Using the Internet to Export Another way of exporting is through the Internet. The Internet has made it easier to do business with other countries. Anyone who has Internet access, can visit your web site. Businesses can translate and change their web sites to appeal to foreign customers.

Shahid Mahmoud's business manufactures puzzles. He recently began promoting his products abroad over the Web. Research showed that Japanese buyers like puzzles. To target this market, he created an e-commerce web site written in Japanese.

Imports

Products and services that are brought in from another country to be sold are **imports**. The United States imports automobiles from Europe, Japan, and Korea. It imports oil from the Middle East and China.

Two main reasons for entrepreneurs to import products to sell are price and quality. Inexpensive imports sell well because consumers like low prices. Some consumers prefer to buy high-quality products even though they are more expensive. Japanese automobiles are popular imports because they have a reputation for high quality.

Some entrepreneurs use imported products to make their own products. James Sutton owns a business that makes African-style clothing. He imports all of his fabric from West Africa because of its unique colors, designs, and textures.

CHECKPOINT

➡ What effect does buying and selling goods in other countries have on a market economy?

Working Together

Work in small groups. Make a list of products you own that have been imported from other countries.

3.3 LET'S GET REAL

1] **THINK ABOUT YOURSELF** Think about the ways that the government influences your life. Talk to your parents for ideas. Write a paragraph explaining the role of government in your life.

2] **WHAT DO YOU THINK?** Do you think the government should serve as a redistributor of income? Why or why not?

3] **MATH CONNECTION** If a small-town florist takes in $630 a week, how much must be set aside to pay a 15 percent income tax? How much must be set aside to pay a 40 percent income tax?

4] **COMMUNICATION CONNECTION** Interview a small business owner in your community. Find out how the government influences the activities of the business. Also ask the owner whether the business imports or exports any products. Write a one-page report summarizing what you learn.

How They Started

Tommy Hilfiger

Tommy Hilfiger is a world-famous fashion designer. He is best known for the brand that carries his name. Hilfiger was born in 1951 in the small town of Elmira, New York. He was the second of nine children. He knew early that he wanted a career in the fashion industry. Instead of going to college, at age 18 he decided to work in retail. His first experience in fashion was at a store called The People's Place in upstate New York.

In 1969, looking for products "for the people," he traveled to New York City. He bought fashionable jeans and bell-bottom pants. He then sold them in his store to college students. By the time he was 26, Hilfiger owned ten shops across New York. He decided to teach himself how to design the clothes he thought customers really wanted. This business went bankrupt!

With his beginning in design, he headed to New York City in 1979. Hilfiger was offered jobs with such notable fashion designers as Calvin Klein and Perry Ellis. He turned them all down. With some financial partners, Hilfiger founded Tommy Hilfiger, Inc. He began designing clothes under the Tommy label in 1984.

As principal designer, he took what started as men's jeans and sportswear to a half-billion-dollar empire of menswear, women's wear, children's wear, footwear, and eyeglasses. Tommy Hilfiger, Inc. is considered one of the top clothing companies in the world. The company's clean-cut clothing is sold in major department and specialty stores. It also is sold in some 165 Tommy Hilfiger shops and outlets. With licensing deals, Hilfiger also offers products such as fragrances, belts, bedding, home furnishings, and cosmetics.

Hilfiger was awarded the *From the Catwalk to the Sidewalk* award at the first VH1 Fashion and Music Awards in 1995. That same year, he also was named Menswear Designer of the Year by the Council of Fashion Designers of America.

Hilfiger describes his casual approach to fashion as "traditional with a twist." His line of clothing continues to be worn by everyone from yuppies to rappers.

Think Critically

1. What do you think contributed to Tommy Hilfiger's early success?
2. What has contributed to the company's continued growth?

How Are Economic Wants and Needs Satisfied?

1. Economics is about satisfying the wants and needs of consumers. Wants are things you would like to have. Needs are things you must have to survive.

2. In a command economy, the government determines what, how, and for whom goods and services are produced. In a market economy, individuals make these decisions.

3. Factors of production are resources used to produce products or services. They include land, labor, capital, and entrepreneurship.

4. The functions of business include production, marketing, management, and finance. They are dependent on each other in order for a business to be successful.

How Do Entrepreneurs Set a Price?

5. In competitive markets, prices are similar for like products.

6. Fixed costs must be paid no matter how much of a good or service is produced. Variable costs go up and down depending on the quantity of the good or service produced.

7. An opportunity cost is the value of the next best alternative you must pass up.

8. Supply is how much of a good or service a producer is willing and able to produce at different prices. Demand is an individual's need or desire for a good or service at a given price.

9. When supply and demand meet, supply equals demand. This point is referred to as the equilibrium price and quantity.

What Affects a Market Economy?

10. The government plays many roles in a market economy. The government may serve as a regulator, a provider of public goods, a provider of social programs, and a redistributor of income.

11. In a market economy, entrepreneurs are free to export or import their products or services.

Choose the term that best fits the definition.

1. Making choices and satisfying the wants and needs of consumers

2. The government determines what, how, and for whom goods and services are produced

3. Occurs because people's wants and needs are unlimited while the resources needed to produce goods and services are limited

4. How much of a good or service a producer is willing and able to produce at different prices

5. Costs that must be paid no matter how much of a good or service is produced

6. Individuals decide what, how, and for whom goods and services are produced

7. An individual's need or desire for a product or service at a given price

8. The value of the next best alternative

9. Costs that go up and down depending on the quantity of the good or service produced

10. Products and services that are brought in from another country to be sold

a. command economy
b. demand
c. economics
d. exports
e. fixed costs
f. imports
g. market
h. market economy
i. monopoly
j. need
k. opportunity cost
l. scarcity
m. subsidies
n. supply
o. utility
p. variable costs
q. want

Review What You Have Learned

11. What is the difference between a want and a need?

12. Explain why a consumer has fewer choices of products in a command economy?

13. How are decisions made in a market economy?

14. Why does scarcity occur?

15. Describe each of the factors of production and its role.

16. Name the four types of utility. Why are they important?

17. What happens when the functions of business do not work together?

18. What happens to price when there is a monopoly?

19. Explain why businesses with mostly fixed costs are at higher risk?

20. Describe one opportunity cost of becoming an entrepreneur? Why should you consider opportunity cost?

21. In what three ways does the government affect production of goods and services in the U.S. economy?

22. What is a public good? Give an example of a public good and describe how it benefits you.

23. Why are exports and imports important to entrepreneurs?

Are You Suited for Entrepreneurship?

Using the *Activities* CD, open the Chapter 3 folder. Open the activity, You Be the Government. Print a copy and complete the activity.

Think About It

1. You plan to start a pet-sitting/dog-walking business. Analyze the demand for such a service by brainstorming. Who is likely to hire a dog walker? What other kinds of services could your business offer?

2. You plan to start a day-care business for children. What government regulations might impact your business? How might you get additional information about these regulations?

Project: Making Entrepreneurship Work for You

This activity will help you develop the business opportunity that you identified in Chapter 1.

1. Make a chart showing the fixed and variable expenses for your business. How much money must you make each month to cover these expenses? Do you need to adjust the original price of your product to make a profit?

2. A supply and demand graph can help you determine the price to charge for your product or service. Complete the Supply and Demand Graph activity in the Chapter 3 folder on the *Activities* CD.

3. Brainstorm and write down all the ways that you think the government may affect your business.

4. Identify global opportunities that exist for your business. Could you export your products or services? Are there products or services you could import?

Chapter 4

How Do Entrepreneurs Get Started?

© DIGITAL VISION

I'm the Boss? Sweet!

People who start their own businesses get to make decisions about everything. They decide what to make, when to work, and what to charge. As an added bonus, they often get to do what they love. Many entrepreneurs have turned a personal interest or ability into a successful business. Brad Sweet of Relay, Maryland is one example. As a ninth-grader on summer break, Brad considered taking a part-time job to earn a little cash. But when his mom's friends began admiring a birdhouse he had made for her as a gift, he had a better idea. He thought of a way to make money on his own terms.

Brad received many compliments for his first birdhouse. So he decided to make several more for a local craft show. He quickly sold them all, and a new business was born. Every birdhouse he sold was like a tiny, traveling advertisement. Everyone who saw one of his creations wanted to buy one.

Brad's birdhouses are made entirely from recycled and recyclable products. High-grade exterior paint makes the houses weather-resistant. The easy-to-remove bottom makes cleaning easy. Each birdhouse's design is unique. Most of Brad's ideas come from his imagination. He also takes special orders. Many customers request a birdhouse miniature of their own home.

Brad continued to operate his craft business through high school and into college. He did most of the work on school breaks and summer vacations. Most part-time jobs don't allow such flexibility. Being your own boss lets you arrange your own schedule.

Of course, running a business has its challenges. You have to motivate yourself to get the work done. Still, Brad would rather be his own boss than work for someone else. Like many entrepreneurs, Brad has found personal satisfaction in starting his own business.

WHAT DO YOU KNOW?

1] What challenges has Brad faced in running his business? What other types of challenges do you think are commonly faced by business owners?

2] What do you think would be the greatest benefit to running your own business? How do you think Brad would answer that question? Explain.

DO YOU WANT TO RUN AN EXISTING BUSINESS?

Terms

business broker
assets
valuator

Goals

* Identify the advantages and disadvantages of purchasing an existing business.

* Describe the steps to take to purchase a business.

* Recognize the advantages and disadvantages of joining a family business.

Purchase an Existing Business

Thinking about starting a new business is exciting. But it also is a great deal of work. Before starting your own business from the ground up, you might consider some other options. One option is to purchase a business that already is open that the owner would like to sell.

Business owners sell their businesses for different reasons. They may have low sales or profits. They may fear new competition or economic conditions. Owners may be ready to retire or may have lost a partner due to death or illness. Partners also may not get along. Another reason is that an owner may just want to do something different.

There are many ways to find out which businesses are for sale. You may find advertise-

© DIGITAL VISION

ments in the classified section of the local newspaper. You might decide to use a business broker. A **business broker** is a person who sells businesses for a living. People with similar businesses might know of other businesses for sale. You may find businesses for sale through sources such as landlords, leasing agents, lawyers, and bankers. You may even locate businesses through bankruptcy announcements. The Small Business Administration and Chamber of Commerce offices also may provide information about businesses for sale.

Advantages of Buying an Existing Business

For entrepreneurs, there are many advantages to buying an existing business.

1. **The existing business already has customers, suppliers, and procedures.** The business may have already built up customer loyalty, which is also called *goodwill*. In addition, you can continue to use the same suppliers that have provided good service in the past. As the new owner, you may want to change some of the policies and procedures set up by the former owner. But fine-tuning a business that is already in operation is usually easier than creating a new business.

2. **The seller of a business may help train a new owner.** The current owner and experienced employees may be willing to help the new owner learn about the company.

3. **There are prior records of sales, expenses, and profits.** Financial planning will be easier and more reliable than it would be for a new business. Business records will give you a history of what has taken place in the past.

4. **Financial arrangements can be easier.** The seller of the business may accept a down payment and allow the rest of the purchase price to be made in monthly payments. This arrangement can reduce or eliminate the need for bank financing. If bank financing is needed, it may be easier to obtain a loan for an existing business. Banks are more likely to lend to an established business with a financial history.

Disadvantages of Buying an Existing Business

Buying an existing business sounds like an easy way to become an entrepreneur, but it can be risky. There are disadvantages to buying a business.

How could the seller of this business help the new owner?

Working Together

Work in small groups. Make a list of reasons that you think a business owner might decide to sell a business. Explain how these reasons could affect the success of the new business owner.

Did You Know?

One of the most common problems that young entrepreneurs face is getting the respect of customers and employees. Many people assume young entrepreneurs are less responsible.

1. **Many businesses are for sale because they are not making a profit.** Owners often try to sell businesses that are not financially profitable.

2. **Serious problems may be inherited.** Businesses can have poor reputations with customers. They may have trouble with suppliers. They also may be in poor locations. If you buy the business, you will have to overcome all of these problems.

3. **Capital (money) is required.** Purchasing an existing business can be expensive. Many entrepreneurs do not have the money needed to purchase a business.

CHECKPOINT

➡ What are some of the advantages and disadvantages of buying an existing business?

Steps to Purchase a Business

Buying a business is a complicated process. It requires a lot of thought. If you are considering buying a business, you will want to follow these steps.

1. **Write down specific information about the kind of business you want to buy.** Identify businesses for sale that match your interests. This will help you find the right business.

2. **Meet with business sellers or brokers to look into specific opportunities.** Ask about the history of the business. Review its financial performance. Find out why the business is for sale. Ask how much the owner wants for the business.

3. **Visit during business hours to observe the company in action.** Inspect the facility closely to make sure that it meets your needs. It helps to see how the business operates when it is open to customers.

4. **Ask the owner to provide you with a complete set of financial records for at least the past three years.** Reviewing these reports will help you see how much profit you can make. It also will help you determine how much you probably will be paying in expenses.

5. **Ask for important information in writing.** Get a list of all assets that will be transferred to the new owner. **Assets** are things of value that are owned, such as furniture and equipment. Obtain a statement about any past or present legal action against the business. Request a copy of the business lease or mortgage and a list of all the suppliers. Have an accountant and a lawyer help you review all of the material. Be suspicious if the owner refuses to provide all of the information you request.

6. **Determine how you would finance the business.** Contact lending institutions for information on a loan. Also, ask if the seller would be willing to finance part or all of the purchase.

7. **Get expert help to determine a price to offer for the business.** You may want to seek help from an accountant or a valuator. A **valuator** is an expert on determining the value of a business. Present the offer in writing to the seller. If an agreement is reached, have a lawyer draw up a sales contract.

CHECKPOINT

→ What steps should you take when purchasing a business?

Enter a Family Business

Does your family own a business? Do you know someone whose family owns a business? Family businesses are a large part of the U.S. economy. According to some estimates, as many as 90 percent of all businesses are owned by families. This percentage includes the majority of small- and medium-sized companies. Even many large companies, such as the Ford Motor Company, continue to be owned largely by people who are related to the company founder.

Advantages of a Family Business

Entrepreneurs who work for their family business enjoy the pride and sense of mission that comes from being part of a family enterprise. They also like that their business remains in the family throughout the generations. Some enjoy working with relatives. They like knowing that their efforts are benefiting the people they care about.

Josh Morgan runs Morgan's. The restaurant has been in his family for three generations. In his grandfather's time, Morgan's was a simple coffee shop. It largely served people in the neighborhood. Later, Josh's mother, Mary, made some changes to the restaurant. Morgan's became a popular lunch spot for people from all over town. When Mary retired two years ago, Josh took over. He carried on some of Morgan's traditions, but he also added some new services. One new service is a gourmet carryout department. Josh takes great pride in seeing how the restaurant has changed since his grandfather's time. He also enjoys the thought that one day his grandchildren may hang pictures of him at the restaurant that will then belong to them.

Why is Josh making changes to his family's restaurant?

© GETTY IMAGES/PHOTODISC

Disadvantages of a Family Business

Family businesses can have several drawbacks. Senior management positions often are held by family members, regardless of their ability. Sometimes they make poor business decisions. It also may be difficult to keep good employees who are not members of the family. Family politics often enter into business decision making. Sometimes, it is hard to separate business life and private life in family-owned businesses. As a result, business problems may end up affecting family life.

Entrepreneurs who do join their family business must be prepared to compromise. Unlike those who start or buy their own companies, people who work for their families cannot make all decisions themselves. They also may be unable to set policies and procedures as they like.

Another challenge for a family-owned business is what to do

How can a family-owned business affect family life?

© GETTY IMAGES/PHOTODISC

when there is no family member to take over the business. Sometimes the individual who is expected to take over decides to follow other opportunities. The family then must decide whether to continue the business or sell it to a nonfamily member.

CHECKPOINT

→ What are some of the advantages and disadvantages of entering a family business?

4.1 LET'S GET REAL

1] **THINK ABOUT YOURSELF** Think about the members of your family. If your family owned a business, you would have to work with them daily. Make a list of the advantages and disadvantages of working with each of your family members daily.

2] **WHAT DO YOU THINK?** When buying an existing business, why is it important to know the owner's reason for selling?

3] **MATH CONNECTION** In 2003, there were approximately 23.7 million businesses in the United States. If 90 percent of them were family businesses, how many family businesses were there?

4] **COMMUNICATION CONNECTION** Think of the different kinds of businesses in your neighborhood. Choose one that you would like to buy. Write a letter to the owner expressing your interest. Include a list of questions to ask the owner.

DO YOU WANT TO BUY A FRANCHISE OR START A NEW BUSINESS?

Terms

franchise
initial franchise fee
start-up costs
inventory
royalty fees
advertising fees

Goals

* **Evaluate franchise ownership.**

* **Identify the advantages and disadvantages of starting a new business.**

Franchise Ownership

Have you ever eaten a sandwich at Subway? Do you know someone who exercises at Curves? Maybe you've mailed a package at The UPS Store. These businesses are some of the top franchises in the United States. Purchasing a franchise is another way you can become an entrepreneur.

A **franchise** is a legal agreement that gives a person the right to sell a company's products or services in a particular area. A *franchisee* is the person who purchases a franchise. A *franchisor* is the person or company that offers a franchise for sale.

More than 500,000 people in the United States own franchises, and that number is growing. Franchising opportunities are available in almost every field. They range from motels to pet stores to video rental outlets.

© GETTY IMAGES/PHOTODISC

Top Five Franchises for 2005

Franchise	Description	Total Investment	Franchise Fee	Ongoing Royalty Fee	Term of Agreement
Subway	Submarine sandwich restaurant chain	$70,000–$220,000	$12,500	8%	20 years, renewable
Curves	Women-only fitness center	$36,400–$42,900	$39,900	5%	5 years, renewable
Quizno's Franchise Company	Quick-service sandwich shop	$208,400–$243,800	$25,000	7%	15 years, renewable
Jackson Hewitt Tax Service	Income tax preparation	$51,700–$85,400	$25,000	15%	10 years, renewable
The UPS Store	Communication and postal service centers	$138,700–$245,500	$29,950	5%	10 years, renewable

The Franchise Opportunities Handbook is a publication of the U.S. Department of Commerce. It lists more than 1,400 franchise opportunities by category. It also provides information about costs and capital requirements.

There are many other sources for finding out about franchise opportunities, including the following:

- *A Consumer Guide to Buying a Franchise*, published by the Federal Trade Commission

- Books on franchising available at your public library

- Newspapers such as *The Wall Street Journal*

- Magazines such as *Forbes*, *Barron's*, *Business Start-Ups*, *Entrepreneur*, and *Inc.*

The table above lists the top five franchises in the United States for 2005.

Operating Costs of a Franchise

If you decide to purchase a franchise, you will have certain expenses. These expenses include an initial franchise fee, start-up costs, royalty fees, and advertising fees. You also may be asked to help pay for nationwide advertising of the franchise.

The **initial franchise fee** is the fee the franchisee pays for the right to run the franchise. The fee can run from a few thousand dollars to a few hundred thousand dollars. It is usually nonrefundable. **Start-up costs** are the costs associated with beginning a business. They include the costs of renting a facility, equipping the business, and purchasing inventory. **Inventory** includes the products you have on hand to sell to customers. **Royalty fees** are weekly or monthly payments made by the franchisee to the franchisor. These payments usually are a percentage of the franchise's income. **Advertising fees** are fees paid to support television, magazine, or other advertising of the franchise as a whole.

Lydia Martinez purchased a Jani-King franchise. Jani-King is a company that provides cleaning services for businesses. In return for the right to use the Jani-King name and logo, Lydia paid a franchise fee of $12,500. In addition to this fee, Lydia spent $10,000 leasing vehicles and purchasing equipment. She will operate the business from her home, so she did not have to rent office space.

During its first year of operation, Lydia's company earned $36,000 in profits. She paid ten percent of those earnings, or $3,600, to Jani-King in royalty fees. During Lydia's second year in business, her company earned $51,000. That year, she paid $5,100 in royalty fees. The royalty fees will change year to year based on the profits of her business. She also will have to determine the amount of money to budget for advertising.

© GETTY IMAGES/PHOTODISC

Why might a business hire Jani-King to do its cleaning?

Advantages of Owning a Franchise

Franchises are becoming more popular. There are four main advantages of owning a franchise.

1. **An entrepreneur is provided with an established product or service.** Having a recognized product or service allows entrepreneurs to compete with other large, well-established companies.

2. **Franchisors offer management, technical, and other assistance.** There are many ways that franchisors can provide help. They can offer on-site training or classes. They can provide help with starting the new business and handling daily operations. They can present tips on how to handle problems that may occur. Some franchisors even offer help on everything from location selection and building design to equipment purchase and recipes. Most franchisors also have toll-free telephone numbers so that franchisees can call for advice.

3. **Equipment and supplies can be less expensive.** Franchises are parts of large chains that are able to purchase supplies in huge quantities. Some of the savings these chains get as bulk purchasers are passed on to the franchisee.

4. **A guarantee of consistent quality attracts customers.** A franchise contract requires a certain level of quality. Consumers know that they can walk into a franchise anywhere in the country and receive the same product or service. The cheeseburger sold at a SONIC Drive-In restaurant in Fresno, California, will be very similar to the cheeseburger sold at a SONIC Drive-In restaurant in Huntsville, Alabama. The quality of a room at a Red Roof Inn in New Jersey will be much like the quality of a room at the Red Roof Inn in Oregon.

Disadvantages of Owning a Franchise

Although franchising sounds like a great idea, there are four main disadvantages that you need to consider.

1. **Franchises can cost a lot of money and can cut down on profits.** The initial capital needed to purchase a franchise business often is high. Also, some of the profits you earn as a franchisee are paid to the franchisor as royalty fees.

2. **Owners of franchises have less freedom to make decisions than other entrepreneurs.** Many business decisions have already been made for franchisees. Franchisees can offer only certain products or services. They must charge prices set by the franchisor. Many entrepreneurs dislike this control. It takes away much of the freedom they sought as independent business owners.

3. **Franchisees are dependent on the performance of other franchisees in the chain.** A franchisee can benefit from the successes of other franchisees. If customers have a good experience at one franchise, then it is more likely that they will visit the same franchise in different locations. But if other franchisees run sloppy operations, customers' opinions of the chain will be negative. As a result, customers may stop going to a franchise, even if a particular store maintains high standards.

Chapter 4 How Do Entrepreneurs Get Started?

4. The franchisor can terminate the franchise agreement. If the franchisee fails to pay royalty payments or meet other conditions, the franchise can be lost. Similarly, when the franchise agreement expires, the franchisor can choose not to renew it.

Evaluating a Franchise

There are many things to consider when purchasing a franchise. You should ask yourself these questions to evaluate a specific franchise.

1. What is the estimated demand for the franchised product or service in the area where I want to locate?

2. Will I be guaranteed that I will have the only franchise in the area for the full term of the franchise agreement, or can the franchisor sell additional franchises in the same area?

3. What are the costs and royalty fees associated with the franchise?

4. How profitable have other franchises in the area been? What do other franchisees think of the franchisor?

5. How long has the franchisor been in business? How profitable is the franchisor?

6. What services does the franchisor provide? Will the franchisor help me with advertising, selling, and location selection?

7. Are the benefits provided by the franchisor worth the loss of independence and the cost of purchasing the franchise?

8. What happens if I want to cancel the franchise agreement?

Some franchisors make false or misleading claims about their franchises. To make sure that you are not being cheated or misinformed, carefully study the documents the franchisor gives you. Be suspicious of any company that will not back up its claims with written financial records. Also beware of high-pressure sales tactics. A franchisor that tries to get

Why must you carefully review a franchise contract?

you to sign a franchise agreement right away is probably not offering you a good deal. Buying a franchise is a big decision. Never allow yourself to be pressured into making the decision too quickly.

Franchise agreements are complicated legal documents. Because they can be difficult to understand, you should never sign one without consulting a lawyer. Let your lawyer know what promises were made to you orally. Then ask your lawyer to make sure that the same promises appear in the written contract before you sign it.

> **CHECKPOINT**
> → Describe the advantages and disadvantages of purchasing a franchise.

You can say that again!

From a relatively early age, I got interested in business. I'm not sure I knew what an entrepreneur was when I was ten, but I knew that starting little businesses and trying to sell greeting cards or newspapers door-to-door…there's just something very intriguing to me about that.

—**Steve Case,** founder of America Online

Starting Your Own Business

You may not have the money required to purchase a franchise, and your family may not own a business. So in order for you to be an entrepreneur, you will have to start a business of your own. You need to consider the many advantages and disadvantages of starting your own business.

Advantages of Starting Your Own Business

Entrepreneurs who start their own business get to make all the decisions. They decide where to locate the business, how many employees to hire, and what prices to charge. They are completely independent and responsible for their own future. Many entrepreneurs find great satisfaction in starting their own businesses. Many are attracted to the challenge of creating something entirely new. They also get a feeling of success when their business earns a profit.

David Srivastava started his mail-order business, In a Jam, from his home. David started out selling dried fruit through the mail. After a year and a half, sales were disappointing. So David began offering preserves and jams. He felt these products had greater sales potential. He also put more effort into packaging. He designed the labels for the jars himself. His instincts proved correct. Eight years after starting his business alone in his basement, David now has 14 full-time employees. His company does business with several large retail stores. Because this was David's business, he made all the decisions himself. He decided which products to offer and how they would be packaged. His success is a result of his efforts alone.

Disadvantages of Starting Your Own Business

There are many risks to consider when you start your own business. You must estimate demand for your product or service. There is no certainty that customers will purchase what you offer. Entrepreneurs who join family businesses, buy an existing business, or buy franchises do not have this uncertainty. They already know that customers will buy their product or service.

Entrepreneurs who start their own business must make some decisions that other entrepreneurs do not have to make. They must decide what product or service to offer. They must choose a location and decide whether to hire employees. What may seem like a good decision may not turn out that way in the end.

Lucy Donnelly realized how difficult it is to start a new business when she opened a kitchen accessories store. Lucy had considered purchasing a store franchise. She ruled it out because of the high franchise fee. Lucy's problems began when she

learned that the location she chose for her business was not convenient for customers. As a result, Lucy had fewer customers than she had estimated. Also, getting suppliers was more difficult than Lucy had expected. Many of them proved to be unreliable. So, she was often out of stock of certain products. Lucy also discovered that some of the high-priced items she purchased were not selling well. This lowered profits.

Working Together

Work in small groups. Compare the differences between starting a submarine sandwich shop from the ground up and purchasing a Subway restaurant franchise.

CHECKPOINT

→ Why is it more difficult to start a new business than to take over an existing business or purchase a franchise?

4.2 **LET'S GET REAL**

1 THINK ABOUT YOURSELF Think about challenges involved in starting a business from the ground up. Do you think you could handle the pressure and the challenges? Write a paragraph telling why you think you are or are not up for the challenge.

2 WHAT DO YOU THINK? In your opinion, what would be the greatest advantage of starting a new business? What would be its greatest disadvantage? Do you think the advantages outweigh the disadvantages? Why or why not?

3 LANGUAGE ARTS CONNECTION Identify a franchise that interests you. Using the Internet or library, research the franchise. Evaluate the franchise using the eight questions in this lesson. Write a short report on your findings. At the end of your report, tell whether you think this franchise is a good opportunity.

4 MATH CONNECTION Juan and Molly Gonzales want to save enough money to purchase a cleaning service franchise in five years. How much will they need to save in equal amounts each year if the franchise fee is $19,500 and start-up costs are $15,200? If estimated company sales are $35,100 and estimated expenses are $11,290 in the first year, how much profit will they make?

WHO WILL OWN YOUR BUSINESS?

Terms

sole proprietorship
partnership
corporation
incorporate
share of stock
board of directors
dividends
liability

Goals

* **Describe the advantages and disadvantages of a sole proprietorship.**

* **Describe the advantages and disadvantages of a partnership.**

* **Describe the advantages and disadvantages of a corporation.**

© DIGITAL VISION

Types of Business Ownership

There are many decisions you will have to make when you decide to start your own business. First, you must decide what kind of business you will start. Then, you must decide what type of ownership your business will have. There are three main types of business ownership.

A business that is owned only by one person is a **sole proprietorship**. A business owned by two or more people is a **partnership**. A business with the legal rights of a person and which may be owned by many people is a **corporation**. A table at the end of this lesson compares these three types of business ownership.

Sole Proprietorship

If you open a business alone, then you are a sole proprietor. Sole proprietorship enables you to be in complete control of the business. Sole proprietorships may be very small businesses with no employees or large businesses with hundreds of employees. The government has very few rules that affect sole proprietorships, so they are simple to establish and operate. Accurate tax records and certain employment laws must be met. But these are usually the only forms of government regulation on a sole proprietorship. For this reason, the sole proprietorship is the most common form of ownership in the United States.

Disadvantages It can be difficult to raise money for a sole proprietorship. You are the only person contributing money. Also, owners of sole proprietorships face a risk that owners of partnerships or corporations do not. If a sole proprietorship fails and there are unpaid debts, the entrepreneur's personal assets (such as a house) may be taken to pay what is owed.

Rachel Gibson learned this lesson the hard way. Last year, her clothing store went out of business, leaving $42,000 in debt. Because Rachel had set up the business as a sole proprietorship, she had to sell some of her personal assets, including her car, to pay off this amount.

CHECKPOINT

→ Why are sole proprietorships the most common form of business ownership?

Partnership

If you decide to open a business with one or more of your friends so that you can share the work and the responsibilities, then you have formed a partnership. Running a business as a partnership means that you will not have to come up with all of the money to start the business. It also means that any losses the business has will be shared by all of the partners. Like sole proprietorships, partnerships face very little government regulation.

Disadvantages Some entrepreneurs do not like partnerships because they do not want to share decision making and profits with other people. They fear being held legally responsible for the errors of their partners. Partnerships can also lead to disagreements and can end bitterly.

© GETTY IMAGES/PHOTODISC

Why might entrepreneurs prefer to have a partner?

GENERAL PARTNERSHIP AGREEMENT FORMING WEB DESIGN 4 U

By agreement made this 28th day of August 20—, we, Andy Russell and Will Barr, both of Chuckey, Tennessee, hereby join in general partnership to conduct a Web design business and agree to the following terms:

1. That the partnership shall be called Web Design 4 U and shall have its principal place of business at 14 Eades Road, Chuckey, Tennessee. Full and accurate records of partnership transactions shall be kept at this address and made available to any partner at any reasonable time.

2. That the partnership shall continue in operation for an indefinite time until terminated by 90 days' notice, provided by one of the partners indicating a desire to leave. Upon such notice, a division of the partnership assets will be made unless the other partner wishes to purchase the whole business by paying a price that is agreed to by both partners. The price shall include goodwill and entitle the purchaser to continue the partnership business under the same name.

3. That each partner shall contribute to the partnership $2,500 for initial capital and supplies and equipment.

4. That in return for the capital contribution in Item 3, each partner shall receive one-half interest in the partnership and its assets.

5. That a fund of $10,000 be set up from the profits of the partnership business as a backup fund. Not less than 15 percent of the monthly profits will be added to this fund until the amount of $10,000 has been accumulated.

6. That the profits and losses of the business shall be divided equally between the partners. The profits and losses will be determined and profits will be paid to each partner on a monthly basis.

7. That the partnership bank account shall be kept in the Tennessee National Bank and that all withdrawals from the account shall be by check containing the signature of at least one of the partners.

8. That each partner shall devote his or her full efforts to the partnership business and shall not participate in another business without the other partner's permission.

9. That no partner shall enter into any agreements representing the partnership outside the normal operations of the Web design business without notice to the remaining partner and the permission of the other partner. All managerial and employee decisions not covered by another section of this agreement shall be made only with the consent of both of the partners.

IN AGREEMENT HERETO, WE ARE

Andy Russell   Will Barr

Andy Russell   *Will Barr*

When two or more entrepreneurs go into business together, they generally sign a partnership agreement such as the one shown on page 92. The purpose of the partnership agreement is to set down in writing the rights and responsibilities of each of the owners. It identifies the

- name of the business or partnership
- names of the partners
- type and value of the investment each partner contributes
- managerial responsibilities to be handled by each partner
- accounting methods to be used
- rights of each partner to review accounting documents
- division of profits and losses among the partners
- salaries to be paid to each of the partners
- duration (length of time) of the partnership
- conditions under which the partnership can be ended
- division of assets after ending the partnership
- procedure for dealing with the death of a partner

CHECKPOINT

➡ What are some of the advantages and disadvantages of a partnership?

Corporation

When you see the word *Incorporated* or *Corporation* or the abbreviation *Inc.* or *Corp.* after a business name, it means that the business is incorporated. To **incorporate** means to set up a business as a corporation. Unlike a sole proprietorship or a partnership, a corporation operates independently of its owners. A corporation has the legal rights of a person. The corporation, not the owners, pays taxes, enters into contracts, and may be held responsible for negligence.

Ownership of a corporation is in the form of shares of stock. A **share of stock** is a unit of ownership in a corporation. People who own stock in the corporation are called *stockholders* or *shareholders*.

Jim Munroe set up his company, Munroe Office Supply, as a corporation. He created 100 shares of stock worth $1,000 each. Jim then sold 15 shares of stock to each of three outside investors. They each paid $15,000,

Be Your Own Boss

You have a large collection of CDs, and you know a lot of your friends have CDs that they would like to sell. You think it would be a good idea to start a business selling CDs over the Internet. Now, you must consider the type of ownership that will work best for you. You must decide if you can operate the business alone or if you will need the help of a partner. Create a list of advantages and disadvantages of running your business as a sole proprietorship or a partnership. What type of ownership would you choose? Why would you choose this form of ownership?

Working Together

Work in small groups. Compare the advantages and disadvantages of each type of business ownership.

for a total of $45,000, to be shareholders in Jim's company. Jim kept the remaining 55 shares of stock worth $55,000 for himself. So Jim owns 55 percent of his company while outside investors own 45 percent. The individual or group that owns the most shares of stock has control of the company.

Every corporation has a **board of directors**. This group of people meets several times a year to make important decisions affecting the company. The board of directors is responsible for electing the corporation's senior officers and determining their salaries. The company's officers, not the board of directors, are responsible for the day-to-day management of the corporation. The board of directors sets the corporation's rules for conducting business. The board of directors also decides how much the corporation should pay in dividends. **Dividends** are payments of profits to shareholders by corporations.

Disadvantages Setting up a corporation is more complicated than setting up a sole proprietorship or a partnership. To incorporate, you will need the assistance of a lawyer. The lawyer will help you file the necessary paperwork with the state official responsible for registering corporations. Because of this process, setting up a corporation can be expensive. A business must be careful when it decides to incorporate. A document called *articles of incorporation* must be written that fully explains the purpose of the business. If the articles are not well written, the corporation's business activities may be affected.

Corporations are subject to more government regulation than are sole proprietorships or partnerships. A lot more paperwork is involved in running a corporation. Another drawback of incorporation is that income is taxed twice. A corporation pays taxes on its income. Shareholders then pay taxes on the dividends they receive from the corporation. So the corporation's profits are taxed as corporate income and again as individual income.

Why Incorporate? If the corporate form of ownership is complicated and costly, why do entrepreneurs set up corporations? Liability is the main reason. **Liability** is the amount owed to others. The shareholders' liability is limited to the amount of money each shareholder invested in the company when stock was purchased.

Munroe's Office Supply has gone bankrupt, leaving $150,000 in debt. Each shareholder loses only the amount he or she invested in the corporation. Therefore, the three outside individuals who invested a total of $45,000 would lose their investment. Jim would also lose his investment of $55,000. If Jim had set up his business as a sole proprietorship, he would have been liable for the full $150,000 of debt. If the business had been set up as a partnership between Jim and his three friends, all four partners would have been liable for the $150,000 debt.

Incorporation allows businesses to raise money by selling stock. Shareholders do not affect the management of a corporation. The main shareholders of the company can change when stock is bought or sold. These changes do not have an impact on the day-to-day operation of the business. Lenders also are more willing to lend money to corporations than to sole proprietorships or partnerships.

CHECKPOINT

→ Why would someone want to set up a business as a corporation?

Comparisons of the Legal Forms of Business

Feature	Sole Proprietorship	Partnership	Corporation
Simple to start	✓	✓	
Decisions made by one person	✓		
Low initial cost	✓	✓	
Limited liability			✓
Limited government regulation	✓	✓	
Easy to raise capital			✓
Double taxation of profits			✓

4.3 LET'S GET REAL

1 THINK ABOUT YOURSELF Think about your *assets*, the things that you own. How much do you think they are worth? If you opened a business as a sole proprietorship and your business failed, how would you pay off any remaining bills of the business? Describe how you would handle this situation.

2 WHAT DO YOU THINK? Why do you think the government has more regulations for corporations than for sole proprietorships or partnerships?

3 MATH CONNECTION Caren McHugh opened The Ruby Slipper, Inc. To raise money, she set up her business as a corporation. She created 500 shares of stock. Each share is worth $75. Caren held 260 of the shares for herself. She sold the rest in even amounts to six investors. How many shares does each investor own? If The Ruby Slipper, Inc. fails and has $65,000 in debt, how much would each investor be liable for?

4 COMMUNICATION CONNECTION With a partner, write a skit about two people who wish to form a partnership. Decide on a business to enter and the duties each person will perform in the business. In the skit, the partners should negotiate the terms of the partnership agreement.

Chick-fil-A, Inc.

Samuel Truett Cathy is credited with creating the first fast-food chicken sandwich. Born in Georgia in 1921, Cathy's entrepreneurial skills began early. At age 8, he was selling soft drinks. During his high school years, he delivered newspapers and won several awards for signing up customers.

In 1946, Cathy and his brother opened a restaurant in a small town south of Atlanta, Georgia. His brother was killed in a plane crash in 1948, but Cathy kept the business going. He credits his wife for encouraging him to carry on with his faith and entrepreneurial spirit.

Cathy's first restaurant was so small he called it The Dwarf House. He began experimenting with chicken sandwiches there and created the Chick-fil-A sandwich in the early 1960s. A family man, he included his children in the business by dressing them up to entertain customers. They remain in the business today in leadership roles.

As a result of the sandwich's popularity, Cathy trademarked *Chick-fil-A* in 1963. He started Chick-fil-A, Inc. in 1964 and founded the Chick-fil-A restaurant franchise chain in 1967. He promoted his sandwich by giving out free samples at tradeshows and to important people.

Starting with an office of five people, Chick-fil-A, Inc. now has over 540 corporate employees. In 1986, Chick-fil-A opened its first freestanding drive-thru restaurant. Today, more than half of Chick-fil-A's 1,200 restaurants are drive-thrus. Cathy helped pioneer the concept of opening restaurants in shopping malls. He rewards his franchise operators with cars and awards college scholarships to restaurant employees.

Chick-fil-A's advertising is a reflection of Cathy's promotional spirit. "EAT MOR CHIKIN" cows are a theme that has been turned into a long-standing marketing program. Since 1996, it includes billboards, in-store materials, promotions, radio and TV ads, and clothing and merchandise sales of more than $42 million.

Chick-fil-A continues to focus on customer service and product quality. It remains family-oriented with its closed-on-Sunday policy.

Think Critically

1. Do you think the fact that Mr. Cathy has been involved with the business from the beginning has contributed to its success?

2. Do you think it was a good idea for Mr. Cathy to involve his children in the family business at any early age? Why or why not?

Do You Want to Run an Existing Business?

1. An existing business already has customers and relationships with suppliers. The seller may train you to run the business. Existing businesses also have records of past profits.

2. Be careful when buying an existing business. It may not be making a profit. It also may have other problems. A large amount of capital usually is needed to purchase an existing business.

3. There are seven important steps to follow when deciding to purchase an existing business.

4. Joining a family business has advantages, such as pride in the business and enjoyment in working with relatives. But family politics can negatively affect the business. Business problems also can affect family life.

Do You Want to Buy a Franchise or Start a New Business?

5. Costs involved in owning a franchise involve an initial franchise fee, start-up costs, royalty fees, and possibly advertising fees.

6. Purchasing a franchise provides an established product or service for you to sell. Franchises also are recognized by customers. You may be able to purchase supplies at a lower cost. But franchise ownership can be expensive. It also does not allow much room for independent decision making.

7. Many people start an entirely new business. There are risks because there is no guaranteed demand for your product or service. You also must make all the business decisions yourself.

Who Will Own Your Business?

8. Businesses can be set up as sole proprietorships, partnerships, or corporations.

9. There are advantages and disadvantages to each type of business that should be considered when you decide how to set up your business.

Vocabulary Builder

Choose the term that best fits the definition.

1. Weekly or monthly payments made by the franchisee to the franchisor
2. A business owned only by one person
3. Group of people who meet several times a year to make important decisions affecting the company
4. A unit of ownership in a corporation
5. A person who sells businesses
6. Fee the franchisee pays for the right to run the franchise
7. A business owned by two or more people
8. Payments of profits to shareholders by corporations
9. A legal agreement that gives a person the right to sell a company's products or services in a particular area
10. A business with the legal rights of a person and which may be owned by many people

a. advertising fees
b. assets
c. board of directors
d. business broker
e. corporation
f. dividends
g. franchise
h. incorporate
i. initial franchise fee
j. inventory
k. liability
l. partnership
m. royalty fees
n. share of stock
o. sole proprietorship
p. start-up costs
q. valuator

Review What You Have Learned

11. Why is it a good idea to visit a company during business hours before you purchase an existing business?
12. What are some of the compromises that must be made by an entrepreneur who joins the family business?
13. Where can an entrepreneur get information about purchasing and operating a franchise?
14. Why should an entrepreneur consult with a lawyer prior to signing a franchise agreement?
15. Why do franchisors offer training to the franchisees?
16. What decisions need to be made when starting a new business?
17. What are the risks of starting your own business?
18. Why do owners of sole proprietorships face more risks than owners of partnerships or corporations?
19. What is the purpose of a partnership agreement?
20. What decisions are made by a corporation's board of directors?

Using the *Activities* CD, open the Chapter 4 folder. Open the activity Research Businesses for Sale. Print a copy and complete the activity.

1. You are meeting with the owner of an ice cream shop you would like to purchase. What specific questions are you going to ask her? What documents do you want to see? How will you decide whether or not to purchase this business?

2. There are three forms of ownership for businesses—sole proprietorship, partnership, and corporation. Research companies on the Internet and list two real companies that fit into each category.

Project: Making Entrepreneurship Work for You

This activity will help you develop the business opportunity that you identified in Chapter 1.

1. Find franchise opportunities available in your business field. Investigate one of these opportunities. Gather information such as initial franchise fees, royalty fees, estimated earnings, and operating expenses. It may help to visit a franchise and speak to a manager.

2. Think about incorporating your business. How much money would you like to raise through the sale of stock? Decide on a selling price for stock in your company based on what the price of stock is for other companies similar to yours. You can use the Internet to research the price of stock. How many shares of stock will you offer for sale?

3. You have a friend who is interested in being your business partner. Use the Partnership Agreement form in the Chapter 4 folder on the *Activities* CD. Write an agreement for the two of you.

4. Now that you have investigated the different types of business ownership, choose the type of ownership you will use for your business. Write a short paper explaining your decision.

Chapter 5

How Do You Select a Location and Hire Employees?

If You Want It Done Right...Delegate?

Tyler Dikman was a 15-year-old high school student in Tampa, Florida, when he started CoolTronics, a computer supply company. It wasn't long before Tyler realized that he was going to need some extra hands to help with the work. Within 18 months of opening CoolTronics, Tyler had hired his first employees. He assigned them tasks that didn't need his personal attention. The employees answered routine e-mail and phone calls. They also handled mailing and receiving packages. Having employees freed Tyler to concentrate on computer repair—the most profitable side of his business.

Tyler persuaded his friends to work for him by paying them more than they could earn at other jobs around town. He couldn't offer them benefits, but employees got free trips to trade shows in Las Vegas and other cities. At first, Tyler assigned his employees only certain tasks.

But when he turned 18, Tyler added a second CoolTronics location in Santa Clara, California, after moving there to attend college. Having a second location forced Tyler to change his management style. He could no longer oversee how his employees were doing their jobs as often as he would like. It became necessary to allow employees to expand their roles and assume greater levels of authority and responsibility. Tyler admits that his shift in management style has helped increase profits.

CoolTronics continues to do well. The business resells cutting-edge computer products from companies such as Dell, ATI, and Intel. Tyler and his employees also offer a variety of services. They provide computer training, build databases, establish web sites, and create networks. They can get a small business up and running within days. Tyler says that he couldn't have done it without his team.

WHAT DO YOU KNOW?

1] What do you think it would be like working for a friend's business? What do you think it would be like supervising a friend's work? Discuss the possible advantages and disadvantages of each situation.

2] If you ran a business, how would you decide how much responsibility to give your employees? What precautions would you take to ensure that they would perform the tasks you assigned them?

WHERE WILL YOU LOCATE YOUR BUSINESS?

<table>
<tr><th>Terms</th><th>Goals</th></tr>
<tr>
<td>trade area
layout</td>
<td>

* **Explain what to consider when selecting a location for your business.**

* **Describe the layouts for different types of businesses.**

</td>
</tr>
</table>

© GETTY IMAGES/PHOTODISC

Begin Selection of Your Site

Have you ever wanted to go to a store, but your parents would not take you there because it was not conveniently located?

Where a business is located often determines its success. The type of business you have also will help you determine the best location for it.

Location for a Retail Business

Given all of the possible types of locations for retail businesses, how do you decide where to locate? One way of identifying your options is to buy a map of your area and mark the trade area. The **trade area** is the area from which you expect to attract customers. Mark on the map all of the locations that might be appropriate for your business. Also indicate the location of all of your competitors. Using a different color marker or symbol, mark the locations of businesses that do not compete with yours but may attract the same kind of customers. For example, if you want to open a poster store that will attract mostly teens, mark the locations of other stores that also appeal to teens. Examples are trendy clothing stores and music stores.

Location Type and Availability

The next step is to identify which type of location is right for your business. Do you want to locate in a community shopping center? A stand-alone store? Downtown? Determining which type of location you want will help narrow your search.

After deciding on the type of location, you must determine what buildings of this type are available in your trade area. The classified section of your local paper will list available locations. You also can find locations simply by driving around your trade area. Signs advertising an available building will be hung in the front window or will be on the front lawn of the building. Real estate web sites also may be helpful in determining what options are open to you. Mark each possible location you find on your trade-area map.

Questions to Ask After making a list of possible locations, inspect each location. Is the location safe? Is it attractive? Does it seem to attract the kind of customers your business will be targeting? Is it easy to reach? Is there enough parking? Do businesses in the area seem to be doing well? After answering these questions, you should be able to cross some of the locations off your list so that you have only one or two locations left.

Michele Kim is planning to open a fabric store. She is sure that there is a market for her product. Michele starts to search for the best location for her store. She rules out a downtown location because of the lack of parking and the fact that many shoppers are not willing to go downtown in the evenings. After much research, she settles on a community shopping center because of the low rent, the good parking, and the safety of the shopping center at all hours.

> **CHECKPOINT**
> ➡ What are some of the things you should consider when selecting a location for a retail business?

Location for a Service Business

For some service businesses, such as restaurants and hair salons, location is as important as it is for a retail business. Owners of these types of businesses will have to be very careful when choosing a location. Convenience is an important factor for many service businesses.

Eileen Whitman runs a small company that repairs computers. Because most of her customers are businesses, Eileen chose a downtown location for her company. By being close to her customers, in an emergency, Eileen usually can have her customers' computers back in service the same day.

Is Location Always Important?

Location is much less important for other types of service businesses. Customers never actually visit some service businesses,

Working Together

In small groups, brainstorm a list of rules an entrepreneur might make if he or she decides to work at home.

such as plumbing or carpet-cleaning companies. Locating these kinds of businesses in expensive areas does not make sense. Being close to customers may be important, however, because customers are more likely to call a company located nearby.

> **CHECKPOINT**
> → How important is location for a service business?

Operate Your Business from Home

Renting or buying business property is expensive. To avoid such expenses, many entrepreneurs run their businesses from their homes. You may decide that a home-based business is a good option for you, too. You will need to check the zoning laws in your area to make sure you are legally able to operate your business from your home.

Home-based businesses are ideal for small companies whose customers do not need to visit the business. Most entrepreneurs who work from their homes set aside a separate room or area for their business. This part of the home is considered their office. It is generally out of bounds for children and other family members.

Rashid Zerbe runs a computer company from his New York apartment. Starting with little more than a $1,500 computer, Rashid began a web site design firm that now employs five people. Tina Mills runs her one-person jewelry design company from her home in Los Angeles, California. Tina's clients include large retailers. All of her

business is done over the phone or Internet and through express mail.

Advantages and Disadvantages Working at home has many advantages. Rent, utilities (such as gas, electric, and water), insurance, maintenance, and other costs are reduced or eliminated. Some of these expenses may be subtracted as business expenses from income taxes. You also save on the time and cost of getting to and from work when you run a business from your home.

Working at home has several disadvantages as well. Some people find it difficult to concentrate because of interruptions from family members or friends. Others find that they miss working outside the home with other people. Some find that they spend more time working than they really want because their business is located in their home.

Why do you need your own separate work area at home?

CHECKPOINT

→ What are some of the advantages and disadvantages of running a business from your home?

Design the Layout of Your Business

After you have decided where to locate your business, you will need to design your layout. The **layout** is the floor plan for your business. Your layout must include enough space for employees, customers, merchandise, and equipment. It also must have space for restrooms, stockrooms, storage, and offices.

Create the Floor Plan You will need to prepare a drawing of the layout as shown below. Graph paper will help you draw your layout to scale. To create a scale drawing, let 1 inch represent 1 foot of actual space. For example, a 4-foot-by-3-foot room is represented by a 4-inch-by-3-inch rectangle. Show the planned use of each area. Also show the location of furniture, display cabinets, shelves, fixtures, and equipment. Your drawing will help you identify problems in your layout. It also will help you communicate with the people who may do remodeling work.

Choose a layout, an outside sign, and window displays that match your image. If you sell expensive jewelry, you probably will decide on an elegant outside sign and a stylish inside design that will appeal to your target customer. If you sell sporting goods, you will select a very different design for your store.

Layout of a Retail Business

For a retail business, appearance is very important. A store with creative window and merchandise displays sends a positive message. A store with crowded aisles and piles of merchandise does not.

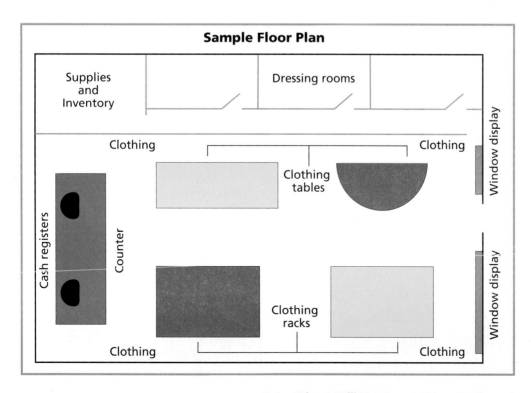

Sample Floor Plan

Supplies and Inventory

Dressing rooms

Window display

Clothing

Clothing

Clothing tables

Cash registers

Counter

Clothing racks

Window display

Clothing

Clothing

Some ways you can send a positive message about your store are:

- **Choose lighting that works best for the kind of merchandise you sell.** Good lighting is important for any business where customers inspect merchandise closely. Avoid fluorescent lighting that creates an unattractive glare.

- **Think carefully about window displays.** Use them as a way to display new merchandise or seasonal items.

- **Make the entrance inviting.** An inviting entrance will draw customers into the store.

- **Use common sense when organizing the merchandise in your store.** Customers should always easily find what they want. Inventory and supplies also should be well organized so that you can find things faster and serve your customers better.

- **Leave at least four feet of aisle space.** You need to make it easy for customers to move around in your store.

- **Create attractive in-store displays.** Customers are drawn to displayed merchandise.

- **Place the cash register in a central location.** Customers should not have to search for a cashier.

Your layout should meet two goals. First, it should attract customers to your store. Second, it should make their experience a pleasant one so that they return. Sending a positive message will attract people to come to your store again and again.

Layout of a Service Business

Service businesses can be divided into two categories:

- service businesses where people visit to receive a service, such as restaurants, hair salons, and tax preparation services

- service businesses that travel to the customer's location and perform the service on-site, such as exterminators, plumbers, and cleaning services

The layout of the first type of service business should be planned just as carefully as that of a retail business. However, on-site service businesses are never visited by their customers, so an attractive layout is not important. Organization is important in the layout of on-site service businesses so that supplies and other items are easy to find.

NET Bookmark

The layout of a store must make it easy for customers to find what they need. The layout is also an important way to stop shoplifting. Access exploringxtra.swlearning. com and click on the link for Chapter 5. Read the article, "Store Layout." What are two ways the store layout can be changed to prevent shoplifting?

exploringxtra.swlearning.com

CHECKPOINT

→ How can the layout of a business send a positive message to customers?

1   **THINK ABOUT YOURSELF** Are you a well-organized person most of the time, or do you let things in your room pile up and get cluttered? As a business owner, it will be important for you to keep your business and workspace neatly organized. Write a paragraph describing your organizational skills and discuss how you would keep your business organized.

2   **WHAT DO YOU THINK?** Location is important for some service businesses and not important for others. Name five types of service businesses for which location is important. Name five types of service businesses for which location is not important.

3   **COMMUNICATION CONNECTION** Design the layout of a bookstore. A small coffee shop is part of the bookstore. Create a scale drawing of the space and show the placement of all of the equipment. Use pictures from catalogs or magazines to show the type of furniture, fixtures, and equipment you have selected. Present your plan to the class and explain why you think your layout will make your business successful.

4   **COMMUNICATION CONNECTION** Talk to owners of local businesses about their location. Ask them what they see as the advantages and disadvantages of their locations. Write a paragraph with your findings and report them to the class.

© GETTY IMAGES/PHOTODISC

How can stores use window displays to attract customers?

WHO WILL YOU HIRE TO HELP RUN YOUR BUSINESS?

Terms

job description
organizational
    structure
recruit

Goals

* Identify the employees your business needs.

* List ways you can recruit employees.

* Explain the steps involved in hiring employees

Identify Your Hiring Needs

At some point, your business may grow enough that you will not be able to run it by yourself. To succeed, you probably will need to hire employees. Employees can help your business run efficiently. Good employees will help you attract customers and increase sales. But how do you know what kinds of employees you need? How do you go about getting them?

To find out your hiring needs, ask yourself these questions:

- What kind of employees do I need?

- What skills am I missing?

- What skills do I need daily?

- What skills do I need occasionally?

To answer these questions, list all of the duties in your business. Then try to identify how much time is needed to perform each of those duties. Your list should help you identify whether you

© DIGITAL VISION

need part-time or full-time workers. You also can determine whether you need managers or assistants and how many employees you need.

Write Job Descriptions

A **job description** is a written statement listing the duties and responsibilities of a job. It states the education and work experience needed to perform a particular job. It often includes the pay rate for the job.

Writing a detailed job description is important. You will need to understand exactly what every job involves so that you can determine how much money to offer job applicants. A detailed job description will make clear the job responsibilities. If a receptionist objects to ordering supplies, you can remind the employee that this responsibility is included in the job description. Job descriptions also can be used to measure how well an employee does a job.

Create an Organizational Structure

Once your company has several employees, you will need an organizational structure. An **organizational structure** is a plan that shows how all the jobs in a company relate to one another. Many businesses use a chart to represent the organizational structure.

In some small businesses, all employees may report directly to the company owner. In larger companies, lower-level employees usually report to a supervisor who then reports to the owner. This kind of organizational structure ensures that the owner

---

SAMPLE JOB DESCRIPTION

Title: Receptionist

Duties and responsibilities: Receives and directs phone calls, greets visitors, receives and sorts mail and packages, orders office and kitchen supplies, keys documents when required.

Qualifications: High school graduate. Needs good communication skills and must get along well with people. Keying speed of 45 words per minute. Experience desirable but not necessary.

Salary: $15,000–$20,000, depending on experience.

---

of a company is not called upon to deal with unimportant issues that could be handled more easily by a lower-level manager.

Sandra Wilson owns Fabulous Flowers. The company's organizational chart is shown below. Sandra has an organizational structure where the sales and purchasing departments have managers that oversee employees. The managers report to the vice president, Robert

Working Together

Working in a small group, talk about the way your school administration is organized. Create an organizational chart for the school.

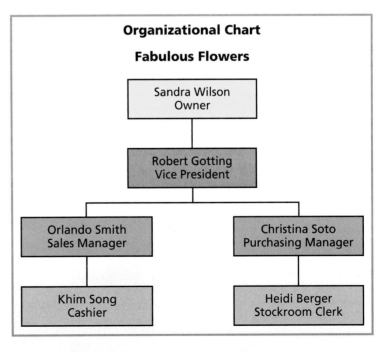

Organizational Chart

Fabulous Flowers

- Sandra Wilson — Owner
- Robert Gotting — Vice President
  - Orlando Smith — Sales Manager
    - Khim Song — Cashier
  - Christina Soto — Purchasing Manager
    - Heidi Berger — Stockroom Clerk

Gotting. Robert, in turn, reports directly to Sandra. This structure helps Sandra focus her time on more important business issues.

CHECKPOINT

→ How do you determine the hiring needs of your business?

Recruit Employees

To **recruit** is to look for people to hire. You can recruit employees in a variety of ways.

Classified Advertising

A want ad is a type of classified ad that announces a job opening. It can be a good way to recruit employees. Your want ad should briefly describe the job, the educational requirements, and the experience needed. It also should identify any special job requirements, such as a willingness to travel or to work evenings.

SAMPLE WANT AD

RECEPTIONIST needed for advertising firm. Good organizational and communication skills a must. Key 45 WPM. High school graduate. Office experience helpful. Salary $15,000–$20,000. Call Ms. Brown, 312-555-8797.

© GETTY IMAGES/PHOTODISC

Why is a want ad a good way to recruit employees?

Employment Agencies

Employment agencies find employees for businesses. These firms try to match people looking for jobs with businesses looking for employees. They charge businesses or the job seekers a fee when a match is made.

College Placement Centers

Most colleges and universities operate job placement centers. These offices collect information on career and employment opportunities, which they make available to their students and graduates. Generally, no fee is charged for using a college placement center. If college students or graduates might be suitable for your business, contact local colleges and universities and ask them how you can have your business listed with their placement centers.

Other Ways of Recruiting Employees

One of the best ways entrepreneurs find employees is by getting referrals from friends, other employees, or other people they know. You can also try to recruit employees by putting a help wanted sign in your store window or posting your job opening on the Web. If your company already has employees, the ideal person for a job you need to fill might already be working for you in a different position.

CHECKPOINT

→ List five ways you can recruit employees.

Hire Employees

Hiring employees is often difficult because you have to make important decisions based on very little information. How should you decide whom to hire?

Know What to Look for in an Employee

The job description identifies the skills and experience an employee needs to do a particular job. You also should look for personal characteristics that would make a person a good employee. Good employees are:

- friendly
- dependable
- honest
- enthusiastic
- good listeners
- always on time
- fast learners

Screen Job Applicants

The first step in the hiring process is to screen the candidates that applied for the job. Screening will help you sort through your list of job applicants and remove the ones that are not right for the job. This step allows you to focus on the most qualified candidates.

Evan Johnson, the owner of Johnson's Medical Supply, ran a want ad in his local newspaper. He was looking for a person with at least five years of experience selling medical equipment. He received more than 150 letters in response to his ad. However, 120 of the letters he received were from people with no experience in the field. Evan immediately removed those letters from the stack. Next, he carefully examined each remaining letter and selected ten candidates to interview, based on their experience.

Interview Job Applicants

The job interview helps you decide whether the job applicant can help you meet customer needs. Making the most of the job interview is as important for you as it is for the job candidate. To make sure that the interview goes well, follow these basic rules.

1. **Be prepared.** Make a list of questions you want to ask, such as those on the next page. Review the job candidate's letter or application just before the interview.

What is the purpose of the job interview?

© GETTY IMAGES/PHOTODISC

SAMPLE INTERVIEW QUESTIONS

1. What interests you about the job?

2. How can your skills and experience help the company?

3. What are your career plans? How does this job fit in with those plans?

4. What other jobs have you had? What did you like and dislike about those jobs?

5. What were your accomplishments at your previous jobs?

6. Why did you leave your last job?

7. How do you think your education has prepared you for this job?

8. What kind of work do you enjoy most? What makes a job enjoyable for you?

9. Describe a difficult situation at your last job or at school and explain how you handled it.

2. **Be courteous.** Be on time for the interview. Avoid taking phone calls during the interview. Try to put the job candidates at ease by offering them something to drink. Make them feel welcome in your office.

3. **Avoid taking over the interview.** Remember that the interview is your chance to get to know the job candidate. To do so, be sure to allow the applicant plenty of time to speak.

4. **Take notes.** Throughout the interview, jot down your thoughts about the candidate as well as any interesting information the candidate gives you.

5. **Look for warnings that the person may not be a good worker.** Warnings include many job changes, unexplained time off between jobs, and negative comments about previous employers.

6. **Don't make quick judgments about a candidate.** Don't rule out someone until the interview is over.

7. **Remain pleasant and positive throughout the interview.** At the end of the interview, thank the candidate for coming and let the candidate know when you plan to make a decision.

8. **Write a summary of your thoughts about the candidate.** You should write this summary right after the interview while your thoughts are still fresh. Put this document in the candidate's file so you can review it later.

Check References

Once you have two or three very qualified candidates, you need to check references. With the permission of the job applicant, call the person's most recent employers to make sure that the applicant held the jobs listed on the

You are going to hire someone to work as your assistant in a car cleaning business. Write a want ad for this job. Then, make a list of questions you will ask the job applicants to help you decide who is the right person for the job.

job application. Ask previous employers about the person. Describe the job the person has applied for. Ask the previous employer if the candidate would perform well in such a job. Other questions may be about the personal qualities of the candidate, such as people skills.

Make a Job Offer

When you have decided to make a job offer, contact the person by phone. Let the person know you were impressed with his or her qualifications. Be sure to state how much you would like the applicant to join your company.

Clearly state the starting salary, benefits, and terms of employment. If the first applicant does not take the job, make the offer to your second choice and then to your third choice, if necessary. Once a candidate accepts your offer, contact all of the other candidates you interviewed. Thank them for interviewing with your business, and politely let them know that you have given the job to another applicant.

> **CHECKPOINT**
> ➔ What steps are involved in hiring employees?

5.2 LET'S GET REAL

1 **THINK ABOUT YOURSELF** As an entrepreneur, you will be the person at the top of the organizational chart. Are you comfortable with the responsibility that will come with being in charge? Write a paragraph describing the way you feel.

2 **WHAT DO YOU THINK?** Why do you think it is important to write a summary of your thoughts about a job applicant after the interview?

3 **MATH CONNECTION** You are thinking about adding a part-time job to your business. You could pay the employee $6.50 per hour. How much would you pay if the employee works 15 hours per week? How much would you pay if the employee works 20 hours per week?

4 **COMMUNICATION CONNECTION** Look through your local newspaper or on the Internet and find a want ad for a job that you think you might want to apply for some day. Write a paragraph telling why you think you would like this job and would be a good candidate for it.

HOW DO YOU MANAGE YOUR STAFF?

Terms

management
policies
motivate
delegate

Goals

* **Describe the three levels of management and desirable leadership qualities.**

* **List ways to motivate employees.**

* **Explain why you should evaluate employees' job performance.**

© GETTY IMAGES/PHOTODISC

Lead Your Employees

Once you have people working for you, you will become a manager. You will no longer focus all of your efforts on doing your own job. Much of your time will be spent managing others. As a manager, you have to be a good leader and motivate your employees. **Management** is a way to achieve goals by using resources. Resources include people, technology, and equipment.

To manage your staff well, you need to understand the different levels and styles of management. You also need to develop leadership qualities. A good leader will encourage employees to do the best they can.

Levels and Styles of Management

There are three basic levels of management—supervisory-level, middle-level, and top management level. The amount of responsibility is different at each level of management. As the manager moves up, the amount of responsibility increases. The number of managers at each level will depend on the size of a company. In a new business, the entrepreneur may take on the role of all levels of management. A large corporation may have many people working as middle- and supervisory-level managers.

Supervisory-level managers work directly with the workers on the job. They are responsible for carrying out the plans of middle management. *Middle management* serves as a link between the supervisory-level and top management. Middle management is responsible for carrying out the goals of top management. *Top management* is responsible for developing the plan for a company and has the highest level of responsibility.

Management Styles Managers will develop a *style* or way of working with their employees. Management styles have changed over the years as the workplace has changed. Successful managers today often *empower* their employees by allowing them to make decisions on their own. Empowerment gives employees a sense of responsibility. It helps speed up the flow of work. It also reduces the manager's workload.

Not all managers use this style. Some managers use fear and threats. These managers treat their employees as if they are lazy and cannot be trusted. Other managers trust and respect their employees and value their hard work. Some managers

What management style is this manager using?

reward employees for good work.

In your working career, you probably will see many different management styles. As you become a manager, you will need to remember what you liked about managers you worked for so that you can develop your own style.

Leadership Qualities

There are many personal characteristics that can help you be a good leader. Desirable leadership qualities include the following.

- **Judgment** makes decisions carefully and fairly

- **Honesty** is ethical when making decisions and is truthful with others

- **Enthusiasm** makes work fun

- **Cooperation** works well with others

- **Communication** listens, speaks, and writes well

- **Dependability** follows through on promises

- **Understanding** respects feelings and needs of people

Developing these leadership qualities has helped Adam Stevenson create a team of hard-working employees at the busy tool rental shop he owns. Every month, Adam posts the work schedule for the following month. He makes sure to assign the unpopular night and weekend shifts evenly among all of his employees. Adam encourages employees who want to make schedule changes to discuss their needs with him. He tries to meet all reasonable requests. Adam encourages employees to come to him with suggestions for improving customer service. He praises employees who have good ideas. He also lets others know that their work is valued.

> **CHECKPOINT**
> → Why is it important for a manager to be a good leader?

Write Employee Policies

As the owner of your own business, you will write policies about vacations, holidays, work schedules, dress codes, and other issues affecting your workers. **Policies** are rules for the workplace. You will need to make sure that all of your employees know these policies. You may need to remind employees of policies if they fail to follow them.

Many companies share policies with the staff by creating an employee handbook. These handbooks can be just a few pages long, or they can fill a small binder, depending on the size of the company and the number of policies.

Train Your Employees

Well-trained employees perform their jobs better. They know what is expected of them. You will need to develop a training program for your new employees. This program should begin as soon as they are hired. Training will continue as things change in your business. For example, you may get a new cash register and will have to train employees how to use it.

There are different ways to train employees. You will need to decide which is best for you, your business, and the employee.

- **On-the-job training** Employees learn new responsibilities by actually performing them at their place of business.

- **Coaching** Employees get instruction from their manager on a regular basis.

E-mail and Internet policy

Important warnings for use of e-mail

...arnings listed below are of critical importance and no... ...rtain circumstances constitute a serious disciplinary... ...y in e-mail messages. Improper statements can give ri... ...y liability. Work on the assumptions that c... ...ssages that are abusive, sexist, raci... ...dential messag...

© DIGITAL VISION

Why are employee policies needed?

- **Mentoring** One employee teams up with another more experienced employee to learn a job.

- **Off-site training** Employees attend a class or workshop to learn something new from an expert in the field.

Safety Procedures Your employees should also be trained in safety issues. They should know how to operate equipment safely and be instructed to wear protective gear when needed. Employees should know emergency plans for fires, tornadoes, and other disasters.

Roberto Rios owns a lawn-mowing service company. He shows all new employees how to operate the lawn mowers and weed trimmers. He provides the employees with safety glasses to wear while using the equipment. Employees are also required to purchase safety boots to wear on the job.

CHECKPOINT

➡ What are the different training techniques?

Motivate Your Employees

To get the most out of your employees, you will have to **motivate** them, or give them a good reason to do something. There are several ways to do this.

1. **Pay them well.** When employees feel that they are paid well, they will be happier and will perform to the best of their ability.

2. **Treat them fairly.** Everyone wants to be treated well. Be sure to treat everyone the same.

3. **Recognize them for the work they do.** Thank employees and reward them for their good work. Praise them often.

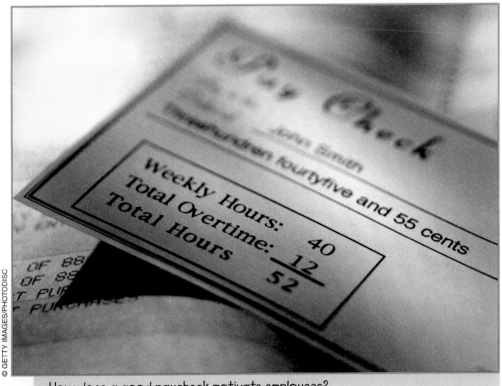

How does a good paycheck motivate employees?

4. Give them some responsibility. Employees who are allowed to make their own decisions often work harder. They take pride in the fact that their work is important to the business.

Delegate Responsibility

Many entrepreneurs have trouble delegating responsibility. To **delegate** is to let other people share workloads and responsibilities. Employees who are given more responsibility are better motivated and usually do a better job. Delegating work to employees allows them to show off their talents.

Delegating allows an entrepreneur to focus on more important things, such as developing ideas for new products. Paperwork and tasks that someone else can perform will free up your time.

Finally, delegating responsibility is necessary if a company is to grow. When your business is small, you may be able to handle everything yourself. If the company is to grow, you will have to let others take on more responsibility to help you keep things running smoothly.

Listen to Employees

Some entrepreneurs fail to listen to their employees. By doing so, they miss out on valuable information that could help them increase sales.

The people who work for you are very familiar with your business. They may be able to offer fresh ideas on how to improve your business. Listening to their points of view may help you come up with new solutions to problems. If you listen to your employees, they will feel that they are valuable to your company and will more likely do a good job for you.

CHECKPOINT

→ Why should you delegate responsibility and listen to your employees?

Work as a Team

In many activities, teamwork is necessary. A ball club cannot win if its players do not work together as a team. Astronauts working on the space station cannot complete their mission if crew members do not work together.

Teamwork is important in many businesses. Employees work as a team to meet company

How can you be a good team leader?

© GETTY IMAGES/PHOTODISC

How can you evaluate employees?

goals. Teams help employees learn from one another. They teach employees how to work together to complete a task. Teams are more likely to work harder and to come up with good ideas for the business.

As the owner of your own business, you will provide the leadership for the team. To be a good team leader, you will need to do the following:

* Build trust among team members and gain their trust.

* Respect and get along with all team members.

* Make sure that all team members understand the goals you have set.

* Encourage team members to share their ideas.

* Make team members feel like partners in your business.

* Motivate the team to meet the goals you have set.

CHECKPOINT

→ Why is teamwork important in many businesses?

Evaluate Your Employees

At least once a year, you need to evaluate, or review, how well employees are doing their jobs. Evaluating job performance will help you decide whether an employee should be given a raise. It also will help you identify good employees who should be promoted and problem employees who should be fired.

Create an Evaluation Procedure

Most businesses perform employee reviews once a year. They review each employee's work and determine the increase in the employee's pay. The job description should be used when reviewing how well an employee has done on the job. If the employee has met all of the job responsibilities in the job description, that employee should receive a pay raise.

You should record the review on a performance evaluation form. The form should include the employee's name and job title, as well as the manager's

Working Together

In small groups, brainstorm a list of personal qualities that team members need to have to help them work well with others.

name, and the dates of the review period, such as 1/1 to 12/31. It also should include job responsibilities, places for comments, goals for the next year, and a section for how the employee can improve. A ranking system can be used to mark how well the employee has done. For example, you can rank an employee's work as below average, average, or above average.

The manager should set up a meeting with the employee to go over the review. A written summary of the review should be kept in the employee's file.

CHECKPOINT

→ Why should you evaluate the people who work for you?

Promote or Terminate Employees

Promoting good employees will help keep them interested in working for your business. Promoting one employee over another one may cause problems.

Be sure you make all decisions fairly. You should base decisions on solid reasons, such as the amount of sales employees made and the quality of their work.

Some employees may not work out. They may end up hurting your business. How will you handle such situations? As soon as you notice an employee not performing well, you should discuss the problem with the employee. If performance does not improve, you should give a written warning. If there still is no improvement, you will need to terminate, or fire, the employee.

Once you decide to terminate an employee, you should do so immediately. Meet with the employee privately and explain why you are letting him or her go. Ask the employee to leave the workplace the same day. Record the date of the termination and the reason for it in the employee's file.

CHECKPOINT

→ Why is it necessary to promote or terminate employees?

© DIGITAL VISION

How should you deal with employees who are not performing well?

It is important for managers to know how to motivate their employees. Managers are learning that it can be difficult to motivate Generation Y workers. Those born after 1980 make up Generation Y. This generation is different from previous generations in many ways. Generation Y is well educated and comfortable with technology such as computers, cell phones, video games, and digital music. These people look for a fun workplace and can grow bored easily.

To attract and keep Generation Y workers, companies have started offering special benefits. Some businesses offer on-site massage and fitness programs or gym memberships. Others offer hair-cutting, dry-cleaning, and car-washing services. Some break rooms now have reclining chairs and beanbag chairs for the comfort of the employees. Or instead, workers may want to take a break in the recreation room and play a round of ping-pong, pool, or video games. Don't be surprised if you see a dog walking around your office because some businesses now allow owners to bring their dogs to work!

Think Critically

1. Why do you think Generation Y workers are harder to motivate?
2. Do you think it is a good idea for a company to offer special benefits? How do these benefits motivate employees?

5.3 LET'S GET REAL

1 THINK ABOUT YOURSELF Review the desirable leadership qualities. Which of these qualities do you have? Do you think you would be a good leader? Explain why or why not.

2 WHAT DO YOU THINK? Why do you think some managers have a hard time delegating work to others?

3 COMMUNICATION CONNECTION Using the *Activities* CD, open the Chapter 5 folder. Open the Performance Evaluation activity and print out a copy of the form. With a partner, role play an employee being evaluated who deserves a promotion. Make up the employer and job. Fill out the performance evaluation form. Summarize the meeting in writing.

4 MATH CONNECTION You own a restaurant, and you have one employee. You pay him $5.50 an hour for a 40-hour week. You pay him an overtime rate of $8.25 an hour for any hours worked beyond the 40 hours a week. Last week, he worked a total of 40 hours. This week he worked a total of 45 hours. How much do you owe your employee for these two weeks?

Harley-Davidson

Harley-Davidson is a company that claims it makes dreams come true, and many customers agree. The thrill of motorcycling on a Harley actually began in 1901 when William S. Harley, age 21, completed a blueprint drawing of an engine designed to fit into a bicycle. In 1903, he and 20-year-old Arthur Davidson built the first Harley-Davidson® motorcycle in Milwaukee, Wisconsin, and made it available to the public. Their first "factory" was a 10-by-15-foot wooden shed with the words "Harley-Davidson Motor Company" written on the door. A childhood friend bought one of the 1903 models from them. The first Harley-Davidson dealer to sell motorcycles was C.H. Lang of Chicago, Illinois.

The company began entering motorcycle races, and word of Harley-Davidson's tough motorcycle spread quickly. Expansion began with a new factory in 1906. It measured 28 by 80 feet, and staff increased to six full-time employees. The location where the factory was built is the same as the present-day headquarters of the company. The first motorcycle catalog also was produced in that year.

In 1907, staff size increased to 18 employees. The factory size was doubled, and dealers were being recruited to sell the motorcycles. The first motorcycle for police duty was sold in 1908 to the Detroit, Michigan, Police Department.

Harley-Davidson went international in 1912, exporting motorcycles to Japan. The number of dealers had grown to over 200 nationwide. In 1916, Harley-Davidson began the *Enthusiast*, the longest published motorcycle magazine in the world.

Harley-Davidson's business grew during World War I, with an estimated 20,000 motorcycles used in the war. After the war ended, the first American to enter Germany after its defeat was riding a Harley-Davidson motorcycle.

Today, with over 1,300 dealers, Harley-Davidson now offers service, products, and clothing. It continues to practice the values that began its business: to tell the truth, be fair, keep promises, respect the individual, and encourage curiosity.

Think Critically

1. How did recruiting dealers allow Harley-Davidson to grow?
2. Why do you think the values that began Harley-Davidson's business are still important today?

Where Will You Locate Your Business?

1. Selecting a trade area for a business is an important part of choosing the right location for a retail business.

2. If a service business performs the service away from the business location, the location is not important.

3. An advantage of working at home is that certain costs can be reduced or eliminated. A disadvantage is that interruptions during the day can make it difficult to concentrate on work.

4. For retail businesses, the purpose of a layout is to attract and keep customers. For service businesses, organization of supplies is an important part of the layout.

Who Will You Hire to Help Run Your Business?

5. You should write job descriptions that list the responsibilities of each job. You also should create an organizational structure to show how jobs in your company relate to each other.

6. Use classified advertising, employment agencies, college placement centers, referrals, and the Web to recruit employees.

7. When hiring employees, you first will need to screen applicants. Then, you will interview those who seem qualified for the job. After you have interviewed several candidates, you should check their references and offer the job to the most qualified candidate.

How Do You Manage Your Staff?

8. Having good management and leadership qualities will help you manage your staff. By writing policies and offering training, you will help your employees perform better.

9. There are several ways to motivate employees, including treating them fairly and listening to them.

10. Teamwork is very important in businesses. A team will work together to meet company goals.

11. You should create a procedure for evaluating employees. Good employees should be promoted. Problem employees should be fired.

Vocabulary Builder

Choose the term that best fits the definition.

1. Area from which you expect to attract customers
2. Plan that shows how all the jobs in a company relate to one another
3. Written statement listing the duties and responsibilities of a job
4. To let other people share workloads and responsibilities
5. To look for people to hire
6. A way to achieve goals by using resources
7. The floor plan for your business
8. Rules for the workplace
9. To give an employee a good reason to do something

a. delegate
b. job description
c. layout
d. management
e. motivate
f. organizational structure
g. policies
h. recruit
i. trade area

Review What You Have Learned

10. Why is it important for a retail business to map out its trade area?
11. Why is the location for a service business not always important?
12. What are some reasons an entrepreneur might want to operate a business from home?
13. What do you need to consider when designing the layout of your business?
14. Why does the layout of a business differ based on the type of business?
15. Why is it important to write detailed job descriptions for all jobs?
16. Why is it important for a business to create an organizational structure?
17. What type of information should a classified want ad contain?
18. What are some of the characteristics of a good employee?
19. Why should you screen job applicants?
20. What are the three basic levels of management? Explain what each type of manager does.
21. Why should a company have employee policies? Give an example of a policy that a company might have.
22. Why is it important to give employees some responsibility?
23. What are some reasons that you might have to fire an employee?

Using the *Activities* CD, open the Chapter 5 folder. Open the activity, Evaluate the Layout of a Business. Print a copy and complete the activity.

Think About It

1. Can you think of successful retail businesses that do not have convenient locations? Why do you think they are successful even though they don't have the best location?

2. Getting referrals from people you know is one of the best ways to recruit employees. Why is this true? Are there any reasons you might not want to use a referral from someone you know?

3. Are good leadership qualities something that can be learned, or are you born with them? Explain your answer.

Project: Making Entrepreneurship Work for You

This activity will help you develop the business opportunity that you identified in Chapter 1.

1. Using a local map, mark the trade area for your business. Mark the locations for your business and for your competitors. Mark any businesses in the trade area that do not compete but that attract a similar type of customer. For each area, write a summary stating why it would or would not be a good place to locate your business. Choose the best location for your business. Explain your decision.

2. Design the physical layout of your business. Create a scale drawing of the space and show the placement of all of the furniture, fixtures, and equipment. Indicate the planned use of each area. How does this layout meet your goals? Calculate your square footage requirements.

3. Write a job description for a new job at your business. Describe the duties and responsibilities of this job. Then, write a want ad for this job that describes the skills and experience needed. Write the interview questions that you will ask the job candidates. Finally, write the questions that you will ask their references.

4. How do you plan to motivate your employees? List one way you could reward employees for their work.

5. What parts of your business require training, and what type of training is the best? Explain how you will train employees.

Chapter 6

How Do You Compete?

© DIGITAL VISION

She's Cleaning Up!

Like lots of kids, 13-year-old Jessie Heenan of Raymore, Missouri, wanted to make some extra money. She decided to start a business. But she didn't know what kind of business to start. Plenty of kids in Raymore cut grass or sold homemade candles. Then Jessie noticed new homes being built in her neighborhood. She got the idea of keeping those houses clean after the work crews left. So Jessie started Neat & Pretty. Her business cleans houses during the construction process.

Jessie believed that builders would be interested in her services, but first she needed to let them know that she was in business. So she set up a marketing campaign. Most of her advertising is word-of-mouth, but she also sends letters and business cards to builders in her area. A few days after mailing out information, Jessie phones the builders. She explains what she does and how she can help. She also cleaned a few houses for free to prove that she could do a good job.

Before setting prices, Jessie contacted several local cleaning companies to find out what they charged. Jessie then set her price slightly lower than her competition. She also gives special discounts.

Neat & Pretty offers three stages of cleaning. The initial cleaning is done after the frame of the house has been built. It includes collecting bits of wood and shingles. The drywall cleaning is done after the sheetrock has been installed. It includes picking up scrap insulation and electrical wire. The final cleaning takes place after the building is completed. It includes picking up carpet pieces. It also includes vacuuming, mopping, and cleaning fixtures. A recent final cleaning took Jessie about three hours. She earned $100.

Jessie expects business to slow during winters and resume during the warm weather months. But slow spells give her time to plan for the next busy season. In fact, building a solid plan is Jessie's best advice to potential entrepreneurs. She recommends that you always plan ahead.

WHAT DO YOU KNOW?

1 How did Jessie use the competition to her advantage? What else might she have done?

2 How did Jessie spread the word about her business? What do you think is the best way to promote a new business like Neat & Pretty? Why?

WHY DO MARKET RESEARCH?

Terms

target market
marketing concept
customers
demographics
market research
secondary data
primary data
focus group

Goals

✳ **Describe a target market and ways to understand your customers.**

✳ **Explain how to use secondary and primary data for market research.**

✳ **Identify the five steps in primary data market research.**

What Is a Target Market?

© DIGITAL VISION

Entrepreneurs with exciting new ideas are so busy thinking about their products or services that sometimes they forget about the customer. But a good business idea will go nowhere without customers. Before opening your new business, you will have to determine who your main customers are. You also will need to find out whether these customers are willing to buy your product or service.

A **target market** includes the individuals that are interested in a particular product or service and are able to pay for it. Identifying your target market helps you reach the people you most want to sell to. As an entrepreneur, you will need to estimate demand for your products or services. You do this by identifying your target customers. Target customers are the customers you would most like to attract. A car dealer selling mid-priced minivans would target middle-class families with children. A car dealer that offers expensive sports cars might target single people with very high incomes.

The **marketing concept** focuses on the needs of customers when planning, producing, distributing, and promoting a product or service. Three activities must be completed by businesses in order to use the marketing concept successfully.

- Identify what will satisfy the customers' wants and needs.

- Create and sell products or services that customers consider better than other choices.

- Operate profitably.

There are some products that don't have a target market. These products appeal to all customers for the same reason. The products are basically the same among all competitors. For these types of products, businesses can use a mass marketing approach. *Mass marketing* uses one marketing plan to reach all customers. Energizer uses mass marketing when marketing batteries using the Energizer Bunny® advertisements. Everyone uses batteries for the same reasons. So, businesses don't need to identify a target market.

Understand Your Customer

Customers are the people who buy the products and services companies offer. The customer should be your most important

Why is it important to understand your customers?

focus. Without customers, companies cannot remain in business. Understanding people's wants and needs will help you to identify business opportunities. The more you know about your customers, the better you will be at giving them what they need and want.

Customers want goods and services to satisfy wants and needs. A *want* is an unfilled desire of a customer. Customers want things such as designer clothes, luxury cars, and vacations to exotic places. A *need* is anything that is required to live. Basic needs must be met before a customer can think about satisfying wants. Food, shelter, water, air, and sleep are needs for all people.

Part of understanding your customers is knowing their demographics. **Demographics** are data that describe a group of people in terms of their age, marital status, family size, ethnic background, gender, profession, education, and income. Using this information can give you an idea of the size of your market. It will tell you how many people would be willing and able to purchase your product or service.

Working Together

Break into small groups. Determine the demographics of the individuals in your group. Make a list of products that are commonly marketed to your demographic group.

6.1 Why Do Market Research? 129

Identify Your Target Market

Businesses that identify their target markets are more successful. If you focus on selling to a certain type of individual, you can more likely give those individuals exactly what they want. To identify the target market for your product or service, you will need to answer the following questions:

- Who are my customers—individuals or companies?

- If my customers are individuals, how old are they? How much money do they earn? Where do they live? How do they spend their time and money?

- If my customers are companies, what industries are they in? Where are those industries located?

- What needs or wants will my product or service satisfy?

- How many potential customers live in the area in which I want to operate?

- Where do these potential customers currently buy the products or services I want to sell them?

- What price are they willing to pay for my products or services?

- What can I do for my customers that other companies are not already doing for them?

As an entrepreneur, you should put yourself in your customers' shoes. You should think about your customers every day. Your customers' needs and buying habits may change. Competitors may change their products and services. By continually studying your market, you will be ready to respond to these changes.

Understand the Competition

Knowing a lot about your competition will help you define your target market. Businesses enter into areas where there is competition all the time. But they have to identify some special customer need or want that is not being met by competitors. Customers may be happy with the products or services being offered, but they may be unhappy

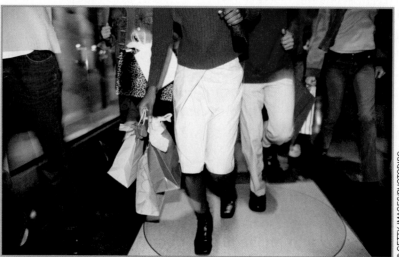

How can demographics help you target your market?

with the prices being charged. Customers might be dissatisfied with the quality of a product or service. They might be willing to pay more for better quality. In either case, a customer need is not being met by a competitor. An unmet need is a possible opportunity for an entrepreneur.

> **CHECKPOINT**
> → What questions should you ask to help identify your target market?

Market Research

For your business to succeed, you need to find out who your customers are. You also need to know what they want or need and how much they are willing to pay for your product or service. To collect this information about your customers, you will conduct market research. **Market research** is a system for collecting, recording, and analyzing information about customers, competitors, goods, and services. Market research can help a business decide which marketing strategies will work the best. Market research can be expensive and time-consuming, but it is definitely worth doing when major decisions are being made. You will use secondary data and primary data to gather your information. Both types of data will help you identify ways in which you can meet customer needs.

Secondary Data

Entrepreneurs usually begin research of their target market by using secondary data. **Secondary data** are found in sources that are already published. Information on population, family size, household income, economic trends, industry forecasts, and other information can be found in secondary data resources. Places to find secondary data include:

- Publications issued by government and community organizations, such as the U.S. Census Bureau, the Small Business Administration, and the Chamber of Commerce
- Books about specific industries
- Information on web sites for government and businesses
- Specialized magazines and journals for particular fields of business
- Newspaper articles

Kisha Nichols wanted to expand her family-owned chain of retail shoe stores. She decided to perform some secondary data research. Kisha visited the local Chamber of Commerce web site. The site provided her with demographics on population for her city and county. It also contained industry forecasts for communities in her area. This information allowed Kisha to identify the largest retail markets. She also was able to discover the retail markets that were expected to grow the most over the next ten years. Kisha also found information in a book about the average income of retail shoe store owners in her state. Newspaper articles gave Kisha data about the lifestyles of people in her area.

You can say that again!

I think it's very important that whatever you're trying to make or sell or teach has to be basically good. A bad product and you know what? You won't be here in ten years.

—Martha Stewart

Most of them worked in professional office settings. This information showed that they had a need for comfortable dress shoes. Studying secondary data gave Kisha a good idea of which community might provide the best sales for one of her shoe stores.

Primary Data

Most market researchers also collect primary data. Information collected for the first time for a specific purpose is **primary data**. A researcher collects primary data to help identify and understand the target market. Primary data can provide the most up-to-date and useful information. But it can be time-consuming and more expensive to collect than secondary data. As an entrepreneur, you will need to determine how much primary data you need to collect for market research.

There are a few different ways to collect primary data. The most common type of primary market research is a *questionnaire*, also called a survey. It is a list of questions you would like to ask your customers to find out demographic and other information. A questionnaire can be presented by mail, over the phone, or in person. Other ways to collect primary data are through observation and focus groups.

Observation Market research can involve observation. If you are considering opening a juice bar in a shopping mall, you might want to see how many customers you could attract. You could go to the mall and count the number of people purchasing drinks at various food outlets. An entrepreneur interested in starting a motorcycle repair shop might count the number of motorcycles at a busy intersection.

Focus Groups Another way in which you could find out about the market is by conducting interviews with small numbers of people. A **focus group** is an interview with groups of target customers who provide valuable ideas on products or services. You can ask the same kinds of questions in a focus group that you would ask in a survey or questionnaire. The benefit of focus groups is that they allow for more discussion than a questionnaire does. So, you can collect more information. The person leading the focus groups asks questions about buying habits, likes and dislikes, and interest in particular products and services. The focus group session is recorded. Then the comments can be reviewed after the session.

NET Bookmark

A focus group can provide an advertiser with information about customers' reactions to a product or even to an advertisement. Access exploringxtra.swlearning.com and click on the link for Chapter 6. Read the article entitled *Basics of Conducting Focus Groups*. According to the article, about how long should a focus group session last? What are the three essential ground rules for conducting a focus group?

exploringxtra.swlearning.com

CHECKPOINT

→ What is the difference between primary and secondary data?

Steps of Primary Data Market Research

Primary data is very useful. It provides you with information you may not find with secondary data. Primary market research involves five steps. Those steps are:

1. Define the question
2. Select a research method
3. Collect data
4. Analyze data
5. Draw conclusions

What should you consider when creating a survey?

© GETTY IMAGES/PHOTODISC

Define the Question

In the first step of the market research process, you need to define exactly what it is that you are trying to find out. Maggie Blandin is thinking about starting a dog-walking service. Before she invests in her business, Maggie would like to know how many dog owners live in the area. She also wants to find out how many of them don't have the time to walk their dogs. Finally, she would like to know how much they might be willing to pay to have someone walk their dogs for them.

Select a Research Method

Once you have defined the market research questions, you are ready to decide how you will get the answers. Should you use a survey? Should you use an observation method? Would a focus group help? The method you use will depend on what type of information you want to gather. For example, you can get people's opinions in a survey or focus group but not by observation. You should perform some secondary data market research first to become familiar with your market. You can then choose the best research method to use to get the information you still need.

If you choose a survey, you should think carefully about how long it should be. You will need to decide what questions it should include and how it should be given. You also will need to determine how many people you should survey. If you use observation to do your research, you need to determine where and when to get the best information. If a focus group is needed, you should think about what kind of customers to include and what questions to ask them.

Maggie decides that a survey is the best way for her to find information about customer preferences for a dog-walking service. Maggie thinks that in addition to a survey, an observation method could give her more information about how many people in her area walk their own dogs.

Collect Data

When you begin collecting data, you will first gather information from secondary data sources. You will need demographic data and information about your specific type of business. This information will help you determine what kind of primary data research to perform.

Maggie Blandin found that 60 percent of the households in her area owned one or more dogs. She also learned that the average annual household income was $75,000. Most households had one or more adults working in a professional field and putting in overtime each week. She also found that dog ownership was on the rise in her area. Based on this information, Maggie put together a survey that would help confirm household incomes. It also would ask specific questions about the lifestyles, opinions, and choices of dog owners.

What kind of data did Maggie collect in her survey?

© GETTY IMAGES/PHOTODISC

Design a Survey

Design a Survey Making a good questionnaire is very important. Questionnaires should be kept to one page in length when given over the phone or mailed. Longer questionnaires can be used if an interview is face-to-face. Questions should be clear and easy to answer. Only the most important questions should appear. If the response to a question serves no specific purpose, the question should not be used.

Analyze Data

Once you have collected all your data, you will need to analyze or interpret the information you have found. You should write a summary of the data so that you can refer to it later. When you analyze the data you have collected, you should look for customers that have things in common. This can help you determine which customers to target.

Through her secondary data market research, Maggie found that 2,500 dogs live in her area. In her primary data research, she found that 30 percent of dog owners in her area would pay $20 to have their dogs walked for 30 minutes. Many would pay to have them walked two or three times a week. This means she could easily have 750 dogs to walk each week.

Be Your Own Boss

You are going to start a house-cleaning business in your neighborhood. You think it would be good to do some market research first. Explain what you hope to find from your market research. Decide which form of market research you will use to gather primary data. Why do you think this form of research will be the best one to use? What kind of secondary data might already be available that you could use for market research?

Draw Conclusions

Once you have analyzed your data, you will need to determine how to use them. You will develop a plan of action based on the information you found in your market research.

Maggie Blandin's market research has helped her conclude that her idea for a dog-walking service is profitable. Her market research has identified her target market as people 31 to 50 years of age who travel often. They work long hours and earn $50,000 to $100,000 a year. She now knows the amount of money people would be willing to pay for her service. She also knows how much income she can expect to make.

In her first effort to get customers, Maggie plans to create a flier aimed at her target market. She will distribute the flier in neighborhoods and veterinary offices. She also plans to distribute the flier downtown and in other business areas where many of her target market customers work.

> **CHECKPOINT**
> → Describe the steps involved in conducting market research.

6.1 LET'S GET REAL

1] **THINK ABOUT YOURSELF** Have you ever been asked questions by someone conducting market research? If not, find out if your parents have ever taken part in a market research study. Using your or your parents' experience, write a paragraph about what you think the researcher was trying to find out.

2] **WHAT DO YOU THINK?** Why is it important to define the questions you want your market research to answer?

3] **LANGUAGE ARTS CONNECTION** Using the *Activities* CD, open the Chapter 6 folder. Select the Market Research Evaluation activity. Review and evaluate the market research survey that Maggie Blandin created for her dog-walking service. Then, use what you've learned to create your own survey. Describe a new product that you think will be successful in the marketplace. Write a survey that will help you learn if there is an interest in your product.

4] **MATH CONNECTION** Marcel wants to open a car wash. For several days, he observed the cars being washed at a competitor and recorded the information below. What is the average number of cars he counted each day? Based on this data, if his car wash was open five days a week, how many cars might he expect to wash per year? (Hint: There are 52 weeks in a year.)

Day 1	Day 2	Day 3	Day 4	Day 5	Day 6
50 cars	45 cars	48 cars	26 cars	47 cars	55 cars

WHO IS YOUR COMPETITION?

Terms	Goals
competitors customer feedback card	✳ **Explain how businesses evaluate the strengths and weaknesses of competitors.** ✳ **Describe strategies for building customer loyalty.**

Study Competitors

Have you ever looked at the same item in two different stores? The prices may have been the same, or one store may have sold the item

© DIGITAL VISION

at a lower price. How did you decide which store to buy the item from? The two stores you were shopping at are competitors. **Competitors** are companies offering similar or identical products and services to the same group of customers. As the owner of a new business, you will have to persuade customers to buy from you and not from your competitors. To do this, you must collect information about your competition. This information will help you see how your business is different or the same from your competitors' businesses.

Evaluating the strengths and weaknesses of your competition will help you figure out what you can do to get customers to buy from your business. Some of the things that you should look at when evaluating your competition are:

- **Price** What do they charge? Are your prices higher or lower?

- **Location** Where are your competitors located?

- **Facility** Is the building nice? Does it have a good location? Is it appealing to customers?

- **Strengths** What does the competitor do that no one else does? What does it do better than everyone else?

- **Weaknesses** What are some disadvantages of your competition?

- **Strategy** How will you attract customers to your business? How will you get customers to come to your business instead of a competitor's business?

Looking at your competition in these key areas will help you find out what other companies are doing that is good or bad. It also will help you figure out the best ways to attract customers.

Hector Lopez has learned about raising fish. He would like to stock his family's lake with fish and open it as a public fishing lake. He decides to visit several fishing lakes in the area where he lives to find out how much they charge and what special features they offer. Hector puts this information in the chart shown below to help him compare his competitors. This research will help him develop a marketing strategy to beat his competition. He has decided that he will get his sister to help him. He also will offer refreshments and restroom facilities at his lake. None of his competitors offer both of these services. He thinks this will help attract customers to his lake.

CHECKPOINT

→ Why should you evaluate your competitors?

Comparison of Competitors

Competitor	Price	Location	Facility	Strength	Weakness	Strategy
Season's Lake Resort	$11.50	Excellent	Good	Excellent location	High price	Offer lower prices
Lakeland Fishery	$5.50	Fair	Good	Low price	Location, no refreshments	Offer more convenient location and refreshments
Carl's Creek	$5.00	Good	Fair	Low price	Facility, no restrooms or refreshments	Offer nicer facilities with restrooms and refreshments
Royal Fishing Lake	$7.00	Fair	Excellent	Excellent facility	Location, no refreshments	Offer more convenient location and refreshments

Strategies for Building Customer Loyalty

Do you have a favorite store where you always shop? Maybe you keep going back because you like what they sell or you like how you are treated. Maybe you earn rewards for shopping there. Getting customers to buy products or services from a business and not its competition is only one step in running a successful business. Businesses also must make sure their customers keep coming back.

Listen and Respond to Your Customers

To keep customers, you will need to find out what they think about your business. Ask your customers questions about your company and respond to the answers they give. Companies that ignore customer concerns will not stay in business long.

Different companies stay in touch with their customers'

needs in different ways. A cosmetics manufacturer may call customers the day after they receive a makeover to ask if they are happy with the products they purchased. Car repair shops also call customers the day after their car was serviced to see if they are pleased with the service. Other companies have a **customer feedback card**, which is a short survey asking customers for their opinions about the company. Customers can write in complaints or positive comments about the business on the customer feedback card. Businesses also can design longer questionnaires for customers to complete.

Jason Rose's business, the Olympic Athletic Club, closed because of his failure to respond to customer feedback. Club members had repeatedly complained about the dirty locker rooms. They also were unhappy with the long wait time for exercise machines during busy hours. Jason ignored his customers' complaints. He believed that the good location of his business and the low monthly fee he charged would ensure his success.

Jason learned from his mistakes. When he opened his next athletic club, he immediately conducted a study to find out what customers wanted. His study revealed, among other things, that he should offer more aerobics classes. He also learned that customers wanted high-speed hair dryers in the locker rooms. Due to his focus on customer satisfaction, Jason's new club is doing very well. He is attracting new members all the time.

© GETTY IMAGES/PHOTODISC

Why did Jason's first athletic club fail?

Other Customer Loyalty Strategies

To build customer loyalty, businesses use many strategies. The main purpose of these strategies is to keep customers happy and keep them coming back to your business. Some of the most basic strategies include:

- excellent service
- more convenient hours than other businesses
- easy return policies
- store credit cards
- personal notes or cards sent for birthdays or to thank customers for their business
- frequent buyer programs

Li-ming Han, the owner of Java Juice, issues shoppers a frequent buyer card for drinks. She

How could a frequent-buyer card help this business?

stamps the card every time a purchase of $5 or more is made. Once the card has been stamped ten times, customers can redeem the card for a free coffee or a fruit smoothie. The frequent buyer card encourages shoppers to buy all of their drinks from Java Juice.

> **CHECKPOINT**
> ➡ What are some strategies for building customer loyalty?

6.2 LET'S GET REAL

1] THINK ABOUT YOURSELF Think about a store that you like to shop in. What is it about the store that makes you want to keep shopping there? Write a paragraph about this store and why you like to shop there. As a guide, refer to the questions that businesses use when evaluating their competitors.

2] WHAT DO YOU THINK? Why is customer feedback important to a business?

3] PROBLEM SOLVING What do you think would be the best strategy to build customer loyalty for a store that sells music CDs? Why did you pick this strategy?

4] COMMUNICATION CONNECTION Shontel Washington just opened an ice cream shop. He would like feedback from the people who visit his shop. Create a short customer feedback card that Shontel could give to customers to learn more about their opinions of his business.

HOW DO YOU GET THE WORD OUT?

Terms

advertising
public relations
publicity
press release
sales promotion
rebate

Goals

* **Explain how to use advertising to promote your business.**

* **Discuss publicity as a form of promotion.**

* **Describe types of sales promotions.**

Advertising

Have you ever seen an advertisement for a product on television and then wanted to go out and buy it? What was it about the advertisement that got your attention? Businesses spend a lot of time and money planning how to promote a new product in the market. Promotion takes many forms. It includes advertising, publicity, and sales promotion. Your *promotional mix* is the strategy for promoting your business using the different forms of promotion.

Service industries, manufacturers, and retailers all advertise. **Advertising** is a paid form of communication sent out by a business about a product or service. Advertising can be very important for small businesses, particularly new ones. Advertising helps you communicate with potential customers. It lets customers know what kinds of products and services your company offers. It tells them why they should buy from you. Large companies generally use advertising agencies to create their

© DIGITAL VISION

advertisements. Advertising agencies usually develop very creative and effective ads. But using an advertising agency can cost a lot of money. As an owner of a small business, you probably will create your own advertising.

Advertising should help a business communicate a positive image. **Public relations** is the act of creating a positive relationship with customers and the general public. Advertising is a public relations activity because it can make potential customers feel good about your company. Getting involved in your community, making donations to charities, and being friendly with your customers also are public relations activities.

Choose Your Message and Medium Your advertising should clearly communicate the message and image you want. If, for example, your marketing strategy is to have low prices, advertisements that call attention to those prices might be beneficial. If you are trying to target customers that are willing to pay higher prices for excellent service, you could create an advertisement about your well-trained staff.

Once you choose a message, you will need to decide which advertising medium to use. A *medium* is the method used to communicate. This could include television, radio, newspapers, and billboards. To choose a medium, you will have to consider both cost and effectiveness in reaching your target audience.

For television and radio advertisements, you pay the station for the amount of time your advertisement or commercial plays. In addition to the fee you pay to air the commercial, you also must consider the costs of making the commercial. If a one-minute commercial costs $25,000 to make, you pay the television station $2,000 for each minute it airs, and you plan to have it aired 30 times, the cost per minute would be $25,000 + ($2,000 × 30) ÷ 30 = $2,833.33.

Television Advertising

Television advertising reaches millions of people every day. It is the best way to reach a large number of people quickly. Television advertising usually comes in the form of commercials or paid advertisements. *Commercials* are usually less than a minute in length and run during breaks in television programming. They are very short promotions about a product or business. *Paid advertisements* can last a half-hour or more and provide more detail about the product being offered. Television advertising allows businesses to communicate through both sight and sound. It can be creative and informative.

Why are commercials a popular way to advertise?

Disadvantages of Television Advertising Advertising on television is very expensive. Making even a low-budget commercial can cost thousands of dollars. Paying a network or cable station to broadcast the commercial can cost much more.

Television reaches too broad an audience to be effective for most businesses. If, for example, only one percent of the viewing audience is interested in a particular product, advertising on television is not likely to be cost effective. There will be many television viewers who are not interested in the product.

Luisa Ramirez is planning to open Luisa's Gourmet Dishes in her local community. Her shop will offer a large selection of gourmet food products. Because of the high costs and the fact that she may not reach her target customer very effectively, Luisa decides that television advertising is not right for her business.

© GETTY IMAGES/PHOTODISC

What might be a disadvantage of advertising Luisa's business on the radio?

Radio Advertising

Radio advertising can be effective for small businesses. It is less expensive than television advertising. You also can be more certain you are reaching your target market. Radio stations tend to attract a particular kind of listener. Pop rock stations target teenagers and people in their twenties. Classical or talk radio stations usually attract older listeners. You can advertise on a station whose listeners share the same demographics as your target market. You can contact stations and ask for information about the demographics of their listeners to make sure they fit your target market.

Luisa Ramirez is targeting middle-aged, upscale customers. To reach this audience, she decides to advertise on the classical music station in her community. She receives demographic information about the radio station's listeners and determines that her business targets a similar type of person.

Disadvantages of Radio Advertising Radio is only an audio message. It cannot visually show your product. Radio listeners may not remember what they hear. They may not even listen closely to the ads.

Newspaper Advertising

Newspapers are the single largest form of advertising in the United States. Newspaper advertising is good for small businesses because:

- it is relatively inexpensive
- it targets a limited geographic area
- it reaches large numbers of people

© GETTY IMAGES/PHOTODISC

What are the disadvantages of newspaper advertising?

Luisa decides to advertise in several local newspapers. She places quarter-page ads in the morning paper serving the city-wide area. She also puts half-page ads in all of the free newspapers that serve her community. The community papers reach a much smaller audience than the large city newspaper, but they are read by the same audience that Luisa is trying to target. Advertising in newspapers is a cost-effective way for Luisa to reach her target market.

Disadvantages of Newspaper Advertising Newspapers reach a large audience, but much of that audience may not be interested in your business. If, for example, you own a small gift shop that caters to people only in your surrounding neighborhood, advertising in your city newspaper may not make sense. You will be paying to reach thousands of people who will never become your customers.

Another disadvantage of newspaper advertising is the fact that your advertisement will compete with many others. Newspapers carry so many advertisements that yours may be overlooked by readers.

CHECKPOINT

What are the advantages of television, radio, and newspaper advertising?

Telephone Directory Advertising

Telephone directories list the phone numbers of people and businesses in a certain area. Directory ads usually appear on a page close to the listing and phone number of the business placing the ad. Directory ads can look a lot like newspaper ads. Customers look in telephone directories again and again, making them a good advertising medium.

A disadvantage of directory advertising is that people look in the directory only when they are already in search of a particular type of business. It is simply a way to persuade customers to try you instead of a competitor that is also listed in the phone book. But, knowing how important the phone book can be, Luisa decides to place a quarter-page ad in the business telephone directory distributed in her area.

Direct-Mail Advertising

Direct-mail advertising includes fliers, catalogs, letters, and other mailers sent to target customers through the mail. The main advantage of direct-mail advertising is that mailing lists for target markets are available for purchase. If your business sells hospital beds, you can buy targeted mailing lists of people who would need to purchase this product. You also can get lists of people based on geographic area. Companies that specialize in putting together targeted mailing lists can provide almost any kind of list for any kind of business.

Direct-mail advertising can be effective if people read it. But many people throw out direct-mail advertising. They call it "junk mail." To reach as many target customers as possible through direct-mail advertising, you will have to come up with an attention-grabbing design or another way to make people read your advertisement.

Luisa Ramirez decides to use direct mail to target residents living in four zip code areas near her store. She creates an attractive brochure with a catchy slogan on the outside cover. She mails it to residents in the neighborhoods she is targeting.

Magazine Advertising

Magazines are an excellent way to aim products and services at specific markets. Fitness magazines are full of advertisements for athletic shoes and other products purchased by athletes. Magazines targeting teenage girls are full of advertisements for products that appeal to them.

Most magazines are nationally distributed. This can make them inappropriate for businesses that sell in a limited geographic area. Some large cities have local magazines. They would be an effective way to target a certain area.

The city in which Luisa will be opening her gourmet food store has two local magazines. One focuses heavily on restaurants and entertaining. Luisa checks the demographics of the magazine's readers and finds that it targets the same market she is trying to reach. She decides to advertise in the magazine every other month.

Outdoor Advertising

Outdoor advertising includes billboards and signs. Such advertising can be valuable in keeping the name of your business in a place where many people can see it. But people view outdoor advertising quickly as they drive by, so it cannot include much information.

Luisa's advertising needs to provide too much information for outdoor advertising to be useful. Luisa also thinks that outdoor advertising may not work for the type of upscale image that she wants for her business. She rules out this advertising medium.

Transit Advertising

Transit advertising includes signs on public transportation, such as buses and subways. Transit advertising can give more information than a billboard can. Such

What are the disadvantages of advertising on billboards?

advertising can be effective if the market you are trying to reach includes many people who use public transportation.

Luisa's target market lives in the suburbs and rarely uses public transportation. For this reason, she rules out transit advertising. It would not help her reach her target market.

> **CHECKPOINT**
> Why is advertising important to a business?

Publicity

Publicity is free promotion that comes from media coverage. Good publicity can be as helpful as advertising. Publicity is free, but producing an event or bringing in a celebrity to create publicity usually isn't.

Publicity also can be negative if the media coverage is unfavorable. For example, some community newspapers publish listings of restaurants that have violated health code laws. Customers may see this publicity and stop eating at those restaurants.

Luisa plans to have an open house to mark her first day in business. She hopes that the media will do a story on her grand opening. To increase this chance, Luisa hires a popular local jazz band to perform. She also invites her community's leaders. In addition, she writes and sends the press release shown below to all of the local newspapers, magazines, and radio and television

---

FOR IMMEDIATE RELEASE

GALA OPENING OF LUISA'S GOURMET DISHES

Come celebrate the opening of Luisa's Gourmet Dishes on Friday, September 20, at 8:00 P.M. Appetizers, imported champagne, and French pastries will be served at the event. Music will be provided by Glendale's leading jazz ensemble, Jazz Expressions.

The opening of Luisa's Gourmet Dishes marks the realization of a dream by owner Luisa Ramirez. "As a specialty cook," she says, "I could not always find the products I needed. And I was never happy with the selection of produce and baked goods in town." Luisa decided to open a store that would offer the kinds of products she could not find elsewhere in town.

Luisa's Gourmet Dishes offers an incredible selection of products, including 14 different kinds of olive oil, 12 different kinds of rice, and pasta products from several different countries. "Everyone's taste is different," says Luisa, "so I offer a large selection."

For more information, contact:
Luisa Ramirez, Owner
Luisa's Gourmet Dishes
1610 Marbury Road, Glendale, CT
(275) 555-3983

Working Together

Work in small groups. Make a list of all of the sales promotions that businesses in your community use. As a group, decide which sales promotion you think is the best.

stations. A **press release** is a written statement that informs the media of an event or product.

To keep her name in the news, Luisa volunteers to write a weekly cooking column for one of the free newspapers in her community. She likes having the opportunity to educate the public about gourmet cooking. Her newspaper column also will help draw more attention to her store.

> **CHECKPOINT**
> → What are some ways to create publicity for your business?

Sales Promotions

A **sales promotion** is the act of offering an incentive to customers in order to increase sales. Examples include:

- contests
- free samples
- coupons
- frequent purchaser programs
- gifts
- special events

Some companies also offer rebates. A **rebate** is a refund offered to people who purchase a product. Customers who purchase a $12 bottle of olive oil may get a $2 rebate from the manufacturer. To make sure that customers are aware of products on which rebates are offered, Luisa posts a flier in her store that includes a list of all rebates.

As part of her sales promotions, Luisa plans to give away a $25 gift certificate each month. She also offers free samples and gives out coupons good for discounts on selected products.

> **CHECKPOINT**
> → Give three examples of sales promotions.

TREND SPOTTER

Since 1912, Cracker Jacks have come with a prize in every box. Today, some retailers are returning to that tradition. In the summer of 2005, Gap launched a promotion that gave a free song download on iTunes to anyone who tried on a pair of jeans in a Gap store. This type of incentive is considered a value-added promotion. Customers receive additional value in the form of a gift by shopping at certain stores or buying certain products.

Think Critically
1. Do you think customers are attracted to a promotion like the one Gap used? Why or why not?
2. Do you think customers would rather have a value-added promotion like this or a coupon for money off the purchase of a product? Explain your answer.

© GETTY IMAGES/PHOTODISC

How can coupons help a business increase its sales?

1 **THINK ABOUT YOURSELF** Think about publicity that a business in your area has received lately. Was it good publicity or bad publicity? How did this publicity make you feel about the business? Write a paragraph describing your reactions and why the publicity made you feel this way.

2 **WHAT DO YOU THINK?** Why is radio advertising better than television advertising for a small business?

3 **LANGUAGE ARTS CONNECTION** A family in your community has lost everything they own in a house fire. Your school is planning a fundraiser to benefit the family. Write a press release for the local newspaper announcing the fundraiser.

4 **MATH CONNECTION** You have produced a one-minute commercial for $20,000. You plan to air it on the local television station for a cost of $1,000 per minute. You plan to air the commercial 20 times. What is the advertising cost per minute? How much would you save per minute if you could produce the commercial for $15,500?

Mary-Kate and Ashley Olson

Mary-Kate and Ashley Olson make clothes with "the old Hollywood glamour at affordable prices." Young girls are rushing to Wal-Mart to buy them and create their own glamorous looks.

Mary-Kate and Ashley are fraternal twins born on June 13, 1986 in Sherman Oaks, California. Their parents started the twins in show business at age one when they shared the role of Michelle Tanner on the hit television program *Full House*. Their popularity grew even more after the show ended in 1995.

The twins used their popularity to their advantage and sold videos, music albums, a book series, and dolls. They created their own production company to make movies starring themselves for the big screen and home video market. They have also won awards in both business and show business.

Their fame helped create a multi-million-dollar brand that includes their mary-kateandashley clothing line. In addition, products in beauty, school supplies, and furniture give the twins an estimated combined net worth of over $300 million.

At age 18, the twins assumed full responsibility for their business. The mary-kateandashley brand has gone international and is available in nine other countries.

Harper's Bazaar put Ashley on its cover in July 2005. It was her first solo cover without her twin. The magazine thinks Ashley is "Fashion's new 'IT' girl." The article quotes her as saying, "Dressing up is all about fun. My idea of the highest compliment is 'adorable.'"

Both girls went on to college. Mary-Kate worked with a well-known photographer. Ashley's interest in fashion led her to work with a designer.

The twins support each other and live together. They also make business decisions together but follow their own interests separately.

Think Critically

1. What do you think helped build the popularity of Mary-Kate and Ashley?

2. What were the risks that Mary-Kate and Ashley took when they started their own production company?

3. Do you think that Mary-Kate's and Ashley's interests in photography and fashion have played a role in making their business successful? Why?

Why Do Market Research?

1. You must understand your customers' needs and wants. The marketing concept focuses on the needs of customers when planning, producing, distributing, and promoting a product or service.

2. To identify your target market, you need to ask yourself many questions. You should ask, "Who are my customers?" and "What needs or wants will my product or service satisfy?"

3. Market research helps you find out what your customers need and want. It also helps you understand your competition.

4. Secondary data are found in published sources.

5. Primary data are collected for a specific purpose. Primary data can include questionnaires, observation, and focus groups.

6. The five steps of primary data market research are: define the question, select a research method, collect data, analyze data, and draw conclusions.

Who Is Your Competition?

7. As an entrepreneur, you need to research who your competitors are. You must analyze their strengths and weaknesses.

8. There are many ways to build customer loyalty. You should ask for and respond to customer feedback. Offering frequent-buyer discounts and excellent service also promotes customer loyalty.

How Do You Get the Word Out?

9. Advertising is a paid form of communication sent out by a business. Your advertising message should communicate the image and information you want.

10. Advertising media include television, radio, newspaper, telephone directories, outdoor advertising, and more.

11. Publicity is free promotion. It can have positive or negative effects for your business.

12. Sales promotions can give your customers incentives to buy your product or service.

Vocabulary Builder

Choose the term that best fits the definition.

1. People who buy the products and services companies offer

2. Interview with groups of target customers who provide valuable ideas on products or services

3. Offering an incentive to customers to increase sales

4. Uses customer needs as primary focus when planning, producing, distributing, and promoting a product or service

5. System for collecting, recording, and analyzing information about customers, competitors, goods, and services

6. Individuals that are interested in a product or service and are willing to pay for it

7. Refund offered to people who purchase a product

8. Act of creating a positive relationship with customers and the general public

9. Information collected for the very first time for a specific purpose

10. Free promotion that comes from media coverage

11. Data found in sources that are already published.

a. advertising
b. competitors
c. customer feedback card
d. customers
e. demographics
f. focus group
g. market research
h. marketing concept
i. press release
j. primary data
k. public relations
l. publicity
m. rebate
n. sales promotion
o. secondary data
p. target market

Review What You Have Learned

12. When evaluating your competition, what should you review?

13. Why is it important to listen to your customers?

14. Why is customer loyalty important to a business?

15. What is the purpose of conducting market research?

16. Where can you find secondary data market research?

17. List and describe the three types of primary data market research.

18. Explain how to design a good questionnaire.

19. How do you decide which advertising medium to use?

20. What are the advantages and disadvantages of publicity?

21. What is the purpose of sales promotions?

Using the *Activities* CD, open the Chapter 6 folder. Open the Who is the Target Audience? activity. Print a copy and complete the activity.

Think About It

1. You are thinking about opening a lawn-service business. Working with a small group, describe the best demographic market for your business.

2. Choose a product with which you are familiar. For one week, keep a record of every promotional activity that you see or hear for that product. At the end of the week, analyze the promotional activities. Determine the target market for the product and the message of the promotional campaign.

Project: Making Entrepreneurship Work for You

This activity will help you develop the business opportunity that you identified in Chapter 1.

1. Identify the target market for your business. Use secondary data sources to help you determine the demand for your product or service.

2. Using the secondary data that you find, describe the customer demographic for your business and product.

3. Conduct primary data research for your business. Use the five-step method described in the chapter. Develop a questionnaire that will give you the information you need. Ask at least ten people in your target market to complete it. Analyze the results and determine the plan of action you will take.

4. Make a list of at least three companies that will be competitors of your business. Create a comparison chart like the one shown in Lesson 6.2. Determine the strategy you will use to beat your competition.

5. Write down your strategies for building customer loyalty. Describe why you think each one will work.

6. Get advertising rates for a local radio station, television station, and newspaper. Choose the advertising medium that is best for your business. Write an ad for that medium. To generate publicity for your business, write a press release that you will send to the media.

Chapter 7

Where Does the Money Come From?

Start-Up Money—That's What I Want

Chrissy Frentz had the idea of selling snow cones out of her Laurel, Maryland garage. She even had a catchy name for her venture—Snowball City. But she didn't have enough money to get started. So, Chrissy waited until she had saved enough to get her business off the ground. She paid half, and her dad gave her the other half.

Although Chrissy's overhead costs were low, she still needed to pay for business fees and start-up supplies. Because Chrissy financed her business with her own money, she couldn't purchase additional equipment and supplies until she had more money in hand.

Brooklyn artists Jeffrey Rodriguez and John Serrano found a different way to find start-up money for their custom airbrush studio and community art center. Jeffrey had been airbrushing designs for his friends from a storefront in his parents' building. When Jeffrey saw some examples of John's artwork, he invited John to his studio. The two quickly decided to form a business partnership called Latin Artist. But they still needed money to get started.

Jeffrey learned that a group called Youth Venture was awarding $1,000 grants to teens who started businesses stressing community service. To qualify for the grant, Jeffrey and John decided to include free art lessons to neighborhood youth as part of their business. Because there were no youth programs in his neighborhood, Jeffrey wanted to get kids off the streets and get them involved.

To apply for the grant, Jeffrey and John needed to create a business plan showing exactly how the money would be used. Their careful work paid off. Jeffrey and John received the grant, which was used to fix up the store. Their community involvement was one reason Latin Artist was named one of the top 20 youth businesses in New York.

WHAT DO YOU KNOW?

1 What are the advantages of using your own money to finance your business as Chrissy Frentz did? Can you think of some disadvantages?

2 Do you think that Jeffrey Rodriguez and John Serrano could have launched their business successfully if they had not found an outside source for start-up money? Explain your answer.

HOW MUCH MONEY DO YOU NEED?

Terms

pro forma financial
statements
start-up costs
operating expenses
cash flow
assets
liabilities

Goals

* **Explain why business owners prepare pro forma financial statements.**

* **Discuss the purpose of a personal financial statement.**

© GETTY IMAGES/PHOTODISC

Pro Forma Financial Statements

Have there been businesses in your community that have shut down? Many people open a business, and within a couple of years, they have to close. There are many reasons that a business may not succeed and may have to close. One of the main reasons is lack of planning for how much money it will cost to open a business and keep it running. In order to be a successful entrepreneur, you must understand how much it will cost you to start your business. You also must know how long it will be before you start making money. Finally, you must know how you can get money to start your business.

Before you can approach a lender or investor about financing your business, you will have to prepare financial statements. These statements help lenders and investors determine if your business has a chance to succeed. They also help lenders determine whether the financing you are requesting is reasonable.

Most of the financial statements that you need to provide will be estimates of how you think your business will perform in its first year. Financial statements based on estimates are called **pro forma financial statements**. The four pro forma financial statements you will need to prepare include the start-up costs, cash flow statement, income statement, and balance sheet.

Start-Up Costs

One of the pro forma financial statements is a list of start-up costs. **Start-up costs** are the one-time-only expenses that are paid to open a business. Common start-up costs include:

- equipment and supplies, such as computers, telephones, and fax machines

- furniture and fixtures, such as desks, chairs, and lighting

- vehicles, including delivery trucks and other automobiles

- remodeling, such as electrical and plumbing expenses

- legal and accounting fees

- licensing fees

Most entrepreneurs have to borrow the money needed to cover start-up costs. Grayson McGrath has started a band with three of his friends. He plans for the band to perform at parties for pre-teens and teenagers and bar mitzvahs and bat mitzvahs. To help determine how much money he will need to borrow to get his business up and running, Grayson calculates his start-up costs. Each member of the band will provide his own equipment.

START-UP COSTS GRAYSON'S PLAYERS	
Item	**Estimated Cost**
Equipment:	
Microphones	$ 750
Speakers	500
Amplifiers	600
Cell phone	100
TOTAL	**$1,950**

Grayson must provide an estimate of his start-up costs in order to borrow money for his business.

Cash Flow Statement

A *cash flow statement* describes how much cash comes in and goes out of a business over a period of time. The amount of cash coming in is your *revenue,* or cash receipts. The amount of cash going out is your *expense.* The cash flow statement will show how much money you have available to pay your bills. To create a pro forma cash flow statement, you will need to estimate your monthly revenues and monthly expenses.

Forecast Revenues To complete a pro forma cash flow statement, you must first forecast your revenues or cash receipts. When you forecast the amount of your revenue, you need to estimate how many products or services you will sell. Using this information, you can determine how much revenue you think you will make. You also need to know the prices you will charge for each item.

Grayson estimates that his band will begin by performing at four parties a month. He plans to charge $75 for each hour performed. To calculate his total revenues, he multiplies the num-

Working Together

Working in a group, choose a business in your area. Make a list of all the items that you think the business had to have to get started. Determine the cost of each item. Calculate the start-up cost for the business.

FORECASTED REVENUES
GRAYSON'S PLAYERS
JANUARY 20—

Band Performances	Hours Performed ×	Charge for 1-Hour Performance =	Revenue
New Year's Eve	4	$75	$300
Sweet 16 Party for Ginger Martin	3	75	225
Eric Elan's Bar Mitzvah	2	75	150
Winter Formal Dickerson HS	4	75	300
TOTAL			**$975**

ber of hours he expects the band to perform by the price he will charge for each hour of performance. He then adds these amounts to calculate his total revenue for the month as shown in the table above.

Forecast Operating Expenses

Expenses that a business has every month are called **operating expenses**. You will need to forecast your expenses. They may include cost of goods, which is what you pay to buy or make the products and services you will sell. They also may include rent, salaries, payroll taxes, office supplies, utilities (electricity, telephone, and water), insurance, and advertising.

Grayson estimates his operating expenses as shown in the table below.

FORECASTED OPERATING EXPENSES
GRAYSON'S PLAYERS
JANUARY 20—

Type of Expense	Amount
Salaries	$ 800
Advertising	300
Transportation	125
Cell phone	50
TOTAL	**$1,275**

Because Grayson's band is providing a service and all band members supply their own instruments, his expenses will be limited. He will have to pay for advertising, salaries for band members, transportation, and a cell phone that is used for making party arrangements.

Positive or Negative Cash Flow

Cash flow is the difference between revenue and expenses.

$$\text{Revenue} - \text{Expenses} = \text{Cash Flow}$$

If revenue totals more than expenses, your business has a *positive cash flow*. You can put this money in the bank or use it to expand your business. If expenses total more than revenue, your business has a *negative cash flow*. You may have to borrow money. You also may have to ask your *creditors*, those to whom you owe money, to give you more time to pay.

It is important to know that changes in the economy can affect the cash flow of a business. The effects of Hurricane Katrina on the Gulf Coast region caused many businesses to experience an unexpected negative cash flow.

Chapter 7 Where Does the Money Come From?

	Jan	Feb	Mar	Apr	May	June
PRO FORMA CASH FLOW STATEMENT						
GRAYSON'S PLAYERS						
JANUARY–JUNE 20—						
Revenues	$ 975	$1,500	$1,275	$ 975	$1,725	$2,100
Operating expenses:						
Salaries	$ 800	$1,200	$1,000	$ 800	$1,400	$1,600
Advertising	300	300	300	300	150	150
Transportation	125	180	150	125	210	240
Cell phone	50	50	50	50	50	50
Total expenses	$1,275	$1,730	$1,500	$1,275	$1,810	$2,040
CASH FLOW	−$300	−$230	−$225	−$300	−$85	$60

Prepare the Cash Flow Statement   After making forecasts of revenues and expenses, you can prepare your cash flow statement. You should create monthly pro forma cash flow statements for the first year of business and yearly statements for the second and third years to give your lender a good picture of your cash flow over time.

It is normal for operating expenses to be higher than revenues during the first few months of operation. Grayson's cash flow will be negative because the number of performances will be low and advertising expense will be high until people learn about the band. Grayson's pro forma cash flow statement is shown above.

Best and Worst Case   Many entrepreneurs create two types of cash flow statements based on a worst case and a best case. For the worst case, you should forecast lower revenues and higher expenses than you think you will have. For the best case, you should forecast the highest revenues and the lowest expenses your business is likely to have.

A worst-case cash flow statement will help you determine how much cash you will need if your business does worse than expected. A best-case cash flow statement will show you how much cash you will have if your business does better than expected. Together, these cash flow statements will help show you and potential lenders how much cash your business is likely to make in any situation.

CHECKPOINT

→ What is the purpose of a cash flow statement?

© GETTY IMAGES/PHOTODISC

Why does Grayson expect to have a negative cash flow at first?

Income Statement

An *income statement* is a financial statement that shows how much money a business earns or loses during a particular period. The money a business earns is called a *profit*. The money a business loses is called a *loss*. For this reason, the income statement also is known as a *profit and loss statement*. Creating a pro forma income statement for a number of years will help lenders see the long-term growth of your business.

Most businesses choose to prepare an income statement once a year. However, some businesses choose to prepare an income statement more often to keep a closer watch on their revenues and expenses. New businesses often review their income statements monthly in order to determine whether a profit is being made.

Grayson estimates his revenues and expenses over the next few years. He prepares the pro forma income statement shown below.

PRO FORMA INCOME STATEMENT GRAYSON'S PLAYERS, 20—		
Item	**Year 2**	**Year 3**
Revenues	$20,000	$24,000
Operating expenses:		
Salaries	$15,000	$18,200
Advertising	1,500	1,200
Transportation	2,400	2,880
Cell phone	600	600
Total expenses	$19,500	$22,880
Income/Loss	**$ 500**	**$ 1,120**

Difference from a Cash Flow Statement

The cash flow statement deals with actual cash coming in and going out of the business. It shows when you actually make a payment on an invoice or when you receive money from a customer. This is different from the income statement. It shows revenues you have not yet received and expenses you have not yet paid. It is a futuristic look at the financial strength of your business.

Suppose Grayson's Players had enough performances to earn $3,000 in July. The company's monthly income statement would show income of $3,000. But Grayson may not actually have received $3,000. Instead of paying the $3,000, customers may have asked to be billed so they could pay later. Grayson may not receive their payments until August or September. There may be some customers that never pay their bills at all.

Customers are not the only people who postpone payments. Grayson may purchase $1,500 worth of new microphones and speakers from a music store but wait 30 days to pay the invoice. The cash flow statement would show that Grayson still has the $1,500 cash because he has not yet paid it to his supplier. The income statement would show that Grayson has already paid the $1,500.

Because not all business transactions are paid immediately, the income statement and the cash flow statement usually will be different.

Balance Sheet

Another pro forma financial statement you should prepare is a balance sheet. A *balance sheet* shows the assets, liabilities, and owner's equity of a business at a particular point in time.

PRO FORMA BALANCE SHEET
GRAYSON'S PLAYERS, DECEMBER 31, 20—

Assets		Liabilities	
Microphones	$ 750	Melody Music Makers	$ 150
Speakers	500	Verizon Phone Company	50
Amplifiers	600	**Total Liabilities**	**$ 200**
Cell phone	100		
		Owner's Equity	
		Grayson McGrath	$1,750
		Total liabilities and owner's equity	**$1,950**
Total assets	**$1,950**		

The balance sheet is based on an equation called the *accounting equation*.

$$\text{Assets} = \text{Liabilities} + \text{Owner's Equity}$$

Assets are items of value owned by a business. They include items such as cash, equipment, and the goods you will sell. **Liabilities** are items that a business owes to others. They include loans and unpaid invoices. *Owner's equity* is the amount remaining after liabilities are subtracted from assets. It is commonly referred to as the *net worth* of the business.

This financial statement is called the balance sheet because the assets of a business must always equal liabilities plus owner's equity. A business that has more assets than liabilities has positive net worth. A business that has more liabilities than assets has negative net worth.

Grayson creates the pro forma balance sheet shown above. It shows how his business will be doing at the end of the first year. Grayson's pro forma balance sheet shows that total assets are more than total liabilities. Therefore, the company will have a positive net worth after the first year.

> **CHECKPOINT**
> → What does an income statement show? What does a balance sheet show?

Personal Financial Statement

Banks are usually interested in the personal finances of the people to whom they lend money. So, you will have to prepare your personal financial statement if you apply for a loan. A personal financial statement is a balance sheet of your possessions and debts. It shows your personal assets, liabilities, and net worth outside of the business.

As part of the materials Grayson prepares for lenders, he includes his personal financial statement. On his personal statement, his owner's equity is shown as Grayson's net worth. His assets include cash, a savings account, a computer, and video equipment. His liabilities include any amounts he owes. Grayson borrowed $500 from his father last year, and he still owes him $200. Grayson has $3,540 in assets. His liabilities total $200.

Why does Grayson consider his video camera an asset?

Grayson determines his net worth by subtracting his liabilities from his assets. He has a net worth of $3,340.

CHECKPOINT

→ What does a personal financial statement show?

7.1 LET'S GET REAL

1 **THINK ABOUT YOURSELF** Think about items that you own and how much they are worth. Think of any money that you owe others. Using this information, prepare a personal financial statement for yourself and determine your net worth.

2 **WHAT DO YOU THINK?** Why do you think banks require so much financial information from those they are considering loaning money to?

3 **MATH CONNECTION** You are preparing to start a personal fitness trainer business. You will go to client's homes and work with them using exercise programs to help them get physically fit. First you want to determine your start-up costs. Use the *Activities* CD and open the Chapter 7 folder. Open the activity titled Starting a Business: How Much Does It Cost? Complete the table in this activity to help you calculate your start-up costs.

4 **MATH CONNECTION** You start a floral delivery service and estimate sales for the first six months: January, $500; February, $1,500; March, $600; April, $1,000; May, $1,200; June, $600. Prepare a bar graph of forecasted sales.

HOW DO YOU GET THE MONEY YOU NEED?

Terms

debt capital
collateral
equity capital
venture capitalists

Goals

* Identify different types of bank loans.

* Explain Small Business Administration loans.

* Describe other sources that can provide debt capital.

Bank Loans

When you think about starting a business and how much it will cost, it may seem impossible to you. You probably do not have the money you would need and wonder how you could ever get it. Well, there are many different ways to get the money you need to start your business.

Most companies borrow money from banks. **Debt capital** is money loaned to a business with an agreement that the money will be repaid, with interest, in a certain time period. You obtain debt capital when you borrow from a bank. There are different ways that business owners can borrow from a bank.

© DIGITAL VISION

Types of Bank Loans

Banks make two kinds of loans—secured loans and unsecured loans. *Secured loans* are loans backed by collateral. **Collateral** is property that the borrower gives up if he or she does not pay back the loan. Banks demand collateral so that they have some way to get their money back if you fail to repay your loan. Suppose a business owner gets a $25,000 business loan and uses her home as collateral. If she fails to repay the loan, the bank has the right to take ownership of her home and sell it to collect the money she owes. Banks accept different kinds of collateral, including real estate, savings accounts, life insurance policies, and stocks and bonds.

Unsecured loans are loans that are not guaranteed with collateral. These loans are made only to the bank's best customers who have excellent credit. Unsecured loans are usually made for very specific purposes. They usually are paid back within a short period of time, often less than a year.

Reasons a Bank May Not Lend Money

Banks use various guidelines to determine which borrowers are good risks. They reject applicants who do not meet their requirements. Some of the main reasons banks turn down loan applications include:

1. **New business** Banks often do not like to lend money to new businesses because these businesses have no record of repaying loans. New businesses are more likely to fail to pay back their loans than companies that already are in business.

2. **Lack of a solid business plan** Banks evaluate businesses based on their business plans. A company with a poorly written or poorly thought out business plan will not be able to get financing from a bank.

3. **Lack of experience** Banks want to be sure that the people setting up or running a business know what they are doing. They do not require you to have owned a business before to get a bank loan. But they do want you to show that you are familiar with the industry and have the management experience to run your own business.

Why might a bank not loan money to this new bike repair shop?

© GETTY IMAGES/PHOTODISC

You work in a bank, and one of your jobs is loan approval. You have to decide which of two businesses you will loan $10,000. Box Office is a sole proprietorship run by Scarlett Jennings. She is planning to offer a mail-order movie rental service. She has over ten years' experience working in movie rental businesses. She came to you with a well-written plan for her business and is planning to invest $5,000 of her own money in the business. Hats, Hats, Hats is a partnership run by Tim Hudson and his brother Nick. They came up with the idea for their business last week and wrote a one-page plan for their business. Tim just graduated from high school, and Nick has worked for three years in an automobile service business. Which business would you consider to be the best risk for the bank loan? Write a paragraph explaining your decision.

4. **Lack of confidence in the borrower** Even if your business plan looks solid and you have experience, you may fail to get financing if you make a bad impression on your banker. Make sure you dress and behave professionally. Show up on time for appointments and provide all the information that your banker requests.

5. **No investment in the business by the owner** Banks are suspicious of entrepreneurs who do not invest their own money in their business. They are unlikely to lend to them. You will have to be willing to use a large amount of your own money if you want to receive financing from a bank.

Getting bank financing for a new business is difficult. But it is not impossible if you can show that you are confident and well prepared and that you will be able to repay the loan. Being aware of the reasons banks do not lend money can help you overcome the bank's five most common objections.

> **CHECKPOINT**
> → What are the types of loans that banks make?

Small Business Administration Loans

Sometimes banks will not lend money for one reason or another. If this is the case, you can turn to the Small Business Administration (SBA) for help.

SBA Loan Assistance

The Small Business Administration is a federal government agency whose purpose is to help small businesses. It provides management and technical advice to owners of small businesses. The SBA also guarantees loans made by banks. In other words, the SBA agrees to pay part of the bank loan if the business owner cannot. The SBA will guarantee up to 90 percent of a bank loan. So, if a business owner fails to pay off a loan, the SBA will pay a certain percentage of the loan to the bank. This loan guarantee can help small businesses get bank financing. The guarantee makes the loan less risky for the bank.

In addition to guaranteeing loans, the SBA sometimes makes loans to small businesses. These loans are not that common because the SBA does not have much money available to give loans.

When the SBA guarantees a bank loan, it asks that the money be used in certain ways. It should be used to buy assets or used as working capital for the business. *Working capital* is the money needed to meet the day-to-day needs of a business. Businesses usually have five to seven years or sometimes longer to repay SBA-guaranteed loans.

Requirements of SBA Loans

The SBA is the largest source of financing to small businesses in the United States. It helps about one million Americans every year. To qualify for aid from the SBA, your company must meet certain requirements.

1. **Your business must be considered a small business.** The definition of "small" depends on the industry. In some retail industries, for example, a company can have sales of $29 million and still be considered small. To find out if your company meets the definition of "small," you should contact the SBA office in your district.

2. **Your business must not be the leader in its field.** If, for example, you own the most popular restaurant in your town, you will not qualify for SBA financing.

3. **Your business must comply with all federal employment laws.** These laws apply to workplace discrimination, safety, and wages.

4. **Your business cannot create or distribute ideas or opinions.** This requirement means that newspapers, magazines, and schools are not eligible for SBA financing.

5. **You must have been unable to obtain financing from a bank.** You should first determine whether you could get a loan from a bank.

6. **You must invest a reasonable amount of your own money in the business.** Entrepreneurs usually cover 30 to 50 percent of the total start-up costs to begin their businesses.

7. **You must provide collateral.** If the assets of your business are not worth enough, you will have to use personal assets as collateral to get financing.

If you meet these requirements, you can apply for a loan from the SBA. The SBA will review your business plan and decide whether or not to finance your business.

Apply for an SBA Loan

To apply for an SBA loan, you will have to provide the following information about your business:

- type of business
- date business started or will start
- location of business
- product or service offered
- business plans
- geographic area business will serve
- competition
- customers
- suppliers
- management experience
- personal financial statements for all owners, including federal income tax returns
- description of how you plan to repay the loan, supported by cash flow statements
- business financial statements (three years of balance sheets and income statements for existing businesses or pro forma statements for new businesses)
- forecasts for at least one year

You may also be asked to provide the SBA with copies of other documents such as rental agreements, franchise agreements, licenses, letters of reference, partnership agreements, or articles of incorporation.

> **CHECKPOINT**
> ➡ What is the purpose of SBA loans?

Other Sources of Loans

Besides the SBA, there are other government agencies that make debt capital loans.

- **Small Business Investment Companies** SBICs are licensed by the SBA to make loans to and invest capital with entrepreneurs.
- **Minority Enterprise Small Business Investment Companies** MESBICs are special kinds of SBICs that lend money to small businesses owned by members of ethnic minorities.

How can you get money to start a business?

Did You Know?

Two-thirds of new businesses survive at least two years. About half of new businesses survive at least four years.

- **Department of Housing and Urban Development** HUD provides grants to cities to help improve low-income areas. A *grant* is financial aid that does not have to be repaid. Cities use grants to make loans to finance projects in needy areas.

- **The Economic Development Administration** The EDA is a division of the U.S. Department of Commerce. It lends money to businesses that operate in and benefit economically troubled parts of the country. Borrowing from the EDA is similar to borrowing from the SBA, but the loan application is more complicated and the restrictions are tougher.

- **State Governments** Government assistance also may be available at the state level. Almost all states have financial agencies that make or guarantee loans to small businesses.

- **Local and Municipal Governments** City, county, or municipal governments sometimes make loans to local businesses. The loans are usually small—$10,000 or less.

Finance Your Business with Equity Capital

Another way to get money for your business is through equity capital. **Equity capital** is money invested in a business in return for a share in the business's profits. Entrepreneurs may try to get equity capital

when they cannot get bank or SBA loans or when they are unable to finance their business out of their own savings. You can get both equity capital and debt capital. You may provide much of the equity capital for your business yourself. You also may get equity capital through people you know or through others who want to invest in your business.

Personal Financing Many entrepreneurs use their personal savings to finance the start of their business. You can use personal savings to help get debt capital from a bank. If you invest your own money, the bank sees that you have faith that your business will succeed.

Friends and Family Some entrepreneurs ask friends and family for the equity capital they need to start their business. Borrowing from friends or family

Why might you not want to borrow money from your friends?

members is not always a good idea. Before borrowing from people you know, consider how the loan may affect your relationship. You may decide that the risk of losing a friend if you are unable to pay back the borrowed money is not worth taking.

If you do decide to borrow money from friends or family members, clearly warn them of the risks involved in lending money to a new business. Be sure both you and they understand exactly how much money you will repay each month. Also specify how or if you will pay back the loan if your business should go bankrupt.

Venture Capitalists Some companies sell stock to venture capitalists. **Venture capitalists** are individuals or companies that make a living investing in new companies. They carefully research opportunities that they believe will make them a lot of money. They usually are interested in companies that have the possibility of earning hundreds of millions of dollars within a few years. Because of this, many small businesses would have trouble getting venture capitalists to invest in their company.

Carlos Cisneros wants to start a small software company, but he needs money. Two of Carlos' friends are venture capitalists. They have invested $20,000 in the business. If Carlos' company fails, they will lose all of their money. If the company succeeds, Carlos' friends could earn hundreds of thousands or even millions of dollars.

> **CHECKPOINT**
> → What are some of the ways that entrepreneurs can get equity capital?

7.2 LET'S GET REAL

1 **WHAT DO YOU THINK?** Why is a secured loan easier to get than an unsecured loan?

2 **THINK ABOUT YOURSELF** Do you think a bank would take a chance on loaning money to a young person to start a business? Write a paragraph describing what you would tell the banker to convince him or her that you would be a good risk.

3 **COMMUNICATION CONNECTION** You want to apply for an SBA loan to start a music store. Write a letter to the SBA providing information about your business. Provide details about your business plan and how you plan to use the money. Also explain how you plan to repay the loan.

4 **MATH CONNECTION** Tisha Appleton obtained a $45,000 loan for her new business. The SBA guaranteed 75 percent of the loan. How much has the bank risked losing if Tisha's business fails?

WHY IS RECORD KEEPING IMPORTANT?

Terms

- transaction
- account
- check register
- payroll
- breakeven point
- inventory
- perpetual inventory method
- periodic inventory method

Goals

- ✳ **Discuss the importance of keeping business records.**
- ✳ **Define the breakeven point.**
- ✳ **Describe the two different inventory tracking methods.**

Types of Records

Good record keeping can help you make smart business decisions. Incomplete or inaccurate records can cause you to mismanage your business or can cause serious legal problems. Many small businesses use professionals to help them keep their records and prepare their financial statements. Certified public accountants (CPAs) have passed accounting examinations and are often hired to help keep records.

The records that entrepreneurs will keep include journals and ledgers, bank records, payroll records, and tax records. It is likely that you will use a computer to keep your records.

Journals

Journals are accounting records of the transactions you make. A **transaction** is a business activity that causes change in assets, liabilities, or net worth. Accurate journals help you keep track of how much money you have earned, how much you have spent, and how much profit you have made.

© DIGITAL VISION

Journals also show how much money you owe and how much people owe you. They also help you create financial statements.

Types of Journals Most businesses keep five journals for their accounting needs.

1. **Sales journal** This journal is used to record *only* sales of merchandise on credit. Merchandise sold on credit means that your customers receive goods or services now but pay for them later.

2. **Cash payments journal** This journal is used to record *only* cash payment transactions. All cash or check payments that your business makes are recorded in this journal.

3. **Cash receipts journal** This journal is used to record *only* cash receipt transactions. Goods paid for in cash at the time your customers receive them are recorded in the cash receipts journal.

4. **Purchases journal** This journal is used to record *only* purchases of merchandise on credit. If you buy and receive merchandise for your business today but you pay for it later, you should record your purchase in the purchases journal.

5. **General journal** This journal can be used to record any kind of transaction. Some businesses use only a general journal. Businesses that use the four special journals described above record transactions that do not fit in the other four journals in the general journal.

Ledgers

Businesses also use ledgers. Transactions recorded in journals must be posted to ledgers every few days. *Posting* means copying information from a journal to a ledger account.

Journals separate business transactions by *type* of transaction, such as a sale or a purchase. Ledgers separate transactions by *account*.

An **account** is an accounting record that summarizes all financial information for one specific business item. Your business will have accounts for expenses, such as rent and utilities. You also will have accounts for cash and sales.

A ledger allows you to review each account individually. For example, all cash transactions recorded in the journals will be posted to the cash account in the ledger. You can find out your cash balance by checking the ledger. The ledger also helps you prepare the financial statements needed for your business.

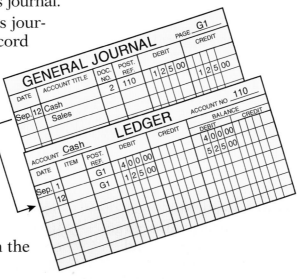

CHECKPOINT

→ Explain the importance of good record keeping for a business.

Bank Statements

Entrepreneurs may need to open a checking account for their business. You should use a business account for all deposits and withdrawals related to your business. If you already have a personal checking account, you will still need a separate one for your business.

When you open your checking account, you will receive a set of checks and a check register. A **check register** is a book in which you record the dates, amounts, and names of people or businesses to whom you have written checks. Computer software that can keep your account records electronically also is available.

Balance Your Account Every month your bank will send you a bank statement. It lists checks paid, deposits and withdrawals made, and bank service charges for the month. When you receive your bank statement, you should balance your check register. Balancing your check register is very important. It will prevent you from accidentally writing checks when you do not have enough money in your account. Writing checks when you don't have enough money in the bank to cover them is illegal. If you write bad checks, your suppliers may stop shipping merchandise to you. Most businesses and banks will charge you a fee for writing a bad check.

Payroll Records

When you have employees working for you, you will have to keep payroll records. A **payroll** is a list of people who receive salary or wage payments from a business. Payroll records show how much your employees earn during a pay period, which could be weekly, bi-weekly, or monthly. Payroll records will include the following information:

- employee's name
- number of hours worked
- regular and overtime earnings
- federal, state, and local taxes deducted
- Social Security and Medicare taxes deducted
- other deductions, such as health or dental insurance

You will use this information to prepare payroll checks for your employees.

Tax Records

As an entrepreneur, you will have to make several different kinds of tax payments. These payments include income tax, payroll taxes, and sales tax.

Income Tax Businesses that earn profits must pay income tax. These taxes are paid quarterly, or every three months. Income tax must be prepaid at the beginning of a quarter, so you will need to estimate your income. If you fail to make these payments or you underestimate how much tax is due, you may have to pay a penalty. You also could face criminal penalties for tax fraud.

Payroll Taxes By law, you are required to deduct taxes from your employees' paychecks and pay these taxes to the government. In addition, your business must pay payroll-related taxes that will help provide Social Security benefits to retired employees.

Sales Tax Most businesses are required to charge sales tax on goods or services they sell. If you own a business that collects sales tax from customers, every month you will have to deposit the tax you collect into a special bank account that belongs to the government.

Sales tax is based on a percentage of sales. The actual percentage charged varies from state to state. You will need to find out the percentage of sales tax to charge in your area.

> **CHECKPOINT**
> → Why should entrepreneurs keep bank, payroll, and tax records?

Computerized Record Keeping

Most small businesses use computer programs to handle their record keeping. Computer software programs can make it easier to keep important business records.

Advantages There are many advantages to using a computer to keep records including:

- **Storing and reporting data** Computer programs allow you to store and examine data more easily than you could with a pencil and paper. They also use the stored data to create reports that help you make business decisions.

- **Linking records** Computerized record keeping links all of the records you keep. Every time you make a sale, the computer program can automatically record the sale on your income statement. It also deducts the item sold from your stock records.

- **Reducing errors** Although computers do not prevent all mistakes, they will prevent calculation errors. Adding up many numbers by hand can lead to mistakes. Computers can perform mathematical calculations much faster than people can, and they are always correct.

- **Correcting errors** If you keep records by hand, you will have to erase any incorrect figures and replace them with correct figures. You also will have to check the other records that were affected by your mistake and change all of those as well. Correcting errors is much simpler when your records are kept electronically. Making a change in one record automatically updates all other records that were affected by the change.

Disadvantages Computers can help you track your business records, but some problems can occur.

- **Staff inexperience** Some employees may have difficulty using computers. For example, they might feel uncomfortable handling sales returns on a computerized cash register. They might not know the correct way to enter special transactions, such gift certificates. This can cause errors in your records.

- **Unauthorized use** Using a computer may make it easier for an unauthorized employee to introduce errors into your records. For this reason, you should limit use of your computer files to trustworthy employees.

- **Computer problems** Your computer hard drive can fail causing you to lose all your records. Viruses can affect the files on your computer. To protect yourself against these kinds of problems, always keep backup copies of your files. Also, install an anti-virus program to check your hard disk for viruses that could damage your files.

> **CHECKPOINT**
> → What are some of the advantages and disadvantages of using computerized record keeping?

Perform Breakeven Analysis

You can determine how increased sales affect your profits by identifying your breakeven point. The **breakeven point** is the amount of sales that must be made to cover all of the expenses, or costs, of a business. If your sales fall below the breakeven point, your costs will be higher than your revenues, and you will be losing money. Once your sales reach the

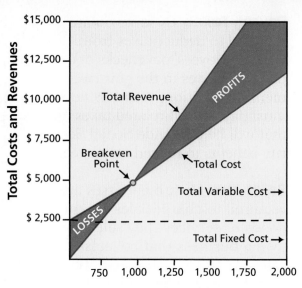

breakeven point, your sales will equal all of your costs. At this level of sales, you will neither make nor lose money. Once your sales are higher than the breakeven point, you will begin to earn profits.

The breakeven point shows the amount of sales you need in order to earn a profit. If your sales are below the breakeven point, you will not earn a profit. You will have to increase your prices, increase the amount you sell, or reduce your costs.

Measure Costs, Sales, and Profits In order to calculate your breakeven point, you will have to know your total fixed costs, your selling price per unit, and your variable cost per unit. You also will have to know the amount of units sold.

Businesses have fixed and variable costs. *Fixed costs* stay the same no matter how many units you sell. For example, the rent you pay on your building will stay the same no matter how many products you sell. So, rent is a fixed cost. *Variable costs* go up or down, depending on the number of units sold. If you sell more of your product, the cost of materials or goods needed to make your product will go up. Cost of goods sold is a variable cost.

Charlene Mason owns a small manufacturing business that produces refrigerator door magnets. The total variable cost of producing magnets depends on her level of sales at any given time. She must figure out her variable costs in order to determine the breakeven point. Her variable costs include the cost of goods needed to make the magnets, salaries of the employees needed to assemble the magnets, and shipping expenses. These variable costs total $28,500 for the year. Charlene divides this number by 30,000, which is the number of magnets she sells each year. Her variable cost per unit then is $0.95.

Calculate Your Breakeven Point The formula for calculating the breakeven point is

> **Total fixed costs ÷ (Selling price per unit − Variable cost per unit) = Breakeven point**

Charlene's fixed costs are $40,000 a year. Her selling price is $3.50 per unit. Her variable cost is $0.95 per unit. Using these numbers in the formula, she gets $40,000 ÷ ($3.50 − $0.95) = 15,686 units.

If she sells 15,686 magnets, she will break even. In other words, Charlene's sales will equal her costs. If she sells more than 15,686 magnets, she will earn a profit. If she sells fewer magnets, she will not cover her expenses and will lose money.

CHECKPOINT

→ What is the breakeven point?

Track Your Inventory

© DIGITAL VISION

Why is it important to track inventory?

Have you ever been to a store to buy something only to get there and find out that the store is sold out of the item? Businesses have to keep the products they sell in stock as a convenience to their customers. If they run out of a product, the customer may buy from a competitor. To avoid running out of items your customers want to buy, you will need to use a tracking method to keep a careful eye on your stock. **Inventory** is the stock of goods a business has for sale. You will need to manage your inventory by determining how much you can afford to keep in stock at any given time.

Every business must track its inventory levels. Tracking your inventory can be done in two different ways. You can use the perpetual inventory method or the periodic inventory method.

Perpetual Inventory Method

The **perpetual inventory method** keeps track of inventory levels on a daily basis. This helps ensure that you never run out of stock on your products. The perpetual inventory method uses stock cards or a computer to keep track of the inventory you have. A *stock card* is a paper record for a single item. Many entrepreneurs do not use stock cards any more. It is much easier and faster to keep inventory records in an electronic format

Working Together

Working in a small group, select a business in your area that sells products or services. Make a list of the items that this business would stock in its inventory. Which items on your inventory list do you think the owner would have to reorder more often?

on a computer. Whether you use stock cards or a computer to track your inventory, you should record:

- a description of the item

- a stock number for identification purposes

- any shipments of inventory, the number of units received, and the date they were received

- any sales of inventory, the number of units sold, and the date of the sale

- the amount of inventory you currently have

- the *reorder point,* which is the minimum amount you want to keep in inventory, so you know when to place an order to get more units

- the maximum amount you want in inventory at any time

Lei Woo owns a toy store. Lei uses her computer to track inventory levels on a daily basis. She makes a list of items that are at the reorder point and then creates a low stock report. That report shows how many units of each item Lei needs to order to restock to the maximum level.

Use a Computer Businesses that sell hundreds of items usually use a computer to track inventory. You will need to purchase special software that connects your electronic cash registers to your computers. Every time a sale is made, the register subtracts the item sold from your inventory. It automatically calculates a new inventory balance.

Take a Physical Inventory

The perpetual inventory method may not be completely accurate. Your actual inventory may differ from that listed in your perpetual inventory system. The difference can be caused by many things, such as failure to record sales, theft, or damage to merchandise. Because of this, you should take a physical inventory at least once or twice a year.

Taking a physical inventory means counting the number of items you have in stock. You will need to record the date on which you are taking the inventory, the stock number of the item, a description of each item, and the actual number of units in stock. At least two people should be involved in taking a physical inventory. One person should count the items on your shelves while the other person records the information. This information can later be entered into a spreadsheet.

Periodic Inventory Method

Some businesses use a **periodic inventory method**, which involves taking a physical inventory of your merchandise. Businesses that use the periodic inventory method take their inventory often. Some check it weekly. Others check it monthly. That inventory will tell you how many units of each item remain in stock. You can then compare your inventory figures to the maximum figures listed on your low stock report to determine how many units of each item you need to order.

> **CHECKPOINT**
> → Describe the two different inventory tracking methods.

Fingerprint technology is now being used by businesses for many reasons. It can be used to increase security. Companies can limit access to their building. The fingerprint technology will identify those employees that have permission to be in the building. If the fingerprint is not recognized, the person cannot enter the building. These systems help keep business records safe by keeping them out of the wrong hands.

Fingerprint technology also is used to make managers more responsible when dealing with financial transactions. During busy times, many managers will give an employee their manager code to use for sales transactions that normally require the manager's approval. If managers must use a fingerprint to access the system, only they can perform those transactions. Fingerprint technology also allows the employer to assign different responsibilities to individual employees. For example, fingerprint technology can be used to control who operates the cash register.

Think Critically

1. How does fingerprint technology help a business increase its security?

2. Can you think of other uses for fingerprint technology?

7.3 LET'S GET REAL

1 **THINK ABOUT YOURSELF** Think about your record keeping habits. Do you keep your school papers well organized? Is your room neat? Write a paragraph describing your habits and how you think they will influence your business record keeping.

2 **WHAT DO YOU THINK?** Why is it important to balance your bank statement with your check register each month?

3 **COMMUNICATION CONNECTION** You own a small business selling skateboards and accessories. You just completed a physical inventory and found that you were missing several items for which you have no record of selling. You have two employees. Write a paragraph explaining how you would talk to them about the missing items.

4 **MATH CONNECTION** Maria Castille owns Castille Imports. The business had $52,200 in sales of 2,088 crystal vases in one year. How much did she charge for each vase? If the variable cost per vase is $2.90 and total fixed costs are $25,056, what is Castille Imports' breakeven point for crystal vases?

John Deere

Y ou may live in the city and never have been to a farm, but you probably know the slogan of the John Deere Company—*Nothing runs like a Deere*. If you live in the suburbs, your Dad's wish list probably includes a John Deere riding lawn mower. Those of you who live on a farm surely know about John Deere agricultural equipment.

John Deere was the founder of a company that began as a one-man blacksmith shop and has grown into a worldwide corporation. The John Deere Company does business in over 160 countries and employs about 46,000 people worldwide. It is one of the oldest industrial companies in the United States.

John Deere was born in Vermont on February 7, 1804. His father, William, was lost at sea when Deere was only four years old. His mother Sarah was left with little money to raise him. He received a common school education and served a four-year apprenticeship learning the blacksmith trade. He gained a good reputation for his workmanship and skill.

Deere eventually moved his family, including five children, to Illinois. As the only blacksmith in the area, he was able to prosper. Deere saw that cast-iron plows would not work well in the heavy, sticky prairie soil. So in 1837, he created a highly polished steel plow using a broken saw blade. The new plow worked much better, and demand for it grew.

Deere came up with the idea of making tools before he had orders for them. This way, he always had an inventory of tools on hand for customers. Ten years after developing that first plow, Deere was producing one thousand plows a year. In 1868, Deere's business was incorporated as Deere and Company. John Deere vowed, "I will never put my name on a product that does not have in it the best that is in me."

The company he founded has followed the same high standards of quality. It uses a large share of its income for product research and development. Deere and Company has grown to become the leading producer of farm equipment in the world. It also is a major producer of construction and forestry equipment and lawn-care products.

Think Critically

1. What do you think of Deere's idea to manufacture tools before he had orders for them?

2. Why do you think Deere and Company uses a large share of its income for product research and development?

How Much Money Do You Need?

1. Your financial plan will consist of five financial statements. All except the personal financial statement will be pro forma financial statements. Pro forma financial statements are estimates of how your business will perform.

2. A cash flow statement shows actual cash coming in and going out of a business over a period of time. An income statement shows how much money a business earns or loses during a particular period. It offers a futuristic look at your finances.

3. A balance sheet shows the assets, liabilities, and owner's equity of a business. The balance sheet must always remain in balance.

How Do You Get the Money You Need?

4. A bank may help you finance your business with a debt capital loan.

5. To help new businesses that cannot get financing from banks, the Small Business Administration (SBA) offers loan guarantees.

6. Besides the SBA, other government agencies may finance your new business. You also can finance your business with equity.

Why Is Record Keeping Important?

7. Journals are accounting records of the transactions you make. Journals separate accounting records by type of transaction.

8. Ledgers separate accounting records by account. Ledgers make it easy to view any one account for your business.

9. Other types of records you will keep are bank statements, payroll records, and tax records.

10. To figure the amount of sales needed to make a profit, you must calculate the breakeven point. If sales are above the breakeven point, the business is making money.

11. To calculate the breakeven point, you must know the total fixed costs, the selling price of an item, and the variable cost per unit.

12. You can track inventory using the perpetual inventory method or the periodic inventory method.

Vocabulary Builder

Choose the term that best fits the definition.

1. Expenses that a business has every month
2. Financial statements based on estimates
3. Book in which you record the dates, amounts, and names of people or businesses to whom you have written checks
4. Items of value owned by a business
5. One-time-only expenses that are paid to open a business
6. Taking a physical inventory of your merchandise
7. Amount of sales that must be made to cover all of the costs of a business
8. Money loaned to a business with an agreement that the money will be repaid, with interest, in a certain time period
9. Money invested in a business in return for a share in the business's profits
10. Individuals or companies that make a living investing in new companies

a. account
b. assets
c. breakeven point
d. cash flow
e. check register
f. collateral
g. debt capital
h. equity capital
i. inventory
j. liabilities
k. operating expenses
l. payroll
m. periodic inventory method
n. perpetual inventory method
o. pro forma financial statements
p. start-up costs
q. transaction
r. venture capitalists

Review What You Have Learned

11. What financial statements can help you get a loan?
12. What is the difference between start-up costs and operating expenses?
13. What is the accounting equation?
14. Why do banks want collateral for a loan?
15. What are the requirements to qualify for an SBA loan?
16. What is the difference between debt capital and equity capital?
17. Why do businesses use accounting journals?
18. Describe the five types of journals that businesses use.
19. What three types of taxes must businesses pay?
20. What information do you need to calculate your breakeven point?
21. Why is it important to know your breakeven point?
22. Why is it important to keep good inventory records?

Using the *Activities* CD, open the Chapter 7 folder. Open the Bank Reconciliation activity. Print a copy and complete the activity.

1. Why do you think the SBA is willing to take a risk on an entrepreneur when a bank will not?

2. What inventory method do you think grocery stores use? Why do you think they use this method?

3. Why do you still need a basic understanding of accounting if accounting professionals do your record keeping?

Project: Making Entrepreneurship Work for You

This activity will help you develop the business opportunity that you identified in Chapter 1.

1. Prepare the following pro forma financial statements for your business: start-up costs, cash flow statement, income statement, and balance sheet. Also prepare a personal financial statement. Make a pie chart of your start-up costs. Which start-up cost is the largest percentage of your total costs? Which start-up cost is the smallest?

2. Determine how much money you need to borrow to start your business. Decide how you will get financing. Explain why this is your best option.

3. Decide what type of journals you will keep for your business. Give an example of a transaction that you will record in that journal. What accounts will your business have? What is the rate of sales tax in your state or county?

4. Contact two local banks and get information about business checking accounts. What type of information do you have to give the bank to open an account? How much will it cost to have a business account? Do the banks offer special services to small business owners?

5. Determine what the selling price of your good or service will be. Using that price and your forecasted expenses determine your breakeven point.

6. If your business has inventory, list all of the items you will have in inventory and your cost for each. Decide if you will use a periodic or perpetual inventory system and explain why.

Chapter 8

Why Do You Need Technology?

© GETTY IMAGES/PHOTODISC

Make Money—And Have Fun Doing It!

Some of the most profitable teen businesses are in computer and technology-related fields. In 2001, YoungBiz.com estimated that its top ten entrepreneurs earned $5.5 million in annual profits. Of those, eight were involved in Internet or computer-based ventures.

None of this will come to any surprise to Pankaj Arora. Pankaj started writing software when he was 12 and moved on to building computers. He now runs his own company, paWare, a provider of Information Technology (IT) business solutions. He admits to being "born a geek." He is quickly becoming a very wealthy geek. By age 18, he was earning up to $300 an hour as a computer consultant. He routinely turns away job offers with six-figure salaries. His company makes a healthy profit. Along the way, he has become a respected author. He has written articles on entrepreneurship and technology in such publications as the *Minnesota Daily* newspaper and *Y&E* and *2600* magazines.

Despite his financial success, Pankaj says that money has never been his primary motivation. He founded paWare to help people and to have fun doing what he liked to do. He credits his success to his ability to consider both the short-term and long-term effects of his decisions, a willingness to keep up with business trends and technology, and his own self-confidence, determination, and enthusiasm for hard work. He also stresses the importance of education.

Pankaj believes that most machinery, even home appliances, will eventually be computerized. For example, an appliance will be able to run a test on itself and let you know what needs to be repaired. Or, your alarm clock may have a wireless connection to the coffee maker to start the brewing process. In some cases, that technology already exists, but in the future it will be commonplace. Pankaj would like to be a pioneer of new technologies.

WHAT DO YOU KNOW?

1] What factors does Pankaj Arora believe contribute to success in business? Do you agree? Would you add anything to his list?

2] How do you think technology will change over the next 20 years or so? Can you think of any ways to turn your ideas into business opportunities?

WHAT TYPES OF TECHNOLOGY WILL YOU USE?

Terms

computer
  hardware
modem
software

Goals

✳ **Describe the types of computer hardware that entrepreneurs use.**

✳ **Identify the computer software you will need to run your business.**

✳ **Discuss other types of technology for your business.**

© GETTY IMAGES/PHOTODISC

Computer Hardware

Computers have changed the face of business. Computers used to be huge machines that filled entire rooms. Only large institutions, such as banks and insurance companies, used them. Today, millions of people use small but powerful computers.

Computers help create documents, store data, and perform calculations. Tasks that once were done manually now are done on computers. These tasks include simple jobs, such as making a sale and calculating taxes. They also include complicated tasks, such as taking inventory and analyzing how much money a business is making.

Computers and the equipment used with them are known as **computer hardware**. Hardware includes desktop computers, laptop or notebook computers, printers, and communication devices.

Desktop Computers

Desktop computers are computers that people use at home or in their offices. Desktop computers are able to meet the needs of almost all small businesses. The type of computer you purchase will depend on the kind of business you own. It also will depend on the ways in which you plan to use computers to run your business. The first decision you will have to make will be to choose between the two basic kinds of computers: personal computers and Macintosh computers.

Personal Computers Most computers used by businesses and individuals are personal computers (PCs), which use the Windows operating system. PCs are ideal for most basic needs, such as word processing, spreadsheets, databases, and Internet access. They also can perform more advanced functions, such as graphics and design.

Macintosh Computers Also known as Macs, Macintosh computers are very easy to use. They provide excellent graphics options and are better than PCs for this special need. Because of their excellent graphics, Macs are used in businesses such as advertising and publishing where graphics and design are a big part of the business.

Laptop Computers

Laptop or *notebook computers* are computers that can be moved easily from place to place. They generally are lightweight and easy to carry. They

What are the advantages and disadvantages of laptop computers?

© GETTY IMAGES/PHOTODISC

can be plugged into an electrical outlet and used at a desk or kitchen table. They also can be operated by a battery pack and used on an airplane or at a coffee shop.

Laptop computers are smaller than desktop computers, but they can be very powerful. Both personal computers and Macintosh computers are available in laptop models.

Advantages of Laptop Computers Laptop computers can be used anywhere. This feature makes them useful for people who travel and need their computers while they are away from their places of business.

Thomas Wilson owns a company that creates web sites. He uses his laptop computer on the subway every morning on the way to his office. The laptop computer lets him work wherever and whenever he wants.

Disadvantages of Laptop Computers Laptop computers may be more expensive than desktop computers. They also have smaller keyboards, which makes typing more difficult. Laptop computer screens are smaller and may not have as clear of an appearance as a desktop model. Also, if there is not a place to plug in your computer and your battery pack is not charged, you cannot use your computer.

Printers

To print the documents you create, you will need to buy a printer. Today most printers are laser or inkjet. The printer that you choose will depend on how you plan to use it and on how much money you want to spend.

Laser Printers Laser printers are the most popular printers for most businesses. They produce high-quality documents in the fastest time. They come in both black-and-white and color models. Because color printers are more expensive to purchase and to operate, most small businesses use black-and-white printers.

Inkjet Printers A popular type of printer for general use is the inkjet printer. These printers are slower than laser printers but may be less expensive. You can purchase a black-and-white or color inkjet printer.

Communication Devices

You will need a communication device that will allow your computer to connect to the Internet.

All computers need a **modem**, which is an electronic device that allows information to be transmitted from one computer to another over telephone lines. There are also cable modems, which connect you to the Internet using cable TV lines.

Some computers have modems built into them. Others need to have an external modem installed. High-speed modems allow you to access another computer's information more rapidly. Low-speed modems are slower, but they cost less.

> **CHECKPOINT**
> → What are the different types of hardware you should consider for your business?

© GETTY IMAGES/PHOTODISC

Why do you need a modem?

Computer Software

In order to run, your computer needs software. **Software** refers to the programs that control computer hardware and direct its operation. The software you purchase will depend on how you use your computer.

Types of Software

Software can be custom-made for a specific use or prepackaged and sold to meet everyone's basic needs. Custom computer programming is very expensive. Larger companies with very special needs generally use custom-built software.

Prepackaged programs include word processing, spreadsheet, database, and other kinds of programs. Most computers purchased today come with software already loaded on them. You can learn about software by taking computer courses in school, reading instruction manuals, using the online help available for the software, or by purchasing "how-to" books. Special training centers and colleges also teach people how to use software programs.

Word Processing Programs

Word processing programs help you create word-based documents, such as business letters and reports. With a word processing program, you can easily make changes to text, create attractive documents, and automatically check and correct spelling. Most word processors also have grammar-checking tools, thesaurus capabilities, graphic options, and more.

Spreadsheet Programs

Spreadsheet programs allow you to easily collect, report, and analyze numerical data. They also allow you to create graphs of your data. They can be used to prepare budgets, measure financial performance, and create financial statements. Spreadsheet programs use formulas to perform basic arithmetic as well as to calculate complex mathematical problems.

Spreadsheets are made up of columns and rows as shown at the right. Columns are labeled with letters. Rows are labeled with numbers. Each column letter and row number identifies a grid box, known as a *cell*. For example, the cell located in column A and row 5 is cell A5.

Jason Waters uses a spreadsheet program to calculate his monthly operating expenses. In the first column, he lists expense categories. In the second column, he enters the amount of each expense. To calculate his total monthly expenses, he adds the six expense categories by entering a formula into cell B8. This formula instructs the program to add cells B2 through B7.

Database Programs Database programs store, sort, and analyze large volumes of data. These programs are very useful for entrepreneurs with a large number of customers. You identify the *fields*, or the information you want to store in your database. Each field contains a certain piece of information. You may want a field for each customer's name, a field for the phone number, and a field for entering what the customer has purchased from you. A collection of fields for a particular customer is known as a *record*. All of your records make up your entire database.

Jane Peterson runs a mail-order business for children's clothing. She keeps a database full of customer information. She decides to mail out a catalog. Because the catalogs are expensive to make, Jane wants to limit the number she sends. Jane has her database sort out customers who have purchased at least $100 worth of clothing in the past.

Sample Spreadsheet		
	A	**B**
1	**Expense category**	**Monthly expense**
2	Salaries	$2,150
3	Advertising	$200
4	Rent	$525
5	Utilities	$195
6	Insurance	$50
7	Other	$125
8	Total	$3,245

CHECKPOINT

→ List three kinds of software and explain what they do.

More Technology for Your Business

Technology is always growing. It seems that every day new developments are being made to make it easier to do business.

Additional Software Programs

Word processing, spreadsheet, and database programs are the most common software programs used by entrepreneurs. Other software programs that meet special needs include:

- **Graphics programs** These programs make it very easy to design fliers, books, advertisements, and more on a computer screen. The images can be loaded into the graphics program, or they can be created with the help of the program.

- **Scheduling programs** Some people prefer to keep their daily schedules electronically.

Working Together

Working in a group, make a list of things a business owner could do with each type of software.

How might a business owner use presentation software?

Scheduling software can be programmed to remind a person of important dates, such as when a meeting has been scheduled.

- **Zip compression utilities** If you send very large files to other people, this software will condense the files so that they can fit easily on disks or CDs or be sent by e-mail. The person receiving the file must unzip the file to be able to use it.

- **Presentation software** This software helps create visually appealing presentations for business meetings. You can use it to create a slide show.

- **Communication software** This software makes it possible to send and receive data over telephone or cable lines. An e-mail program is an example of communication software.

Other Technologies to Consider

There is much more than just computer software and hardware to help you do business more quickly and easily. Some other technology items you should consider using in your business include:

- **LCD projector/panel** This device allows you to project your computer screen onto a wall for presentations. It can be used with presentation software.

- **Fax capabilities** You can use a fax machine or fax software to send copies of documents to people who also own a fax machine or fax software. This is a quick way to send a document to someone.

- **Photocopier** Using a photocopier is a fast, easy way to make copies of documents for your files or for other people.

- **Scanner** Similar to a photocopier, a scanner allows you to copy a document and turn it into a computer file.

- **File transfer protocol (FTP)** Files can be corrupted when sent over e-mail. FTP allows you to post a file to a computer server. The person who needs it then can download the file. FTP can be accessed

Why are cell phones useful to business owners?

only if you know the server name and password.

- **Cell phone** These phones are widely used in business today. They are small and can be carried with you all the time. Customers can easily contact you so you never have to lose touch with them.

Cell phones give you easy access to suppliers and customers when you are away from the office.

CHECKPOINT
→ What other technology items might you use in business?

8.1 LET'S GET REAL

1 THINK ABOUT YOURSELF Talk to your parents about how they use computers in their business and personal lives. Think about how you use a computer at school and at home. Write a paragraph comparing the way you and your parents use computers.

2 WHAT DO YOU THINK? If you owned a small candle-making business, do you think you would need custom-made computer software? Why or why not? What are some of the ways you might use software?

3 LANGUAGE ARTS CONNECTION Write a one-page report about the ways a small business could use computer software to its advantage. Write your report using word processing software, if possible.

4 MATH CONNECTION Using the Internet, an office supplies catalog, or a computer store sales ad, choose a computer system and the additional hardware and software that you would need for a computer repair business. Determine the total cost of the system.

HOW CAN YOU USE THE INTERNET?

Terms

Internet
Internet service
  providers
electronic mail
web page
e-commerce

Goals

* Explain how to send messages and find information on the Internet.

* Discuss how to promote your business over the Internet.

* Describe how you can use the Internet to conduct business.

Log on to the Internet

The **Internet** is a worldwide computer network that allows people to communicate with each other electronically. It allows you to send or receive electronic mail and to access the World Wide Web. In recent years, it also has become a way of buying and selling items.

To access the Internet, you will need to sign up with a service that will allow you to connect to a central computer through your telephone or cable line. Companies that provide this service are known as **Internet service providers**, or ISPs. AOL, MSN, and Earthlink are examples of ISPs.

Choose an Internet Service Provider

All ISPs provide connections to the Internet. Some also provide other benefits, including information services and the ability to post web pages. You can choose from many different ISPs.

© GETTY IMAGES/PHOTODISC

Some are small local providers while others are giant national providers. In choosing your ISP, you will want to consider three main factors:

1. **Will you be able to connect easily to the ISP?** Some ISPs are easier to connect to than others. You can connect by telephone line, through a cable line, or by using wireless technology.

2. **Can you connect to the ISP without interrupting your phone service?** Some ISPs will use your regular phone line to connect to the Internet, so you cannot make or receive phone calls while on the Internet. This could interfere with your business if you miss calls from customers. There are ISP options that do not interfere with your phone service.

3. **What monthly charges will you have to pay?** ISPs may charge based on how much time you actually spend online, or they may have a flat rate charge. If the ISP you choose is based in your home city, you may also have to pay long-distance charges to log on when you are out of town.

Beth Cheng owns a manufacturing company that produces cellular phones. She employs 20 full-time salespeople, each of whom covers a different region of the country. Beth wants her salespeople to be able to connect to the Internet from anywhere in the country. Therefore, she signs up with an ISP that does not charge long-distance rates when her employees use the Internet while out of town.

Use Electronic Mail

Electronic mail, commonly known as *e-mail*, is used to send and receive electronic messages around the world. E-mail addresses are necessary to send or receive these messages. E-mail is a popular form of business communication for several reasons:

1. **E-mail is convenient.** E-mail messages are received almost instantly. By using e-mail, many business problems can be solved on the same day that they occur.

2. **E-mail is inexpensive.** There is no charge for sending or receiving e-mail. The only charges are the fees you must pay to your ISP and the cost of local telephone or cable service.

3. **E-mail is not intrusive.** Telephone calls often catch people at inconvenient moments. But, e-mail messages can be read at the recipient's convenience.

4. **E-mail messages can be saved.** Your e-mail program can save all of the messages you send and receive. You can refer to messages received weeks, months, or even years ago. This acts as an electronic filing system.

5. **E-mail messages are less formal than letters and memos.** Although they should use good business language and grammar, e-mail messages do not need to be carefully formatted. Therefore, they take less time to prepare.

Did You Know?

The terms *Internet* and *World Wide Web* do not mean the same thing. The Internet is a global network that connects millions of computers. It started with four linked computers in 1969. The World Wide Web is a way to locate and view information stored on the Internet.

Chapter 8 Why Do You Need Technology?

Rob Miller runs a small business that provides restaurants with supplies and equipment. Last week, one of Rob's suppliers sent an e-mail to let Rob know that an order could not be filled. Rob then sent an e-mail message to other suppliers to try to find a replacement supplier.

Rob also uses e-mail to communicate with his customers. Many of the restaurants he serves place orders with him over the Internet. He immediately e-mails a response to confirm their orders and let them know when the orders will be filled.

Surf the Web

The Web can be a very valuable resource for entrepreneurs because there are thousands of web pages containing business-related information. A **web page** is a file stored on the Internet that greets visitors and provides information. A software program called a *browser* allows you to view the Web on your computer screen. Microsoft Explorer and Netscape are two popular browsers. Each web page has a special address that no other web page can use. This address tells a browser what file to show on the screen.

There are special web sites called *search engines* that allow you to search, or "surf," the Web using words and phrases. Google™ is one of the most popular search engines. Searching the Web by using a search engine helps you find sources for products and services you need for your business.

Leslie Wells owns a retail store that sells 1920s jewelry and clothing. She searches the Web for products her customers might want to buy. Last month,

Leslie located a web page that described several 1920s evening gowns she thought her customers would like. She used her credit card to buy the dresses over the Internet.

CHECKPOINT

→ What are some of the ways the Internet can be useful to a business?

© GETTY IMAGES/PHOTODISC

How can "surfing the Web" help a business owner?

Promote Your Business on the Internet

Many companies have web sites to promote their business. A web site is a collection of linked web pages. These sites often include information about a company's history, products and services, policies, and staff. They tell customers how to order products or services and can even advertise job openings with the company.

Do You Need a Web Site?

If your business targets only customers who live near you, you probably will not need a web site. If you sell services or products that can be used by people all over the world, you may want to consider electronic marketing. To use the World Wide Web to market your business, you will need to find an ISP that will host your web site. A *web host* will provide you with space and a web address for your web site. Your web site also will need to be designed. You can learn how to design it yourself, or you can hire a web site designer.

What Should Your Web Site Include? Marketing your business online is similar to marketing your business in more traditional ways. Your web site should:

- describe the products and services your business offers
- provide information and graphics that will persuade potential customers to buy your products or services

- let customers know how they can place an order
- allow customers to contact you through e-mail if they have questions about your products or services

> **CHECKPOINT**
>
> ➡ What are some of the things a web site should include?

Do Business over the Internet

Some businesses allow customers to place orders online. Selling products or services over the Internet is known as electronic commerce, or **e-commerce**. This kind of selling is expected to play a growing role in the U.S. economy in the coming years.

Businesses of various types and sizes use e-commerce. Some of these businesses sell millions of dollars' worth of merchandise over the Internet every year. Others are small businesses that sell everything from fresh flowers to used books online.

Gain Internet Customers

Accepting orders over the Internet is much more complicated than promoting your business over the Internet. Creating an e-commerce web site also is costly. Because of the expense involved, you should first focus your efforts on creating a web site to promote your business. After you begin to attract Internet customers, you then can think about changing your web site to make e-commerce possible.

Working Together

Working in a group, make a list of businesses that could benefit from having a web site. Explain why.

Select E-Commerce Software

To set up an e-commerce site, you will have to purchase special software. It will perform three important functions:

1. **Allow customers to charge purchases over the Internet** The software will check a customer's credit card number to verify that it is real. It will then bill the customer's account for the purchase.

2. **Keep credit card numbers confidential** Customers must feel confident that their credit card numbers will not be used to make illegal purchases.

3. **Link to an inventory database** By connecting your inventory database to your e-commerce site, the software

© GETTY IMAGES/PHOTODISC

Why would a business need e-commerce software?

will allow your customers to check whether an item is in stock.

CHECKPOINT

→ How can you use the Internet to sell your products and services?

8.2 LET'S GET REAL

1 **THINK ABOUT YOURSELF** Have you or someone in your family purchased something over the Internet? Did the transaction go smoothly? Are there any reasons why you would not make purchases over the Internet? Explain why.

2 **WHAT DO YOU THINK?** In your opinion, what are the advantages and disadvantages of using e-mail to communicate with coworkers, suppliers, and customers?

3 **COMMUNICATION CONNECTION** Many businesses have their own web sites. Using the *Activities* CD, open the activity Comparing Web Sites in the Chapter 8 folder. After completing the comparison charts, write a letter to one business describing what you liked about its web site. The letter should also include your recommendations for improving the web site.

4 **LANGUAGE ARTS CONNECTION** Write a paragraph explaining how an entrepreneur could use the Internet to conduct business.

HOW DO YOU CHOOSE TECHNOLOGY FOR YOUR BUSINESS?

Terms

technology plan
computer
  consultant

Goals

* **Explain how you can evaluate your business's need for technology.**

* **Determine where to purchase the technology you need.**

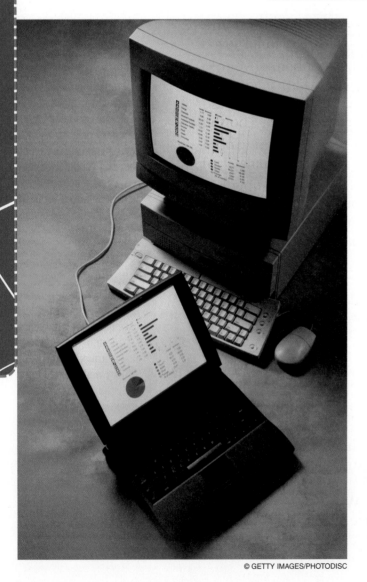

© GETTY IMAGES/PHOTODISC

Determine Your Technology Needs

Before you choose technology for your business, you will have to carefully evaluate your needs. In order to make the right purchasing decisions, you must first determine how you will use technology.

Plenty of technology exists to help you run your business. Some of this technology is very expensive, and much of it may not be right for your business. Your job as an entrepreneur will be to determine which technology will help you best meet your customers' needs and increase your profits.

Select a Computer

Once you decide to start your own business, you probably will want to buy at least one computer. Before you make your purchase, prepare a list of all of the ways you would like to use your computer. Then try to identify hardware and software that will help you do so.

Purchase Hardware Many people who are not computer experts end up purchasing much more than they really need. Some of the resources that can help you determine how much and what kind of hardware to purchase include:

- magazines for entrepreneurs and small businesses
- computer magazines (especially buying guide issues)
- *Consumer Reports*
- the Small Business Administration
- the Service Corps of Retired Executives (SCORE)
- computer salespeople

Technology Plan for RUXTON HEALTH AND RACQUET CLUB

Goal Increase number of customers who pay bills within 30 days.

Solution Purchase database program to track accounts and create billing letters. Use program to identify late payers and create mailing list. Contact late payers, reminding them of importance of paying on time.

Goal Identify most profitable product lines in order to improve marketing efforts.

Solution Purchase spreadsheet program to analyze profits of various product lines (health club memberships, tennis memberships, racquet shop, snack bar).

Purchase Software Your computer requires software to perform the functions you want. To identify the software you need, list all of the tasks you would like to perform on your computer. Then try to find software that will help you perform these tasks.

Write a Technology Plan

A **technology plan** includes specific goals you have for your business and describes how technology could be used to meet those goals. A technology plan will help you avoid wasting money on technology products that you don't need. A plan also will keep you from waiting too long to buy technology products that could increase your sales or reduce your costs.

Enrique Fernandez has identified several ways to use new technology to increase profits at his Ruxton Health and Racquet Club next year. As part of his technology plan, he lists his goals and the technology he plans to use to meet those goals, as shown above.

Stay Up to Date on New Technology

Technology changes at a fast pace. As a business owner, you need to keep informed about advances in technology. New technology may be developed that could change the way that you run your business. For example, the Internet now allows many people to work from home instead of going to an office. If a company has a web site, it can receive customer orders 24 hours a day. This is a change from how businesses used to operate. New technology could even help improve the products or services you offer.

Working Together

Working in a group, brainstorm at least three more goals that Enrique Fernandez might add to his technology plan. Write a solution for each goal stating how technology can be used to help reach the goal.

Technology today allows one device to do what it used to take several different devices to accomplish. Smart phones, digital cameras, and all-in-one printer devices are examples. You can now use smart phones to take and send pictures, record videos, watch movies, access the Internet, send e-mails, and text-message. As more and more electronic devices are being equipped with built-in wireless technology (Wi-Fi), people are going to be able to access the Web from anywhere there is a hot spot. A *hot spot* is a public area where you can connect to the Internet using wireless technology. Hot spots can be found at restaurants, airports, libraries, and even in homes.

Think Critically

1. What effect do you think wireless technology will have on businesses?

2. How available are hot spots in your community?

CHECKPOINT

➡ How can you evaluate your business needs for technology?

You can say that again!

If General Motors (GM) had kept up with technology like the computer industry has, we would all be driving $25 cars that got 1,000 miles per gallon.

—**Bill Gates,** Chairman and Chief Software Architect of Microsoft Corporation

Make Your Purchase

Now you are ready to talk with suppliers about purchasing equipment. You can contact a computer consultant or buy what you need from a retail source.

Computer Consultants

A **computer consultant** designs computer systems for businesses. Consultants make sure that all of the parts of your system will work together properly and that the equipment you buy meets your needs.

Don Hannahs owns a tax preparation service. He wants to upgrade the computers in his office. He wants the new computers to work with the printers he bought several years ago. He also wants to be able to send files directly to the new computerized photocopier he plans to purchase. Don contacts a computer consulting company that specializes in helping businesses purchase the right computer hardware.

Retail Sources

If your business is small and your needs are limited, you can purchase what you need at a retail store that sells office technology. Some of these stores have salespeople who understand the products and can help you determine which products will best meet your needs. However, be aware that some salespeople are not computer experts. For this reason, it is important that you know what you want to buy before you shop. Retail stores also offer service warranties on the products they sell. A warranty will help ensure that your computer gets fixed or replaced if it breaks down. You should find out if the store services the computers itself or if it sends them to another company to be serviced.

Mail-Order and Internet Companies If you know exactly what you need, you can buy computers, computer programs, and other technology products from a mail-order or Internet company. You may find better prices on the Internet or through mail-order catalogs. Just be sure the company has a good reputation. Also, be aware that you most likely won't receive the per-

© GETTY IMAGES/PHOTODISC

What are the advantages and disadvantages of buying technology on the Internet?

sonal attention and service you would at a store.

CHECKPOINT

→ Where can you purchase the technology you need?

8.3 **LET'S GET REAL**

1 THINK ABOUT YOURSELF Think about new technologies that have recently been introduced. Do you use any of them? Write a paragraph telling how new technologies have affected your life.

2 WHAT DO YOU THINK? Why is it important to review the most up-to-date sources of information about hardware and software when you are ready to buy?

3 COMMUNICATION CONNECTION Find various newspaper or magazine advertisements for computer hardware. Write a letter to a computer supplier describing the system you want for a new desktop publishing business. You will be preparing different kinds of documents, such as reports and fliers, for your customers. Ask for price quotes on each part of the system.

4 MATH CONNECTION You are choosing an Internet service provider. One service charges $279 for an entire year of unlimited service. Another provider charges $4.95 per month. This provider gives you five free hours per month. Each additional hour is $2.00. There are no long-distance charges to connect to either provider. You estimate your Internet use to be about 30 hours a month. Which provider should you use?

The Bose Corporation

What do the Olympic Games, the U.S. military, and a NASA space shuttle have in common? Did you guess that they all have a sound system produced by the same company—The Bose Corporation? If you did, then you would be right! If you haven't heard of Bose, you probably haven't been listening. The Bose Corporation deals with the science of sound.

Bose was founded in 1964 by Massachusetts Institute of Technology (M.I.T.) professor Dr. Amar G. Bose. Bose became interested in radios in 1943 at the age of 12 when he bought a radio kit. He learned to repair radios and even started a radio repair business. When he was a student at M.I.T. in the 1950s, Bose purchased a new hi-fi stereo system and was disappointed because it failed to deliver sound like that of a live performance. Using his degree in electrical engineering, he began to conduct research in the field of speaker design.

Bose's findings resulted in new design concepts that help deliver the excitement of live music to the listener. Bose's first product was a speaker that was in the shape of a sphere that reflected sound from the ceiling and walls all around the room. This was different from the traditional speakers that blast sound directly at the listener. Customers appreciated Bose's high standard for lifelike sound reproduction. That was the beginning of a long list of major technologies coming from Bose.

Bose supports research by reinvesting 100 percent of the company's profits back into the company. He believes that research is an important part of producing excellent products. In 1986, the Acoustimass® speaker technology was used in speakers small enough to fit in the hand. Although small, they produced sound quality once thought impossible from speakers. Bose was named the 1987 Inventor of the Year.

Thanks to Bose, we all can enjoy high-quality sound in our homes, stadiums and entertainment arenas, churches, stores, and restaurants. The automobile and airline industries also put Bose sound systems into their products. Bose operates in the United States, Europe, Canada, Australia, Asia, and South America.

Think Critically

1. How has technology played a role in the success of The Bose Corporation?
2. Why is it important that Bose reinvest its profits in new technology?

What Types of Technology Will You Use?

1. Computer hardware consists of desktop computers, laptop computers, printers, and modems. You must determine what types of hardware you will need for your business.

2. Computer software refers to the programs that control the computer. The most common types of software include word processing, spreadsheet, and database programs.

3. Other technological elements you may add to your business include graphics programs, scheduling programs, presentation software, communication software, LCD projectors, fax machines, photocopiers, scanners, and cell phones.

How Can You Use the Internet?

4. The Internet is a computer network that allows people to communicate electronically and access the World Wide Web.

5. To connect to the Internet, you will need to sign up with an Internet service provider. Before choosing an ISP, you should find out how easy it will be to connect to it, whether it will interrupt your phone service, and what monthly charges you will have to pay.

6. You can use electronic mail to send and receive messages. There are many advantages to using e-mail in your business.

7. You can surf the World Wide Web to find information on businesses and other resources.

8. You can promote your business over the Internet by creating a web site. You can also participate in e-commerce—selling products or services over the Internet.

How Do You Choose Technology for Your Business?

9. You should figure out what kind of technology you need to run your business. Then, you should contact suppliers and purchase the needed hardware and software.

10. It is important to write a technology plan for your business. It will help you determine how much equipment you need and when you need to buy each item.

Vocabulary Builder

Choose the term that best fits the definition.

1. A file stored on the Internet that greets visitors and provides information
2. A system used to send and receive electronic messages around the world
3. An electronic device that allows information to be transmitted over telephone lines from one computer to another
4. Computers and the equipment used with them
5. A company that provides connections to the Internet through your telephone or cable line
6. Programs that control computer hardware and direct its operation
7. Selling products or services over the Internet
8. Worldwide computer network that allows people to communicate with each other electronically
9. Describes how technology can be used to meet specific goals of your business
10. An individual that designs computer systems for businesses

a. computer consultant
b. computer hardware
c. e-commerce
d. electronic mail
e. Internet
f. Internet service provider
g. modem
h. software
i. technology plan
j. web page

Review What You Have Learned

11. What is the difference between computer hardware and computer software?
12. What are some of the tasks for which business owners use computers?
13. Why would you use a spreadsheet program?
14. What are some of the ways to learn how to use software?
15. Why might you purchase presentation software or graphics software?
16. What are the three factors you need to consider when choosing an Internet service provider?
17. List at least three advantages of e-mail.
18. What type of information usually is included on a company's web site?
19. Name three functions of e-commerce software.
20. What sources can help you decide what technology equipment to purchase?
21. What do computer consultants do?
22. List advantages and disadvantages of buying technology products at a retail store.

Using the *Activities* CD, open the Chapter 8 folder. Open the activity Deciding on the Technology to Use. Print a copy and complete the activity.

Think About It

1. Why do business owners need to understand the different types of computer hardware and software? What are the advantages and disadvantages of prepackaged software?

2. What type of businesses would benefit from using e-mail? Why?

3. The sports store that you own has been very successful in your local neighborhood. You would like to expand outside your neighborhood and do business over the Internet. What do you need to consider before getting started in e-commerce? What information will your web site contain?

Project: Making Entrepreneurship Work for You

This activity will help you develop the business opportunity that you identified in Chapter 1.

1. Evaluate the technology needs for your business by preparing a list of all the ways you would like to use your computer. Write a technology plan. Research and identify the types of hardware you will need. Compare three hardware products by making a chart that lists each product's features and price. Which product will you purchase and why?

2. What types of software will you need to run your business? Compare three products that may work for your business. Make a chart that lists the features and price of each product. Do you know how to use this software? If not, how will you learn to use it?

3. Explain why it is important that you have Internet access. How can you use the Internet for your business? Based on the research you have done in this lesson, which Internet service provider will you use? How much will it cost you to use this provider for one month? For one year?

Chapter 9

What Do You Need to Grow Your Business?

9.1 How Can Selling Help You Succeed?

9.2 How Can You Protect Your Business?

9.3 What Is Ethical Behavior?

© GETTY IMAGES/PHOTODISC

Kiss Your Pricing Woes Goodbye!

Their mom wouldn't let them wear lipstick, so they decided to make their own. That's how Maggie and Allie Cawood-Smith got the idea for Beet Lips, an organic lip balm made from plants grown in their Auburn, California garden. To set prices, the girls must carefully consider the cost of ingredients to produce their product.

Maggie and Allie grow most of the herbs used in Beet Lips, so their main expenses come from packaging and advertising. They sell their product in tiny, hand-decorated tins at local stores and gift shops. They use fliers and attractive display baskets to appeal to customers. They also operate a web site.

But how did they decide what to charge for their product? First, they calculated how much it costs to make the lip balm. Next, they checked the prices of similar products in stores. Then, they set their prices higher than their costs but lower than the prices of competing products. Half-ounce tins of Beet Lips sell for $3.50. Maggie and Allie make about $1.50 profit for each tin they sell. The sisters also highly recommend online selling. They were able to make $700 in one month during a recent holiday season.

If you sell goods, you need to account for all of your expenses. You also must include "hidden" expenses, such as your time. A good general rule for setting prices is to add the costs of your materials and labor and then multiply that amount by two. You may need to change this figure based on what people are willing to pay and how much profit you want to make.

You also can look at the prices of similar products, like Maggie and Allie did. But if you do your pricing homework, and if your product is as good as Beet Lips, you'll be off to a good start in making your first sale.

WHAT DO YOU KNOW?

1] What sales techniques do Maggie and Allie use to sell their products?

2] Do you think the sisters' technique for setting prices would work for large corporations like Ford Motor Company or Microsoft? Why or why not?

HOW CAN SELLING HELP YOU SUCCEED?

Terms

personal selling
features
benefits
needs assessment

Goals

* **Explain the importance of good selling skills.**

* **Define customer needs and wants.**

Selling

As an entrepreneur, you will need to be a good salesperson. You will have to sell your business idea to people whom you would like to invest in your business. You also will have to sell your products or services to your potential customers.

As your business expands and you need to hire others to work for you, it will be important for them to have good selling skills too. To many customers, the salesperson is the business because this person may be the only representative of the company the customers ever meet. It is important for the salesperson to create a positive image of the company. A salesperson is responsible for selling the products or services of the business. The salesperson's role is very important because the business makes its money from sales.

Personal Selling

When a salesperson talks to potential buyers and tries to persuade them to purchase something, the salesperson is using **personal selling**. It is important

© DIGITAL VISION

You are going to hire a photographer to assist you in your children's photography business. This person will be responsible for selling the photography service to parents of three- and four-year-olds who attend a local day-care center. The person you hire also will help you take pictures of the children during busy times, such as holidays.

You want to be sure you select the right person for the job. What is the most important thing for you to look for in a potential salesperson? What type of training will you provide for the employee?

for the salesperson to identify the customer's needs and concerns so that they can be addressed throughout the sales process.

Product Knowledge

To be good at selling a product or service, a salesperson must know all of the features and benefits of what is being sold. **Features** are what the product or service actually does. For example, if you were going to buy an MP3 player, the features would include the number of songs it can hold and how easy it is to operate. **Benefits** are the advantages gained from the features. A benefit of an MP3 player is that you can hear your favorite song whenever you want.

Customers mainly are interested in the benefits they will receive from purchasing a product or service. But many times, a salesperson builds a sales presentation around the features alone. It is important for the salesperson to help the customer see the benefits and the value of the product or service. In this way, the customer will be less likely to object to the price of the item as the sales presentation

moves along. If the salesperson for the MP3 player talks only about the size of the memory and how easy it is to download songs, the customer might not make the connection between these features and their benefits. If the customers don't clearly see the benefits, they may think the MP3 player is too expensive. But, if the salesperson points out how nice it would be to play favorite songs anytime and anywhere, the customer will see the value and might not object to the price.

A business must spend time training salespeople about the product or service being sold. It also must provide training about the market in which the salespeople are selling. Salespeople also should be familiar with their own company as well as their company's competition. The more salespeople know about the environment in which they are working, the more effective they will be.

Working Together

Working in a group, choose a product that you would like to buy. Make a list of the features and benefits of the product.

CHECKPOINT

→ Why are good selling skills important to entrepreneurs?

Determine Customer Needs and Wants

Customers purchase goods and services in order to satisfy needs. The need being satisfied may be as basic as food, water, or shelter. But it may be a more complicated need related to self-esteem and the desire to feel important. A salesperson must determine what type of need the customer is trying to satisfy in order to sell a product or service to meet the need. Lower-level needs are not usually met through personal selling because customers do not have to be persuaded to purchase items that satisfy their basic needs. Selling skills become more important as customers are trying to meet upper-level needs.

Needs Assessment

Customer needs for a target market are determined through marketing research. This research helps a business decide what type of product or service to offer customers. When a customer goes shopping, it is up to the salesperson to find out as much as possible about the customer's situation. The salesperson should conduct a **needs assessment**, which involves interviewing the customer to determine his or her specific needs and wants. Then, the salesperson should help identify the choices the customer has for satisfying these needs and wants.

Some customers will know exactly what they need. Meeting their needs is referred to as *need satisfying*. Even when the customer knows what he or she

wants, the salesperson must be willing to take the time to help better satisfy the customer's needs. If the customer does not know what he or she needs, satisfying the need is called *problem resolution*. Problem resolution requires the salesperson to take on the customer's point of view. You should ask questions to determine what the customer needs and requires. You will act as an expert to assist the customer in solving the problem.

Buying Decisions

Customers' buying decisions are influenced by rational and emotional reasons. *Rational buying decisions* are based on logic. Reasons for buying include safety, simplicity, quality, reliability, convenience, durability, knowledge, cost, and ease of operation. Customers evaluate their choices and make a purchase only after careful thought. *Emotional buying decisions* are based on the desire to have a specific product or service. Often, little thought or time is spent making an emotional decision. Some reasons

Why is a washing machine likely a rational buying decision?

for emotional buying include fear, protection, appearance, recreation, improved health, comfort, recognition, pride of ownership, imitation, prestige, and popularity.

Customer Decisions

Following a problem-solving process is the best way for customers to make a buying decision. They must define the problem, gather information, identify various solutions, evaluate alternatives and select the best option, take action, and evaluate the action.

A salesperson can assist customers through this process by helping them define their need, showing them all the products or services that could meet the need, explaining the features and benefits of the various options, making the sale, and following up with the customer.

NETBookmark

When entrepreneurs try to sell their products and services to customers, one of the most important parts of the selling process is closing the sale. A sale is closed when the customer decides to purchase. Some buying decisions are hard for customers to make. A good salesperson will persuade the customer to buy without being pushy. Access exploringxtra.swlearning.com and click on the link for Chapter 9. Read the article. What does the term *ABC* mean in sales? If a customer tells you, "I'll be back later," is that a good sign? Why or why not?

exploringxtra.swlearning.com

CHECKPOINT

→ Why is it important to determine the needs and wants of the customer?

9.1 LET'S GET REAL

1 THINK ABOUT YOURSELF Are you a good salesperson? What characteristics do you have that will help you be a good salesperson? What skills do you still need to develop? Write a paragraph telling about your selling skills.

2 WHAT DO YOU THINK? Why do you think personal selling is used in a business?

3 LANGUAGE ARTS CONNECTION As a salesperson, you must learn to sell product benefits—not features—to customers. Using the *Activities* CD, open the Chapter 9 folder. Open the activity Turn Features Into Benefits. Print a copy and complete the activity.

4 MATH CONNECTION Your sales goal for one month is to capture 15 percent of the market. Sales in your area for the previous year averaged $180,000. Based on this average, how much will you have to sell to achieve your goal?

HOW CAN YOU PROTECT YOUR BUSINESS?

Terms

security precautions
shoplifting
bounced check

Goals

* **Describe a business risk.**

* **Identify types of business theft.**

* **Explain how risks are classified.**

* **Describe the types of insurance that protect a business from risks.**

Business Risk

As an entrepreneur, you will face many risks. For example, there is a risk that the business will fail or lose money. **Security precautions** are the steps that you take to protect yourself against different types of risks. Once you have identified the risks you face, you can determine the security precautions you need to take.

The categories of risks are human, natural, and economic. *Human risks* are those caused by the actions of employees or customers. Some of the human risks you face involve theft. Shoplifters or employees may steal your merchandise. Burglars may break into your business and steal your equipment. People may use stolen credit cards or may write checks when they don't have money in their account.

Natural risks are caused by acts of nature. Examples are storms, fires, floods, and earthquakes. The occurrence of any of these natural disasters could

© GETTY IMAGES/PHOTODISC

bring about tremendous loss to a business. Hurricane Katrina, a natural risk, delivered a devastating blow to the Gulf Coast region of the United States in September 2005. The loss of homes and businesses in Louisiana, Mississippi, and Alabama led to many people being displaced and having to start their lives over in new locations.

Economic risks occur because of changes in business conditions. Changes can result from an increase or a decrease in competition, changes in population, inflation or recession, and government regulations. World events also can result in economic changes. The terrorist attacks on September 11, 2001, caused a huge downturn in the U.S. economy. This resulted in major layoffs and cutbacks by businesses and decreased the income of many Americans. As a result, many entrepreneurs lost their businesses.

Why is shoplifting a problem for businesses?

© GETTY IMAGES/PHOTODISC

CHECKPOINT

→ What are some examples of human, natural, and economic risks?

Types of Theft

All business owners must be aware of the different types of theft. Shoplifting, employee theft, and robbery are all possibilities. There also is the chance that the business could be the victim of credit card fraud or bounced checks. Business owners must learn about ways to prevent the different types of theft.

Shoplifting

Shoplifting is the act of knowingly taking items from a business without paying. Customers shoplift millions of dollars in merchandise every year. The problem exists in almost every type of retail business.

If you own a retail business, you will have to take steps to prevent or reduce shoplifting. Some of the things you can do include the following:

- Instruct your employees to watch for customers who appear suspicious.

- Hire security guards or off-duty police officers to patrol your store.

- Post signs indicating that you prosecute shoplifters.

- Ask customers to leave their shopping bags at the counter.

- Install electronic devices, such as mounted video cameras, electronic merchandise tags, and point-of-exit sensors, to detect shoplifters.

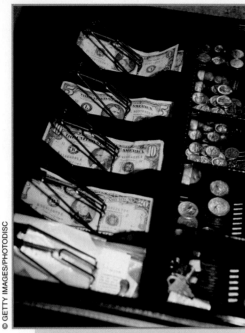

How can a business owner protect against employee theft?

Employee Theft

Most employees are hard working and honest. But there are a few who will take things, such as office supplies, equipment, and even money, from your business. These employees can destroy your business financially.

As an entrepreneur, you need to be aware of the possibility of employee theft. You need to take steps to prevent the problem from occurring. You also need to know how to detect the problem and to handle it once it is detected. The following procedures should help.

- **Screen job applicants to prevent hiring dishonest employees.** Screening can involve verifying a job applicant's work and educational background. You can also check criminal records and credit reports.

- **Install security cameras.** Knowing that they are being recorded can discourage employees from stealing.

- **Establish a tough company policy on employee theft.** The policy should explain the consequences of theft and should be shared with all new employees.

- **Be on the lookout.** Watch for cash shortages in the cash register and missing merchandise and supplies.

Robbery

Almost all businesses could be robbed. You can choose a safe location for your business to guard against being robbed. You also can install special locks and burglar alarms. To limit losses in the event of a robbery, many businesses keep only a small amount of cash in the cash register. Once a certain amount of cash is received, it is moved to a safe. Some businesses also use surveillance cameras. These cameras discourage robbers from entering the business. Be aware that you may be robbed regardless of the number of precautions you take. It is simply a risk of being open for business.

Credit Card Fraud

Business owners lose millions of dollars every year because of stolen credit cards. If a purchase is made on a stolen credit card, a business may not be able to collect the money. To prevent stolen credit cards from being used to buy goods, you can install an electronic credit authorizer. This machine checks to see if a credit card is valid. If the card has been reported stolen or if the cardholder has gone over the credit limit, authorization to use the card will not be granted.

Bounced Checks

A **bounced check** (or bad check) is a check that is written when the checking account does not have enough funds to cover the check amount. Preventing losses from bounced checks is difficult. To minimize losses, you can establish a policy of accepting checks written on in-state banks only. You also can charge a fee if a customer writes a bad check to your business. Asking for identification, such as a driver's license, can help you track down a person who writes a bad check so that you can collect the money due. If bounced checks are a serious problem in your area, you may decide not to accept checks at all.

> **CHECKPOINT**
>
> ➡ What are the different types of theft and what can be done by a business owner to protect the business from them?

How can uncontrollable risks affect businesses?

© GETTY IMAGES/PHOTODISC

Classification of Risk

Business owners face different types of risks—human, natural, and economic. These risks can be further classified based on the result of the risk, control of the risk, and insurability of the risk.

Result of Risk

Pure risks present the chance of loss but no opportunity for gain. If you have a vehicle that is used in your business, every time it goes out on the road there is the risk of an accident. If there is an accident, loss will likely be suffered. However, if an accident is avoided, there is no opportunity for gain.

Speculative risks offer you the chance to gain as well as lose from the risk. Investing in the stock market is a good example of a speculative risk. When you invest money, you have the chance to make money if the stock price rises. However, if the stock price falls, you have the chance to lose money.

Control of Risk

Controllable risks can be reduced or possibly even avoided by actions you take. Installing a security system in your business could control the risk of your business being robbed.

An *uncontrollable risk* is one that actions have no effect on. The weather cannot be controlled, but it can have a huge effect on some businesses. If a hurricane hits a resort town, a decrease in business and loss of profits will result. But, if the weather is sunny and warm,

tourism will grow, and business owners may make a profit.

Insurability of the Risk

A risk is *insurable* if it is a pure risk faced by a large number of people and the amount of the loss can be predicted. The buildings that businesses are housed in face the risk of being destroyed by fire. The value of the buildings can be estimated. So, insurance companies sell insurance to pay for buildings if they are damaged by fire.

If there is a risk that a loss will occur and the amount of the loss cannot be predicted, the risk is *uninsurable*. If a business moves to a new location, customers may not follow. The loss of income that could result from lost customers is not predictable and, so, is not insurable.

> **CHECKPOINT**
>
> → What is the difference between a pure risk and a speculative risk?

© GETTY IMAGES/PHOTODISC

What type of insurance would cover a fire?

Types of Insurance

As a business owner, you are at risk from more than just criminal activity. A fire could destroy your building. An accident could injure an employee. A broken water pipe could ruin your inventory. After identifying risks you face, one of the security precautions you can take is to purchase insurance to protect against some financial losses.

The most important types of insurance you will need for your business include property insurance, casualty insurance, life insurance, and workers' compensation insurance.

Property Insurance

Property insurance insures all business property against normal risks, including fire, robbery, and storm damage. Most businesses purchase property insurance for all three of these risks. Insurance companies usually offer separate policies for buildings, vehicles, and other business property, such as cash, equipment, and inventory.

Property insurance does not cover floods or earthquakes. If your business is located in a part of the country that more often experiences special kinds of natural disasters, you may want to purchase a separate insurance policy that covers these kinds of tragic events.

Casualty Insurance

Casualty insurance protects a business against lawsuits. It can protect you from having to pay damages if an accident occurs on your property. It also can protect your business against lawsuits claiming that a defect in the product you manufactured or sold caused bodily injury to a customer.

Life Insurance

Life insurance is insurance that is paid if the holder of the policy dies. A business owner buys life insurance so that his or her family or heirs have enough money to continue the business.

Workers' Compensation

Workers' compensation is not a type of insurance that a business purchases. It is a government-sponsored insurance program that helps workers who are injured on the job. Business owners are required to contribute to this program. Workers' compensation covers medical expenses for work-related injuries. It provides income benefits to workers who are unable to work as a result of their injuries. All businesses are required by law to provide workers' compensation.

Other Kinds of Insurance

Other types of insurance that you may want to purchase include flood, business interruption, crime, and renter's insurance. Depending on your business and its location, you may or may not decide to purchase these additional kinds of protection.

CHECKPOINT

➡ List all the types of insurance you can purchase for your business.

9.2 LET'S GET REAL

1 **THINK ABOUT YOURSELF** Have you ever known anyone who shoplifted? Write a paragraph about the experience and how you handled it or how you would handle a shoplifting experience if it occurs in the future.

2 **WHAT DO YOU THINK?** You own a pizza shop. You suspect that one of your delivery people is charging customers more than what they actually owe and keeping the difference. How would you handle the situation?

3 **COMMUNICATION CONNECTION** Your friend has decided to open a skateboarding park. She has asked you what types of insurance you think she will need. Prepare a report on the coverage that you think she will need.

4 **MATH CONNECTION** The Old World Café's cash register receipts showed total sales of $884. The cash equaled $534, and the credit card slips equaled $237. How much of the sales are not accounted for? What might explain the difference?

WHAT IS ETHICAL BEHAVIOR?

Terms

ethics
code of ethics
business ethics

Goals

* **Define *ethics*.**

* **Explain the importance of establishing a code of ethics for your business.**

What Is Ethics?

Have you ever tried to make a decision about something when you knew one of your choices was right and the other one was wrong? And even knowing this, was it still a difficult decision for you to make?

Ethics is the study of moral choices and values. Ethics involves choosing between right and wrong. Behaving ethically means that you are behaving in an honest manner.

As the owner of your own business, you will be forced to deal with what is right or wrong. You will have to make ethical decisions about the way you want to run your business. Thinking about ethical issues in advance will help you handle conflicts when they arise.

Culture and Ethics

Different cultures define ethical behavior differently. In some countries, it is considered unethical to take bribes. In other countries, paying bribes may be

© GETTY IMAGES/PHOTODISC

an accepted business practice. In some countries, employers may treat employees badly. In other countries, employers are expected to treat their employees with respect.

Code of Ethics

Even within the same culture, individuals develop different standards, or codes, of ethics. A **code of ethics** is the level of ethical behavior demanded by an individual, a business, or a culture. Some individuals have very high standards of ethics and do what is right in every situation. Other individuals don't develop a standard of ethics at all. They act without thinking whether their actions are right or wrong.

Jan Sommers has a high personal code of ethics. Last week, she received a duplicate refund check from one of her suppliers. Jan knew that the check had been sent to her by mistake. She immediately called the supplier to report the error.

CHECKPOINT
→ What does it mean to have a high code of ethics?

How are recycled bags related to business ethics?

Ethics and Business

Ethical questions arise in every type of business. Large corporations, small companies, and home-based businesses all deal with ethical dilemmas at one time or another. **Business ethics** is the application of the principles of right and wrong to issues that come up in the workplace.

Set High Standards

Business and ethics used to be considered unrelated to each other. Over the past hundred years, this view has changed. Businesses today recognize that they must behave in an ethical manner to keep customers.

Myths About Business and Ethics Some people believe that entrepreneurs need not be concerned with ethical issues. They believe that their only goal should be increasing profits. They might think that acting ethically can hurt their profits. In fact, using ethics in business can help you avoid problems. It also can make customers and suppliers more willing to do business with you.

Consumer Awareness Consumers and business owners are both concerned about business ethics. Because consumers are so aware of ethical issues, businesses find ways to show customers that they practice ethics in their daily operations. Manu-

You can say that again!

At this moment, America's highest economic need is higher ethical standards—standards enforced by strict laws and upheld by responsible business leaders.

—President George W. Bush

The importance of business ethics is growing. It is good business to be ethical. Because of this, there are many trends related to ethics. Ethics is now increasingly being taught in school. Business leaders are supporting ethical behavior by offering ethics training to their employees. Companies are acting more ethically and socially responsible. They often sponsor events that benefit their community or contribute to local or national charities. Businesses also are now more concerned about the environment. They are careful not to use products that may harm the environment.

Think Critically

1. Why do you think ethics is now being taught in school? Do you think this is a good idea? Why or why not?

2. Can you provide an example of a local or national business that contributes to good causes or that uses environmentally friendly products? How does this help the business?

facturers of some shampoos and cosmetics print on their packaging that they do not test their products on animals. Consumers who have strong opinions about animal rights may be more willing to purchase such products.

Establish an Ethical Workplace

As the owner of your business, it will be up to you to inspire your employees to behave ethically. You will want to establish an ethical workplace for several reasons.

- You want to do the right thing.

- You want to serve as a role model to others.

- You want to be proud of the way you conduct yourself, and you want others to be proud of you.

- Ethical behavior is good for business because it gains the trust of customers.

- Employees are more likely to act ethically if they see the business owner acting in an ethical way.

- Acting ethically reduces the possibility of being sued.

Create a Written Code of Ethics One way that you can communicate your ethical beliefs to the people who work for you is by creating a written code of ethics. Such guidelines will help you and your employees make ethical decisions.

You should create a code of ethics as soon as you begin your business, even if you are your business's only employee. You also should establish company policies and procedures to let you and your employees know how to behave in certain situations.

Working Together

Working in a small group, describe an ethical dilemma that a business owner may face. Then, explain how the business owner might handle this dilemma.

To create a code of ethics for your business, think about ethical dilemmas that may arise and come up with solutions for dealing with them. Talk to other entrepreneurs to see what kinds of ethical problems they have encountered.

Jackie Rand owns a large discount store, Dollar Saver. Every month, salespeople from various manufacturing companies come to his company to sell their products or services. They meet with the head of Dollar Savers' purchasing department, Ellen Chao. Last month, a manufacturing salesperson offered Ellen a free vacation. Not sure whether she should accept the gift, Ellen checked the company handbook. It clearly stated that gifts worth more than $100 should never be accepted from manufacturing salespeople. The

What could be included in a company handbook?

© DIGITAL VISION

written guidelines helped her solve an ethical dilemma.

CHECKPOINT

→ Why is it important for entrepreneurs to establish a code of ethics?

9.3 **LET'S GET REAL**

1 **THINK ABOUT YOURSELF** All individuals and businesses should practice ethical behavior. Have you ever experienced unethical behavior from an individual or business? Describe your experience.

2 **WHAT DO YOU THINK?** Is it important for entrepreneurs to always act in an ethical manner? Why or why not?

3 **COMMUNICATION CONNECTION** Interview someone you know who grew up in a different culture or at a different time in your culture. Ask the person if there are any ethical differences between the cultures or times. Write a short report and present your findings to the class.

4 **MATH CONNECTION** You receive your bank statement. In reviewing your deposits, you find that a deposit you made for $110 has been posted by the bank to your account as $1,100. What is the amount of the error? What would be the ethical thing for you to do? If you don't do the ethical thing, what problems might this cause?

Nintendo/Gunpei Yokoi

The spirit of entrepreneurship can arise anywhere on earth. How it begins is often an interesting story as demonstrated by the life of Gunpei Yokoi.

Gunpei Yokoi was born in 1941 in Kyoto, Japan. He excelled in mathematics and science in school and graduated from college with a degree in electronics. In 1965, Nintendo hired Yokoi to maintain the machines used to manufacture its Hanafuda playing cards.

Nintendo had begun in 1889 as a playing cards manufacturer. In 1963, it started to manufacture games as well. Gunpei Yokoi eventually was reassigned as an engineer in the new games division. He soon invented *The Ultrahand*, which sold 1.2 million units during the holiday season in 1970. It was Nintendo's first toy—a toy arm on an accordion-like extension that kids could use as an extendable claw.

Nintendo eventually became very successful in video arcade systems. As microprocessors were introduced in 1975, a partnership with Mitsubishi Electric developed home-use video games. While designing *Game & Watch*, Yokoi invented the famous control cross that is still used on video game consoles today. He also did extensive work on the system we know today as the Nintendo Entertainment System.

In 1989, Yokoi created the Game Boy, which was the first portable, handheld game system with interchangeable game paks. It was the most successful handheld machine ever produced, selling over 60 million units worldwide. In 1996, the Game Boy Pocket was introduced. Yokoi also worked on *Famicon* and the first *Metroid*.

During his 30 years at Nintendo, Yokoi's products were very successful, but success never turned his head. A loyal employee, Yokoi always placed the focus on Nintendo rather than taking all the credit himself.

In 1996, Yokoi left Nintendo to set up his own toy company, Koto Laboratory in Kyoto, but he was tragically killed in a car accident on October 4, 1997.

Nintendo continues with great success, but it might not have been so successful without the contributions of Gunpei Yokoi, the creator of Game Boy, Nintendo Entertainment System, and *Game & Watch*.

Think Critically

1. What skills did Gunpei Yokoi have that helped him contribute to the success of Nintendo?
2. Do you think Yokoi would have been able to create all of these products on his own if he had not been working for Nintendo?

How Can Selling Help You Succeed?

1. Selling skills are important to an entrepreneur. Selling is how a business makes money. In the beginning, you will have to sell your business ideas to investors. Once your business is running, you will have to sell your products or services to customers.

2. Personal selling involves talking to potential customers and trying to persuade them to make a purchase.

3. Good salespeople will know all the features and benefits of the products and services they sell.

4. Customers make purchases based on their needs. They can make rational buying decisions or emotional buying decisions.

How Can You Protect Your Business?

5. Businesses face risks in human, natural, and economic categories. Once you have identified the risks faced by your business, you have to determine the security precautions that you need to take.

6. Human risks include shoplifting, employee theft, robbery, credit card fraud, and bounced checks. Natural risks include storms, floods, and earthquakes. Economic risks include inflation and changes in the population.

7. Risks faced by businesses are based on the result, control, and insurability of the risk. Insurance can be purchased to protect your business against insurable risks.

8. There are many types of insurance needed for your business, including property, casualty, life, and workers' compensation.

What Is Ethical Behavior?

9. Ethics is the study of moral choices and values. A code of ethics is the level of ethical behavior demanded by an individual, a business, or a culture.

10. You should write a code of ethics for your business. It can help determine what to do if an ethical dilemma arises.

11. Businesses should find ways to show customers that they practice ethics in the daily operation of the business.

Vocabulary Builder

Choose the term that best fits the definition.

1. Act of knowingly taking items from a business without paying
2. The advantages gained from the features of a product or service
3. What a product or service does
4. Study of moral choices and values
5. Interviewing the customer to determine his or her specific needs and wants
6. Level of ethical behavior demanded by an individual, a business, or a culture
7. Steps you take to protect yourself against different types of risks
8. Application of the principles of right or wrong to issues that come up in the workplace
9. Occurs when a salesperson talks to potential buyers and tries to persuade them to purchase something
10. A check that is written when the checking account does not have enough funds

a. benefits
b. bounced check
c. business ethics
d. code of ethics
e. ethics
f. features
g. needs assessment
h. personal selling
i. security precautions
j. shoplifting

Review What You Have Learned

11. Why should salespeople have a lot of knowledge about the products they are selling?
12. Describe the difference between features and benefits.
13. How can you conduct a needs assessment for a customer?
14. What influences a customer's reasons for buying?
15. How can a salesperson help a customer make a buying decision?
16. Why is it important to screen job applicants before hiring them?
17. What are some things that could happen that might make a business owner think an employee is stealing?
18. Why are speculative risks uninsurable?
19. Why is buying insurance for your business important?
20. How does culture affect ethics?
21. Why should you establish an ethical workplace at your business?
22. What are some things you can do to establish an ethical workplace?

Using the *Activities* CD, open the activity Ethical—Yes or No? in the Chapter 9 folder. Print a copy and complete the activity.

Think About It

1. You have an employee working for you who does not understand the importance of good selling skills. What can you do to help the employee?

2. Businesses lose millions of dollars every year because of stolen credit cards and bounced checks. Why wouldn't a business owner protect himself or herself by accepting only cash?

3. You are working with a friend to cater a party. The two of you have met with the customer to discuss the menu and the price you will charge. The customer was very specific about the brands of food that she wanted you to serve. When you and your partner go shopping, you find that the brands she specified cost more than what you budgeted. Your friend thinks that you should substitute cheaper brands and not tell the customer. What are the ethical issues you face? What do you think would be the best way to resolve the issue? Why?

Project: Making Entrepreneurship Work for You

This activity will help you develop the business opportunity that you identified in Chapter 1.

1. To increase your product knowledge, create a features and benefits list for each of the products and services you will sell. Explain how you can use these lists to develop selling strategies for you and your salespeople.

2. Develop strategies to protect your business from theft. Describe how your business will prevent shoplifting, employee theft, robberies, credit card fraud, and bounced checks. Present your strategies to the class and be prepared to answer questions.

3. Contact an insurance agent to obtain information on insuring your business. What types of insurance do you need? How much coverage should you buy?

4. Describe some situations specific to your type of business that may pose an ethical dilemma. Write a code of ethics for your business that includes company policies and procedures for dealing with these particular situations.

Chapter 10

How Do You Make A Plan?

Butterflies Are Forever

When she was 13 years old, Kassidy Briles of Des Moines, Iowa hatched an unusual business idea. Kassidy had always been fascinated with insects, but she had never thought of a way to turn her interest into a business. Then she read a newspaper article about someone who raised and sold butterflies. Now Kassidy owns and operates her own company, Dream Wings. She sells butterflies in decorative cages as gifts.

Kassidy wasn't sure the idea behind Dream Wings was possible, so she attended an entrepreneurial seminar. There she learned about the importance of business plans. With her mother's help, Kassidy wrote an 18-page plan. The plan included information about company management and the products and services she intended to provide. It also identified her target markets and strategies for reaching them, and it provided financial details. Kassidy found the most difficult part was estimating future sales. She admits that she made a few changes to the plan after she opened her business.

Kassidy sells most of her butterflies to brides and grooms who release them at their weddings instead of throwing rice. Teachers also buy butterflies for class science projects. Kassidy sells others as all-occasion gifts. She includes instructions for letting the butterflies go. Although Dream Wings has been successful, Kassidy continues to revise her original business plan. For one thing, she wants to expand her customer base. For example, she believes that hospital patients might consider a cage of butterflies to be a more charming gift than flowers.

Kassidy doesn't think that everyone needs a business plan as detailed as hers, but she does recommend including an overall description of the business, estimated start-up costs, and a goal for how soon you plan to break even. The important thing is to start making plans today for where you want your business to be tomorrow.

WHAT DO YOU KNOW?

1] How do you think writing a business plan helped Kassidy determine if her idea was possible?

2] Kassidy's business plan was very detailed, but she doesn't necessarily believe all teen entrepreneurs need a plan as detailed as hers. Do you agree with Kassidy? Why or why not?

WHY DO YOU NEED A PLAN?

Terms	Goals
business plan	✳ **Explain the purpose of writing a good business plan.** ✳ **Describe the importance of a business plan.**

© GETTY IMAGES/PHOTODISC

The Business Plan

Have you ever thought about doing something new, but you could not seem to get started? Perhaps it was because you knew what you wanted to do, but you did not have a plan for how to do it. A plan serves as your guide. It helps you get started and stay focused.

A **business plan** is a written document that describes all the steps necessary to open and operate a successful business. Once you have worked out the details of your business, it is important to put everything on paper. Writing these details will help you visualize all the parts of your business. It also will help you persuade other people and banks to invest in your business idea. A business plan:

- describes what your business will produce, how you will produce it, and who will buy your product or service

- explains who will run your business and who will supply it with goods

- states how your business will win over customers from competitors and what your business will do to keep customers

- provides detailed financial information that shows how your business will succeed in earning a profit

Writing a business plan is one of the most difficult and important things you will do as an entrepreneur. A business plan can make or break your business.

Purposes of a Business Plan

The business plan serves three important purposes.

1. **A business plan explains the idea behind your business.** It spells out how your product or service will be produced and sold. To persuade people and banks to invest in your business, you need to show that your business idea is a good one. So, you will need a completely new product or service or one that is better or less expensive than products or services that already exist. You will need to identify who your target customer is and show how your company will be able to get and keep customers.

2. **A business plan sets specific goals and describes how your business expects to achieve them.** A good business plan includes sales estimates for the short term (the first year), the medium term (two to five years after startup), and the long term (five years in the future). It describes the products and services that will be introduced over the next five years. It also describes future plans, such as expansion of the business.

3. **A business plan describes the backgrounds and experience of the people who will be running the business.** Banks and other lenders make financing decisions based on how well they think a company can meet its goals. Entrepreneurs that have a background related to their business idea are more likely to succeed. If you provide good information on the background and experience of the people who will be running your company, the bank or investor will be more likely to invest money in your business.

© GETTY IMAGES/PHOTODISC

Why would a bank want to know about your background?

CHECKPOINT

→ What are the three main purposes of a business plan?

• • •

Working Together

In small groups, brainstorm the ideal backgrounds and experience of people who could run the following types of businesses:

- sporting goods store
- gift basket company
- clothing store

Importance of a Business Plan

Every new business must have a business plan. The business plan is important for several reasons.

- **A business plan makes you think about all parts of your business.** Don Jung began a graphic design business from his home. He spent many hours thinking about the business and thought he was ready to start it until he sat down to write his business plan. He had not yet made sales and profit estimates. He also had not thought about the possibility of hiring staff if the business grew too large for him to handle alone. Drafting a business plan helped Don gain even more confidence in his business idea. It showed him that building a successful business based on his idea would be possible. Working on his business plan also helped Don think through business strategies, recognize limits, and identify potential problems.

- **A business plan may help you secure financing for your business.** Lenders require a business plan before they will consider financing a business. Without a business plan, you will not be able to get a business loan.

- **A business plan helps you communicate your ideas to others.** By the time you write your business plan, you will have given a lot of thought to the business you want to start. A business plan reassures you that your business can succeed. If you communicate your ideas well on paper, you also can persuade the reader that your business will succeed. The business plan can help you get a loan from a bank. It also may persuade suppliers to extend credit to your company.

- **A business plan can serve as a tool for managing your business.** Once your business is up and running, you can use the business plan in your decision making. Adam Rothwell regularly uses his business plan to help manage his company, Adam's Art. Adam's plan laid out his vision of how the company would grow over time. By fol-

How does a business plan help you think about all parts of your business?

© GETTY IMAGES/PHOTODISC

When McDonald's first opened, one of its goals may have been to provide quality food in a timely manner. Now, due to the demand for healthier menus and the claims that fast food has contributed to the obesity problem, McDonald's has had to change its goals. McDonald's started using new packaging for its food products. The package lists the calories, fat, carbohydrates, protein, and sodium in the item. The package also shows the percentage each element provides of the recommended daily allowance for an average adult on a 2,000-calorie-per-day diet. Businesses must be willing to make changes to their original business plan to meet the changing needs of customers.

Think Critically

1. Do you think this new packaging will increase or decrease McDonald's sales? Why?

2. Do you think it is important for companies to respond to the concerns of the public? Explain your answer.

lowing the strategies in his plan, he has increased sales by offering new products and by targeting a larger area.

CHECKPOINT

→ Why do entrepreneurs need to write business plans?

10.1 LET'S GET REAL

1 THINK ABOUT YOURSELF Putting your business plan in writing helps you communicate your ideas to others. In addition to having others read your business plan, do you think discussing it with them can help get your ideas across? Why or why not?

2 WHAT DO YOU THINK? Why do you think a well-written business plan is so important to an entrepreneur's success?

3 COMMUNICATION CONNECTION You are starting a business caring for people's houseplants. Write a paragraph explaining the idea behind the business. Be sure to spell out how you plan to market your services.

4 MATH CONNECTION If 44 percent of all new businesses last at least four years and there were 500 new businesses that opened in your area last year, how many of those new businesses will still be open in four years?

WHAT GOES INTO A PLAN?

Terms

goals
resume

Goals

* **Identify the seven basic elements of a business plan.**

* **Describe additional elements that may be needed in a business plan.**

© GETTY IMAGES/PHOTODISC

Basic Elements of a Business Plan

All businesses are not alike. Therefore, not all business plans are alike. A business plan for a sole proprietorship business based in a home will differ from a business plan for a large corporation with offices in many cities. But all business plans have the same purposes, so they all should include seven basic elements.

1. history and background of your idea
2. goals for your company
3. products or services you will offer
4. form of ownership
5. management and staffing
6. marketing
7. current and projected financial statements

History and Background

Something must have sparked the idea for your business. Describing how you came up with the idea can help lenders, investors, and others understand how your business will operate.

Nora Ellis and Samantha Richards are qualified childcare workers who worked together at a day-care center for many years. The center often turned away children because it did not have the room or staff to take care of more toddlers. Nora and Samantha realized that they could make a profit running their own day-care center. Their business plan explained that there was a high demand for quality day-care services in the area and that they were well experienced to meet this need.

Goals

Your business plan should outline your short-term, medium-term, and long-term **goals**. This section of the business plan describes your vision of where you want your company to be in the future. Some entrepreneurs are very clear about what they want to do with their business. Others know their short-term goals, but they have not thought further ahead.

Nora and Samantha know what their short-term and medium-term goals are. In the first year of business, they want to get financing that will allow them to buy or lease a building, equip the building, and staff it with eight employees. In their second and third years of business, they want to invest in more equipment and possibly expand their day-care center to take in more children. But they have not decided what their goals are for the long term. Writing a business plan will force them to think about these goals. For example, they will need to decide whether they want to run only one day-care center or whether

they want to expand and have a chain of day-care centers.

Products or Services

This part of your business plan should describe the products or services your company plans to produce and sell. You should explain how these products or services differ from those already on the market. You will need to describe any unique features of your products or services. You also need to explain the benefits customers will gain by purchasing from your company.

Industry In the Product or Service section of your business plan, you should describe the industry in which you will operate. It should include:

- outside factors affecting your business, such as high competition or a lack of suppliers
- estimates for industry growth
- economic trends of the industry
- technology trends that may affect the industry

To find this information, you will need to conduct research. Government documents, newspaper and magazine articles, books on industry leaders, and the Internet are all good places to start. Be sure to name all of these sources in your plan. Listing sources makes a business plan more persuasive.

Location The Product or Service section of your business plan also should describe the location of your business. Because the location of a business often is important to its success, lenders

Working Together

In small groups, set short-term, medium-term, and long-term goals for one of the following new businesses:

- lawn care company
- housecleaning service
- cookie baking business

© GETTY IMAGES/PHOTODISC

Why is the location of a business often important to its success?

want to know exactly where your business will be located.

Writing the Products or Services section of the business plan was easy for Nora and Samantha because they had a clear idea of what services they wanted to offer. In the Industry section of their plan, they included population data for their area. This information showed that demand for their service could grow over time. They also listed government sources that reported an increasing demand for day-care services as more women with young children join the work force. For the Location section of the business plan, Nora and Samantha wrote that they planned to start the business in an ideal location—in the heart of a community where most families have young children and both parents work outside the home.

Form of Ownership

In your business plan, you should have a section describing your form of ownership. Provide information that relates to your form of business, such as whether you

have partners or how many shareholders you have. This section of the business plan is important because each form of business ownership has a different effect on how the business works and makes profits. If you use your business plan to obtain financing, the lender will be interested in this information.

Management and Staffing

You and the people you hire to help run your company are responsible for its success. Even the best business plan will not help your company succeed if it is carried out by people who are not capable. The Management and Staffing section of the business plan should show that you and the people who will be working for you have the experience, maturity, and knowledge to operate your business.

Nora and Samantha have college degrees in early childhood education. Together, they have more than 35 years of experience in day care, including 15 years in management. To show readers of their business plan that they are well qualified to run a day-care center, they included copies of their resumes. A **resume** is a summary of your education and work experience.

Marketing

In your business plan, you also should include information on marketing your business. You will explain who your target customers are, how large the market is for your product or service, and how you plan to enter that market. You also should explain how you plan to deal with competition.

You should list your company's advantages over the competition. These advantages may include:

- performance
- quality
- reliability
- location
- price
- promotion
- public image or reputation

Nora and Samantha's target customers are the parents of the 1,000 to 1,500 children between the ages of two and five who live in their area. Nora and Samantha determined that 90 percent of the families would be able to afford their services. To enter the market, Nora and Samantha will advertise in local newspapers. They will send out fliers to families in the target market. They also will offer two months of care at a discounted rate for new customers.

Current and Projected Financial Statements

The financial section of your plan consists of three elements.

1. **Identification of risks**
   Lenders and investors will want to know what risks your business faces and how you plan to deal with them. Do not be afraid to list potential problems. Lenders know that every business faces risks. They will be reassured to see that you have clearly thought through the potential problems and have developed a plan for dealing with them. Examples of risks that you could face are competitors lowering prices, costs running

higher than estimated, and demand for your product or service declining over time.

2. **Financial statements** A new business must include projected financial statements, known as pro forma financial statements, in its business plan. A business already in operation must include current financial statements as well as projected financial statements.

3. **Loan request and return on investment** You also must state how much you need to borrow and how you plan to use the money. You should give investors an idea of how much money they could expect to earn on their investment in your business. You also should state how much of your own money you are investing in the business.

Nora and Samantha know the main risk is that parents will think their center is unsafe. They have prepared a pamphlet entitled "Safety and Your Child." They plan to use this as part of their marketing package. They included a copy of the pamphlet in the appendix of the business plan.

Nora and Samantha have included projected financial statements, which show how much money and profit they expect to earn. They require $140,000 to start their business. Together, they are contributing $85,000 of their own money. They need a loan of $55,000. They included this information as well.

> **CHECKPOINT**
> → List the elements of a business plan and explain why each element is important.

Additional Elements

All business plans should include the seven basic elements. Some businesses need to provide additional information in their business plans. A business that has licensing requirements or must meet legal restrictions and regulations, such as a restaurant, would include a section on legal issues in its business plan. To identify any special sections that you should include in your plan, ask yourself what you would want to know about a business before you would lend it money.

As part of their business plan, Nora and Samantha devote a section to health and safety issues. They describe their procedures for dealing with allergies, illnesses, and injuries. They also outline plans for dealing with emergencies, such as broken water pipes or fires.

CHECKPOINT

→ Why should some businesses include additional information in their business plans?

10.2 LET'S GET REAL

1 THINK ABOUT YOURSELF When writing a business plan, it is important to think about the competition. Think of a product or service you use often. What are the advantages it has over competing products?

2 WHAT DO YOU THINK? Why should you include management and staffing issues in your business plan?

3 MATH CONNECTION You plan to start a corporation. You have $67,500 in savings, but you need $165,000 total to begin your business. How much money will you need from investors? What will be your percentage of ownership?

4 COMMUNICATION CONNECTION Write what you think the short-term, medium-term, and long-term goals would be for a person who has just purchased a toy store.

HOW DO YOU CREATE AN EFFECTIVE PLAN?

Terms

trade associations
cover letter
statement of
    purpose
executive summary

Goals

✳ **Identify resources to help develop your business plan.**

✳ **Explain how a business plan should be organized.**

Research the Business Plan

Your business plan needs to persuade readers that you have a good, realistic business idea. To do this, you will have to do some research. You must use resources that provide information and data based on facts rather than opinions. This will show the reader that your idea is based on solid evidence.

Researching and writing a business plan takes lots of time. Most entrepreneurs spend 50 to 100 hours developing their business plans. Pulling together the information you will need to write your business plan involves researching all parts of your business, from leasing space and deciding what you will charge for your product or service to dealing with competitors. Researching all the parts of your business will teach you a great deal about running a business. It also may provide you with specific ideas for starting your company.

© GETTY IMAGES/PHOTODISC

Print Resources

Information for your business plan may come from many sources. Your public library should have many books on entrepreneurship. In addition, books on marketing, financing, hiring and managing a staff, purchasing a business, and operating a franchise may be helpful. The library also should have books devoted specifically to writing a business plan. Some books have sample business plans. These books will provide you with valuable information on running your business.

Magazines also may be helpful, especially magazines devoted to small business ownership and to your specific industry. Ask your librarian to help you find magazines that contain information that may be useful for your business plan.

Government documents may provide you with useful information. You should review publications issued by the Small Business Administration (SBA) and other federal agencies. The SBA office nearest you should be able to provide you with publications to help you complete your business plan.

What kind of print resources can help you prepare your business plan?

© DIGITAL VISION

Online Resources

Much of the information you can find in print resources also is available on the Internet. The SBA web site contains much of the same information that the SBA provides in print. Many magazine articles and even some books can be found on the Internet. In addition, there are many web sites specifically for entrepreneurs and small businesses that may offer detailed information. Several web sites walk you through writing a business plan step by step. You can even ask questions on some web sites.

People Resources

People from many organizations can help you with your business plan. Counselors from Small Business Development Centers provide free one-on-one assistance in developing a business plan. They also provide inexpensive workshops on topics that may help you develop your plan.

Another source of valuable assistance is the Service Corps of Retired Executives (SCORE). More than 12,000 retired executives volunteer their time with SCORE to help young entrepreneurs. They provide free advice that may be helpful to you as you prepare your business plan. You can set up a personal meeting with a SCORE volunteer, or you can work with a SCORE volunteer over the Internet.

Working Together

In small groups, make a list of questions about writing a business plan that you could ask a SCORE volunteer.

Additional Resources

Your local Chamber of Commerce and Small Business Development Centers have information on trends affecting local businesses. **Trade associations** are organizations that support certain types of businesses. These associations also can be valuable sources of information.

Some entrepreneurs hire experts to help them write their business plans. Professional business consultants can be found in directories at your library or on the Internet.

Nora and Samantha began their business plan by taking books out of the library. They also read information on childcare businesses that they received from the Small Business Administration. Once they had an outline prepared, they met with a counselor from their local Small Business Development Center. The counselor helped them prepare their pro forma financial statements.

> **CHECKPOINT**
> → Why do you need to conduct research to write a business plan?

Organize Your Business Plan

Your business plan is your best opportunity to let other people know what you want to do with your company. It gives you the chance to persuade them that your idea is good and that you have the talent and resources to make your idea a successful business venture.

To make the best impression on people who will read your business plan, you will want to create an attractive document that is neat, well organized, and easy to read. Handwritten business plans are not acceptable. All business plans must be word processed and printed on standard-sized white paper. In addition, your business plan should follow a standard format. There are certain things that should be included in the business plan. These things include introductory elements, the main body of the plan, and an appendix.

Introductory Elements

Every business plan should begin with a cover letter, a title page, a table of contents, a statement of purpose, and an executive summary. These elements

Be Your Own Boss

You are going to start Green Thumb, a plant-growing business. You will grow herbs, flowers, and other garden plants to sell in your community. You have done the research and found that there is a market for this business. There is only one hardware store that sells garden plants in your community.

In order to get the business started, you will need $250 to buy supplies. Write a cover letter for your business plan.

THE MT. WASHINGTON CHILDREN'S CENTER

5813 NORTH AVENUE, BALTIMORE, MARYLAND 21205
(410) 555-4445

April 11, 20—

Ms. Jane Stewart
Vice President
First National Bank
E. 35th Street
Baltimore, Maryland 21212

Dear Ms. Stewart

Enclosed please find a copy of the business plan for the Mt. Washington Children's Center, a proposed new day-care center in northwest Baltimore that will serve approximately 50 young children. We believe that the shortage of high-quality day care in this part of the city will allow us to earn significant revenues for the center and that we will be making a profit within three years of opening.

To establish the kind of center we envision, we plan to invest $85,000 of our own money. We will need additional financing of $55,000. As you will note from our pro forma financial statements, we plan to repay the loan within five years.

Please let us know if there is any additional information you would like to receive. We look forward to hearing from you.

Sincerely yours,

Nora Ellis   *Samantha Richards*

Nora Ellis   Samantha Richards

help set the tone for your business plan.

Cover Letter A **cover letter** is a letter that explains or provides more information about a document or a set of documents. The cover letter for your business plan should include your name, the name of your business, and your address and telephone number. It should briefly describe your business and its po-

tential for success. It also needs to tell the reader how much money you need to borrow.

Nora and Samantha prepared the cover letter shown above.

Title Page Your business plan should have a title page that indicates the name of your company, the date, the owner(s) of the company, and the address and phone number of the company.

STATEMENT OF PURPOSE

The Mt. Washington Children's Center will operate as a private day-care center serving approximately 50 children in northwest Baltimore. The Center will offer excellent supervision in a clean, safe, learning environment.

The project is requesting $55,000 in financing. This money will be used to:

- rent and remodel 4,000 square feet of indoor space
- prepare 18,000 square feet of outdoor space for use as a playground
- purchase equipment such as swings, jungle gyms, sandboxes, and supplies
- pay salaries of eight employees until cash flow can cover operating expenses

Table of Contents A table of contents is a listing of the material included in a publication. It shows the reader what each page covers. The table of contents needs to be accurate, so you need to make sure that the sections are in the correct order. You also should check the page numbers to make sure that they are shown correctly in the table of contents.

Statement of Purpose The **statement of purpose** briefly describes why you are asking for a loan and what you plan to do with the money if you receive it. It should be no more than one or two paragraphs.

Nora and Samantha's statement of purpose is shown above.

Executive Summary An **executive summary** is a short restatement of a report. It should capture the interest of its readers and make them want to read more. If the executive summary is unconvincing, a lender may decide not to read your entire business plan. A strong executive summary is important to the success of your business plan.

The executive summary should be no longer than one or two pages. It should be written in a clear, simple style. Your executive summary should:

- describe your business idea and communicate what is unique about your idea
- include your estimates for sales, costs, and profits
- identify your needs, such as inventory, land, building, and equipment
- state the amount you are interested in borrowing

Although the executive summary appears before the main body of the business plan, it should be written after the business plan has been completed. To write the executive summary, go through the business plan and find the most important and persuasive points you have made. Then write an outline of an executive summary based on these points.

EXECUTIVE SUMMARY

The Mt. Washington Children's Center (MWCC) will be formed as a partnership in Baltimore, Maryland. It will be owned and operated by Nora Ellis and Samantha Richards, highly respected child-care professionals with more than 35 years of experience in the field. Three experienced teachers and three teacher aides will supervise approximately 50 boys and girls between the ages of 2 and 5. A receptionist and a cleaning person will also be hired.

MWCC is being established in response to the shortage of high-quality childcare in northwest Baltimore. Only two small day-care centers now serve a population of 45,000 upper-middle-class families. In 75 percent of these households, both parents work outside the home. The convenient location of the Center will make it an attractive day-care option for parents in the area. When completed, it will include four large outdoor play structures and eight personal computers. It will be staffed by the finest day-care professionals in Baltimore and led by a management team that is well recognized.

Market research indicates that the MWCC could expect to fill 90 to 100 percent of its student positions immediately upon opening and that the center would be profitable as early as the third year of operation. Expansion could begin in the third year. To finance the start up of the company, its owners are seeking $55,000 in financing, which they would expect to repay within five years.

Once you have created a draft of your executive summary, ask people who do and do not understand your business to read it. If readers do not come away with a clear sense of what you plan to do and how you will succeed in doing it, your executive summary needs more work.

Nora and Samantha wrote the executive summary shown above. They asked several of their friends and business associates to review it. One day-care professional suggested they state that the center would be equipped with video monitors that allow supervision at all times. Another reader said that Nora and Samantha needed to add that they planned to invest $85,000 of their own money.

Main Body of Your Plan

The main body of your plan should include the seven basic elements of a business plan. It also should include any additional elements that you think are necessary.

Lenders do not have time to read business plans that are long or hard to understand. Your plan should be short and to the point. Do not include unnecessary information. Use simple language to present a clear idea of what you want to do and how you plan to do it. Use charts and tables to illustrate your point.

Why should you ask someone else to read your executive summary?

Appendix

The appendix is the part of the business plan that contains any supporting evidence that was not included in the body of the report. Documents that might be included in the appendix are your resume, personal financial statements, income tax returns, copies of any large sales contracts you already have negotiated, letters of recommendation, and legal documents.

CHECKPOINT

→ What is the purpose of each part of a business plan?

10.3 LET'S GET REAL

1] **THINK ABOUT YOURSELF** It is important to use people resources when you write your business plan. Think about people you know. Who would be a good resource for you to talk to about your business plan?

2] **WHAT DO YOU THINK?** Why is it possible to write an executive summary only after you have written your business plan? Why might the executive summary be more important than the body of the plan?

3] **COMMUNICATION CONNECTION** You want to open a new bike messenger service business, but you need $2,500 to get started. Write a statement of purpose for a business plan that will be read by a group of investors.

4] **MATH CONNECTION** You need a total of $174,500 to start your business. If you plan to get a loan for 20 percent of the total, how much of your own money will you have to invest?

The Coleman Company

The slogan of the Coleman Company—"The Greatest Name in the Great Outdoors"—actually had its beginning indoors. In 1900, W. C. Coleman, a young man who needed money for his last year of law school, decided to sell lamps in Kingfisher, Oklahoma. He had first seen the lamp that would change the course of his life in a drugstore window in Alabama. Even with his poor vision, he could read small print by the bright light from that lamp.

The lamp had a mantle, not a wick, and it was fueled by gasoline under pressure. The light was clean and white. Coleman bought the inventory from the company that made the lamps. He was sure he could sell the lamps to shopkeepers who wanted to keep their stores open in the evening. But merchants in Kingfisher had just purchased a product from another salesman, so they would not buy from Coleman.

Being resourceful, Coleman decided to sell a light service instead of the lamps themselves. He drew up contracts with a "no light, no pay" clause. That offer persuaded his customers to do business with him, and the Hydro-Carbon Light Company began to grow.

From Kingfisher, Coleman expanded to San Diego and Las Vegas. In 1902, he relocated to Wichita, Kansas. He began manufacturing his own lamps, which he named the Coleman Arc Lamp. And he changed the name of the company to the Coleman Lamp Company.

A lantern produced in 1914 was the beginning of Coleman's camping business. The U.S. government declared the lantern an "essential item" of World War I. During World War II, upon government request, Coleman developed the G.I. Pocket Stove. Soldiers used it to cook food, heat drinks, purify water, and even to keep warm in foxholes.

As rural areas began to use electricity, lanterns no longer were needed to light homes and businesses. The Coleman Company began to expand its product line. It began manufacturing gas floor furnaces and heaters that enabled it to survive the Depression years.

After World War II, the Coleman Company followed trends and expanded its inventory to include leisure products. By the end of the 1960s, it was the biggest name in the camping business. Today, the company continues to introduce new products for camping.

Think Critically

1. How did Coleman overcome a challenge as he started his business?
2. Do you think that getting government contracts contributed to the success of the Coleman Company? Why or why not?
3. How has the Coleman Company's ability to follow trends helped it be successful today?

Why Do You Need a Plan?

1. A business plan is a written document that describes what your business will produce, how you will produce it, and who will buy your product or service.

2. A business plan discusses issues such as who will run your business, how you will keep customers, and how your business will earn a profit.

3. Writing a business plan will help you to think about all parts of your business, to secure financing, to communicate your ideas, and to manage your business.

What Goes Into a Plan?

4. Business plans should include basic information in the following areas: history and background of your business idea, goals, products or services, form of ownership, management and staffing, marketing, and financial statements.

5. Some business plans also should include information on licensing requirements, legal issues, and other items needed for a specific business.

How Do You Create an Effective Plan?

6. You should research your business plan through print resources, online resources, and people resources. Books, magazines, and other printed resources can be good reference materials for your business plan. Some organizations, including the Small Business Administration, offer assistance in writing a business plan.

7. Your local Chamber of Commerce and Small Business Development Centers are good sources for researching your business plan. Trade associations also may have helpful information.

8. Your business plan should be neat and well organized. It should always be word processed.

9. Your business plan should include the following elements: cover letter, title page, table of contents, statement of purpose, executive summary, main body, and appendix.

Vocabulary Builder

Choose the term that best fits the definition.

1. A written document that describes all the steps necessary to open and operate a successful business
2. Organizations that support certain types of businesses
3. A short restatement of a report
4. A letter that explains or provides more information about a document or a set of documents
5. A brief description of why you are asking for a loan and what you plan to do with the money if you receive it
6. A summary of your education and work experience

a. business plan
b. cover letter
c. executive summary
d. goals
e. resume
f. statement of purpose
g. trade associations

Review What You Have Learned

7. Who is a business plan written for?
8. How can a business plan help you run your business?
9. What is the difference between short-term, medium-term, and long-term goals? Why should entrepreneurs identify each of these goals?
10. Why would lenders want to know the form of ownership for your business?
11. What advantages can a business have over its competitors?
12. Why is it important to identify the risks you face and include them in your business plan?
13. Why might it be necessary to include additional elements in your business plan?
14. Where can you find industry data you might need for your business plan?
15. What information might you want to research when writing your business plan?
16. Why should a business plan be word processed and follow a standard format?
17. What are the introductory elements that every business plan should include?
18. What should the cover letter of your business plan do?
19. Why is an executive summary important to a business plan?
20. What should be included in the main body of your business plan?
21. What kind of items might be included in the appendix of your business plan?

Using the *Activities* CD, open the Chapter 10 folder. Open the activity, Business Plan Resources. Print a copy and complete the activity.

Think About It

1. You want to open a business that makes advertising fliers for local businesses. You need to borrow money to buy a new printer and computer. What research do you need to do before you write your business plan? To whom will you present your business plan?

2. Writing a business plan is an important part of starting your own company. Do you think entrepreneurs ever need to update their business plans? Why or why not?

3. How do you think a business plan for a home-based business differs from that of a large corporation?

Project: Making Entrepreneurship Work for You

This activity will help you develop the business opportunity that you identified in Chapter 1.

1. Focus on the history and background element of your business plan. Describe how you came up with the idea for your business project.

2. List your short-term, medium-term, and long-term goals for your business. How can you achieve each of these goals?

3. Prepare a one-page report that fully describes your product or service and how it differs from other products or services currently available.

4. Explain why there is a market and a need for your product or service. Interview five or more people about your product or service. How many of them would buy it?

Did any of them make suggestions for improvement? Describe how you will beat your competition.

5. Begin the financial section of your business plan by identifying the risks your business faces. Explain how you will overcome each risk.

6. Now you are ready to write your own business plan using all the information you have gathered from the activities in the *Making Entrepreneurship Work for You Project* at the end of each chapter. Use the Business Plan Checklist on the *Activities* CD to help you prepare your business plan.

Glossary

A

Account an accounting record that summarizes all financial information for one specific business item (p. 169)

Advertising a paid form of communication sent out by a business about a product or service (p. 140)

Advertising fees fees paid to support television, magazine, or other advertising of the franchise as a whole (p. 86)

Agenda a list of things to be discussed or done during a meeting (p. 31)

Alternatives choices (p. 44)

Aptitude the ability to learn a particular kind of job (p. 20)

Assets things of value that are owned (p. 80); cash, equipment, and the goods you will sell (p. 159)

B

Benefits advantages gained from the features of a product or service (p. 205)

Board of directors group of people elected by stockholders who meet several times a year to make important decisions affecting the company (p. 94)

Bounced check a check that is written on a checking account that does not have enough funds to cover the amount of the check (p. 211)

Brainstorming a problem-solving method often done in a group setting that involves coming up with a large number of fresh ideas (p. 46)

Breakeven point the amount of sales that must be made to cover all of the expenses, or costs, of a business (p. 172)

Business broker a person who sells businesses for a living (p. 79)

Business e-mail a formal type of e-mail used for business communication (p. 30)

Business ethics the application of the principles of right and wrong to issues that come up in the workplace (p. 215)

Business letter the most common form of business writing (p. 29)

Business plan a written document that describes all the steps necessary to open and operate a successful business (p. 224)

C

Cash flow the difference between revenue and expenses (p. 156)

Characteristics qualities that make a person different from others (p. 14)

Check register a book in which you record the dates, amounts, and names of people or businesses to whom you have written checks (p. 170)

Code of ethics the level of ethical behavior demanded by an individual, business, or culture (p. 215)

Collateral property that a borrower gives up if he or she does not pay back a loan (p. 161)

Command economy the government determines what, how, and for whom goods and services are produced (p. 55)

Commitment a pledge to do something (p. 22)

Competitor company that offers similar or identical products and services to the same group of customers (p.136)

Computer consultant a person who designs computer systems for businesses making certain the equipment meets the needs of the business and all the parts of the system work together properly (p. 196)

Computer hardware computers and the equipment used with them (p. 182)

Consumer one who purchases goods or services (p. 13)

Corporation a business with the legal rights of a person and which may be owned by many people (p. 90)

Cover letter a letter that explains or provides more information about a document or a set of documents (p. 236)

Customer feedback card a short survey asking customers for their opinions about a company (p. 138)

Customer person who buys the products and services a company offers (p. 129)

D

Debt capital money loaned to a business with an agreement that the money will be repaid, with interest, in a certain time period (p. 161)

Delegate to let other people share workloads and responsibilities (p. 118)

Demand an individual's need or desire for a good or service at a given price (p. 64)

Demographics data that describe a group of people in terms of their age, marital status, family size, ethnic background, gender, profession, education, and income (p. 129)

Dividends payments of profits to shareholders by corporations (p. 94)

E

E-commerce selling products or services over the Internet (p. 192)

Economics making choices and satisfying the wants and needs of consumers (p. 54)

Electronic mail (e-mail) worldwide system used to send and receive electronic messages (p. 190)

Employee a person who works for someone else (p. 5)

Entrepreneur someone who provides a product or service for someone else (p. 4)

Entrepreneurship the process of running a business of one's own (p. 4)

Equity capital money invested in a business in return for a share in the business's profits (p. 166)

Ethics the study of moral choices and values that involves choosing between right and wrong (p. 214)

Executive summary a short restatement of a report (p. 237)

Expenses costs of supplies that are used in a business (p. 36)

Exports products and services that are produced in one country and sold in another (p. 70)

F

Features what a product or service actually does (p. 205)

Fixed costs costs that must be paid no matter how much of a good or service is produced (p. 62)

Focus group an interview with groups of target customers who provide valuable ideas on products or services (p. 132)

Franchise a legal agreement that gives a person the right to sell a company's products or services in a particular area (p. 83)

G

Goals section in business plan that describes your vision of where you want your company to be in the future (p. 229)

I

Imports products and services that are brought in from another country to be sold (p. 71)

Income money earned from providing goods or services (p. 36)

Incorporate to set up a business as a corporation (p. 93)

Initial franchise fee fee the franchisee pays for the right to run the franchise (p. 84)

Interest an amount that can be earned on money that is invested (p. 38)

Internet a worldwide computer network that allows people to communicate with each other electronically and to access the World Wide Web (p. 189)

Internet service providers companies that provide a connection to the Internet via telephone or cable lines (p. 189)

Interoffice memo a short note written from one person in a company to another person in the same company (p. 30)

Inventory includes the products you have on hand to sell to customers (p. 84); the stock of goods a business has for sale (p. 173)

J

Job description written statement listing the duties and responsibilities of a job (p. 109)

L

Layout floor plan for a business (p. 105)

Liabilities items that a business owes to others including loans and unpaid invoices (p. 159)

Liability amount shareholders may lose, limited to the amount each invested in the company when stock was purchased (p. 94)

Loss occurs when expenses are greater than income (p. 36)

M

Management way to achieve goals by using resources (p. 114)

Manufacturing business a business that makes the products it sells (p. 6)

Markdown an amount subtracted from the retail price to determine the selling price (p. 39)

Market includes the customers and the location that a business wants to serve (p. 56)

Market economy individuals decide what, how and for whom goods and services are produced (p. 56)

Marketing concept focuses on the needs of customers when planning, producing, distributing, and promoting a product or service (p. 129)

Market research a system for collecting, recording, and analyzing information about customers, competitors, goods, and services (p. 131)

Markup an amount added to the cost of an item to determine the selling price (p. 39)

Memorandum a short written form of business communication (p. 30)

Modem an electronic device that allows information to be transmitted from one computer to another over telephone or cable TV lines (p. 184)

Monopoly one company controls all of a market (p. 61)

Motivate to give employees a good reason to do something (p. 117)

N

Needs things you must have in order to survive (p. 54)

Needs assessment a salesperson interviews a customer to determine his or her specific needs and wants (p. 206)

O

Operating expenses expenses that a business has every month (p. 156)

Opportunity cost value of the best alternative you must pass up (p. 63)

Organizational structure a plan that shows how all the jobs within a company relate to one another (p. 109)

P

Partnership a business that is owned by two or more people (p. 90)

Payroll a list of people who receive salary or wage payments from a business (p. 170)

Periodic inventory method involves taking a physical inventory of a business's merchandise (p. 174)

Perpetual inventory method keeps track of inventory levels on a daily basis (p. 173)

Personal selling a salesperson talks to potential buyers and tries to persuade them to make a purchase (p. 204)

Policies rules for the workplace (p. 116)

Press release a written statement that informs the media of an event or product (p. 146)

Primary data information collected for the first time for a specific purpose (p. 132)

Pro forma financial statements financial statements based on estimates (p. 155)

Profit occurs when income is greater than expenses (p. 36)

Public relations the act of creating a positive relationship with customers and the general public (p. 141)

Publicity free promotion that comes from media coverage (p. 145)

R

Rebate a refund offered to people who purchase a product (p. 146)

Recruit to look for people to hire (p. 110)

Resources things that are used to create products and services (p. 21)

Resume a summary of your education and work experience (p. 230)

Retailing business a business that sells directly to customers (p. 7)

Royalty fees weekly or monthly payments made by the franchisee to the franchisor (pp. 84–85)

S

Sales promotion the act of offering an incentive to customers in order to increase sales (p. 146)

Sales tax a federal, state, or local government tax charged on goods (p. 40)

Scarcity occurs because people's wants and needs are unlimited while the resources needed to produce goods and services are limited (p. 56)

Secondary data data found in sources that are already published (p. 131)

Security precautions the steps that a business owner can take to protect against different types of risks (p. 208)

Self-assessment looking within and thinking about your personal strengths and weaknesses (p. 18)

Service business a business that sells services rather than products (p. 7)

Share of stock a unit of ownership in a corporation (p. 93)

Shoplifting the act of knowingly taking items from a business without paying (p. 209)

Software programs that control computer hardware and direct its operation (p. 185)

Sole proprietorship a business that is owned by one person (p. 90)

Start-up costs one-time costs associated with beginning a business (pp. 84, 155)

Statement of purpose section in business plan that briefly describes why you are asking for a loan and what you plan to do with the money if you receive it (p. 237)

Subsidies government payments to producers of certain kinds of goods (p. 67)

Supply how much of a good or service a producer is willing and able to produce at different prices (p. 63)

T

Target market individuals that are interested in a particular product or service and are able to pay for it (p. 128)

Technology plan specific goals for a business that describe how technology could be used to meet those goals (p. 195)

Trade area area from which you expect to attract customers (p. 102)

Trade association organization that provides support for certain types of businesses (p. 235)

Transaction the exchange of goods or services for money (p. 40); a business activity that causes change in assets, liabilities, or net worth (p. 168)

U

Utility present in a good or service that is useful (p. 57)

V

Valuator an expert on determining the value of a business (p. 81)

Variable costs costs that go up and down depending on the quantity of the good or service produced (p. 62)

Venture capitalists individuals or companies that make a living investing in new companies (p. 167)

W

Wants things you think you must have in order to be satisfied (p. 54)

Web page a file stored on the Internet that greets visitors and provides various types of information (p. 191)

Wholesaling business a business that sells the products it buys to someone else (p. 6)

Index